ENJOY !

Designing the Successful Corporate Accelerator

Designing the Successful Corporate Accelerator

Jules Miller

Jeremy Kagan

WILEY

Library of Congress Cataloging-in-Publication Data:

Names: Miller, Jules (Advisor to enterprise startups) author. | Kagan, Jeremy (Growth and innovation consultant) author.
Title: Designing the successful corporate accelerator : how startups and big companies can get with the program / Jules Miller, Jeremy Kagan.
Description: First edition. | Hoboken : Wiley, 2021. | Includes index.
Identifiers: LCCN 2020056295 (print) | LCCN 2020056296 (ebook) | ISBN 9781119709060 (cloth) | ISBN 9781119709084 (adobe pdf) | ISBN 9781119709053 (epub)
Subjects: LCSH: New business enterprises. | Corporations. | Technological innovations—Management.
Classification: LCC HD62.5 .M545 2021 (print) | LCC HD62.5 (ebook) | DDC 658.4/063—dc23
LC record available at https://lccn.loc.gov/2020056295
LC ebook record available at https://lccn.loc.gov/2020056296

SKY10024798_020821

This book is dedicated to all the innovators, disruptors, change agents, and intrapreneurs who are working hard to innovate from within your companies. It's often a thankless job as you try to move mountains with only your bare hands and sheer willpower. We've been there and feel your pain. We hope this book helps you, at minimum, with another supporting hand to move those mountains. We know you can make it happen!

Contents

Foreword

Finding your way through any unfamiliar jungle is always easier with Google or (gasp) even paper maps. That's why this book is so important – it's the map big corporations need to uncover a disruptive innovation powerhouse inside their own companies. *Designing the Successful Corporate Accelerator* first challenges whether you have the right pieces in place to set up an accelerator at all, and if you do, it helps you navigate the road to success along every step of the way. For the best results, consider sharing this book generously with your leadership team and everyone involved in the innovation process.

Successful disruptive innovation is a war that big corporations have been losing for generations. With your determination and the authors' guidance, perhaps the next decade can be the turning point where companies actually get it right. What the heck, it's only been 75 years since we lost Henry Ford, and 90 for Thomas Edison, right?

Over the past century, large companies poured billions of dollars into allegedly disruptive failures with an embarrassing success rate – well below 10%. Remember Edsel, Saturn, Betamax, and New Coke? They're just a whisper of the cast of fallen characters. Each is incrementally innovative, for sure, but all are simply old solutions with a few new bells and whistles.

And, as the authors discuss, many corporations excel at *innovation theater*: putting young people in cool tech-forward office space with foosball and ping pong plus a dozen exotic flavors of fresh-ground coffee. Seldom have these theaters produced any meaningful disruptive innovation, the kind that changes lives, markets, or the way we do things. You know, things like self-driving or electric cars, hydrogen fuel cells, iPhones, or even Amazon.com. It's fundamentally different, far more intense innovation, writ large.

Most of the time, truly disruptive innovation is the province of startups – many founded in the proverbial garages like trailblazers Apple and HP. These smaller, more nimble companies – usually led and nearly always staffed by T-shirted, scruffy 20- to 30-year-olds – consistently deliver the lion's share of disruptive innovations that continuously change our universe. Startups aren't shackled by the constraints or bureaucracy of the dinosaur corporations, which allows them to be creative and try things that bigger companies can't (or won't). And they do it at a blistering speed.

In 1973, when I last worked at a Fortune 1000 company before joining the entrepreneur and venture capital world, I mostly worked the 2:30–9:30 a.m. shift, editing news for Westinghouse Broadcasting. Apple, Microsoft, Oracle, and SAP were born at this time. Tesla, Uber, and others followed in a nonstop recurring pattern readily summarized as "startups innovate, corporations execute." And for the past 50 years or so, with a few notable exceptions, truly disruptive innovation has been seen as antithetical to the common wisdom practiced by the world's leading corporations. "No skateboards, risk-taking or failures in these hallowed halls, sonny!" is the mantra. Corporate managers plan, then execute the plan, and the corporation executes those who don't execute. See, it's simple. But how?

Risk-taking that leads to disruptive innovation is just *so* much easier in a startup. Unlike corporations, startups basically have nothing to lose – no customers to screw up, no reputation to sully, and no rulebook or procedures manual to follow religiously. Most corporate executives described startup operations as chaos theory in action . . . there was no formal process, no roadmap to guide the innovation process. Then in 1999 Steve Blank retired after the $8 billion IPO of E.piphany, the company he founded three years prior, and decided to teach and write down what he'd learned in a career spanning a dozen startups.

Steve spent months developing a "test and iterate, then test again" business innovation model called Customer Development, later rebranded as "Lean Startup." It's often likened to the scientific method as applied to business innovation. Since we'd worked closely together launching his startup, Steve asked me to join him and write the method down in painful detail. Two years and 1,000 revisions later, we published *The Startup Owner's Manual* (Wiley), a bestseller in 23 languages. It translates Steve's principles into a granular, gritty, step-by-step process for turning ideas into repeatable, scalable, and (ultimately) profitable businesses.

WHY CORPORATE ACCELERATORS?

The demand for corporate innovation increases almost daily. Markets and customer needs change at an increasing rate, pandemics notwithstanding. New competitors and innovations emerge, often from startups, intensifying the big company challenge to deliver consistent new product launches, topline revenue growth, and steadily increasing profits in the face of unpredictable enemy forces. If you're even thinking about reading this book, I need say no more.

As the authors quickly point out, innovation requires an organization willing to move fast, ignore process, break rules, and take risks – vital ingredients antithetical to and seldom seen in even the fastest-moving major corporations. Internal accelerators bring the rocket-fueled, rule-breaking, T-shirt-wearing, spunky, devil-may-care entrepreneurs inside the corporation, ideally shielded from many of the processes, rules, and procedures that make big companies successful. Your authors Jules Miller and Jeremy Kagan have seen the movie, fought the battles, and will walk you step by step through the complex decision set that drives a successful corporate accelerator.

Corporate accelerators are hardly a one-size-fits-all proposition, and the book does a great job outlining the choices, pathways, and operating principles in getting the right accelerator launched the first time. And it guides you through the strengths and weaknesses of matching your program with different corporate objectives, environments, industries, geographies, and more.

Now you, too, have a roadmap. In fact, it appears you've already bought it! This wonderfully comprehensive how-to guide is from two seasoned entrepreneurs who have served as "accelerator accelerants" and corporate innovation leaders. With this book, Jules and Jeremy have done exactly the same thing for corporate innovation that Steve Blank and I so proudly created for startups. They've crafted a comprehensive, granular, step-by-step playbook for the process of considering, planning, funding, and executing a successful corporate accelerator.

Use it well, travelers!

Bob Dorf
Serial entrepreneur, startup advisor,
educator, best-selling co-author,
The Startup Owner's Manual.

Acknowledgments

In the preparation of this book, we have been so fortunate to have support and encouragement from colleagues and peers around the world. We are forever grateful to the people who took time to review this book and make it better, and to all of the people we interviewed who shared the good, the bad, and the ugly of running innovation programs.

We'd like to offer particular thanks to our fellow accelerator professionals, who gave us insight into their own struggles and ways of doing things, from colleagues at Columbia University like Daniel Goetzel and Dmytro Pokhilko; Murat Aktihanoglu and Jon Axelrod at Entrepreneurs Roundtable Accelerator; Scott Howard at Share Ventures; Dustin Shay at Village Capital; KJ Singh and Matt Kozlov at TechStars; David Post and Marie Wieck at IBM; and many more.

To other friends who may have spoken with us just once but made an impact: It may have been a short conversation or a simple anecdote to you, but your guidance and confirmation of your own challenges and successes made the book much better. While we couldn't share all of the amazing stories, they absolutely informed our thinking and contributed to the result.

There were several people who provided crucial assistance in the actual writing and research process. We're looking at you, David Golding and Gabi Silver Wolozin. Your dedication and hustle summarizing interviews, researching background information, reading drafts, and keeping us all on track made the writing process smoother and much more enjoyable. Thanks for the meetings, the musings, and the mental muscle. Also many thanks go to our fantastic interns and collaborators who helped with interviews, research, and writing, including Zach Epstein, Austin Chung, Richard Tsay, and Scott Jenkins.

We absolutely must thank our individual partners and families, who tolerated the need for quiet time to write (and write and write) as well as odd hours for calls and meetings. When one person was writing, the others took over double duties on the home front, which we are especially appreciative of in the middle of a global pandemic. We truly thank you and appreciate your support.

Jules is incredibly grateful for everyone at the Kauffman Fellows Program. This research started as my final Thought Leadership Project for the program, and I wouldn't have jumped down the rabbit hole otherwise. I must also thank my mother, Rhonda Miller, who has been a journalist for more than 50 years and helped to refine early drafts of the book and affiliated blog posts. Without you I wouldn't have had the courage to think I could write a book at all, or the grammar and vocabulary skills to communicate my ideas. I'd also like to thank my partner Amir Chaudhri, who is the most loving and supportive human anyone could ever hope to have in their corner. You've always been a rock-solid advocate of my ambitious career plans, and I'm grateful for your patience and love while writing this book, the second most important thing I co-created this year.

Jeremy continues to realize how much successful writing has been a team effort. To my wonderful wife Katherine, so many thanks – every bit of quiet time for writing I could grab depended on you successfully distracting our three kids. That you accomplished this miracle in lockdown from coronavirus and made it look effortless is why we have a book. And to the kids – Alexis, Rose, and Jacob – Daddy loves you, even when he needs some peace and quiet to get the writing done. Thanks for your patience and support!

Of course, there is our talented team of experts, the people at Wiley, who believed in this project and provided amazing professional assistance as we brought the book to life. Special appreciation to Michelle Miller and Ewelina Olechowska for the stellar graphics. And thank you to the editorial team for making us sound better and forcing Jules to use an Oxford comma. We appreciate your patience during the moving target of delivering new chapters as we kept trying to make it perfect.

Last, but certainly not least, we are grateful to the readers of this book who are called to work in the field of corporate innovation. Getting this right is a challenging and often unappreciated task, but we appreciate you and can't wait to see you succeed. We've done the easy part of aggregating the existing wisdom and case studies, then mapping out a course to follow. The hard part is doing it, which is up to you.

About the Authors

Jules Miller has alternated between working in the corporate world and the startup/VC world for nearly two decades in Silicon Valley, New York, and Los Angeles. She started her career at Ernst & Young in the Venture Capital consulting group, then became an "intrepreneur" before she had any idea what that was. She would consistently (and annoyingly) suggest new initiatives to her boss, who thankfully allowed her to work on these projects as long as her core job was prioritized, then supported the initiatives that gained traction. This included completing the Big 4 accounting and consulting firm's first carbon footprint and also launching new business units around cleantech and environmental sustainability.

Miller then founded three companies, a consulting firm and two venture-backed tech companies, one of which is still a thriving, profitable business and one of which was acquired. She went through the process of applying to multiple accelerator programs as an entrepreneur and ultimately decided not to participate when accepted due to a perceived lack of value or long-term support that made it seem not worth it to give up a big chunk of equity.

More recently, Miller tried to address these issues when she launched two highly regarded blockchain accelerator programs for IBM and co-founded the IBM Blockchain Ventures group. She felt the challenges of corporate innovation first hand, and as a result has developed a clear perspective on building and managing accelerator programs that work for both the big companies and the participating startups. She now works with several accelerator programs as a mentor and is an entrepreneur in residence at 500 Startups.

Miller is currently a partner at Mindset Ventures, a venture capital fund investing in early-stage enterprise software companies. Mindset started as a partner fund to a global Microsoft Accelerator program, along with several other corporates, and eventually spun out to be an independent entity. They still source many good investments from Y Combinator, the Microsoft Accelerator, and other accelerator programs, and believe fully in the power of corporate-startup partnerships. Miller spends much of her time working with the founders in her portfolio to help them effectively partner with large enterprises.

Miller is a Kauffman Fellow, a scout for Indie.vc, a venture partner for Republic, and an advisor to several enterprise startups and corporations that want to partner with startups. She moved from NYC to Los Angeles in the middle of the global pandemic (and writing this book!), and she is slowly learning to appreciate this thing called work/life balance.

***

Jeremy Kagan is a growth and innovation consultant, and advisor to corporations, startups, and digital media companies. He is the former managing director of the Eugene Lang Center for Entrepreneurship at Columbia Business School, where he oversaw the entrepreneurial curriculum, student programs, the Lang venture capital fund, and the Columbia Startup Lab. While there, he launched the Columbia Alumni Virtual Accelerator (CAVA) and the corporate innovation program, partnering companies and student entrepreneurs to start businesses in their areas of interest. Kagan remains on the board of the Lang Center, and is a mentor in residence at the Columbia Startup Lab. He is a judge of the Columbia Entrepreneurship annual business plan competition and the SIPA Dean's Challenge for Social Impact startups.

As a Columbia Business School professor, Kagan co-teaches, with Steve Blank, the annual Lean Launchpad class, an intensive one-week boot camp open to all Columbia University students. He is also a professor of digital marketing, faculty director of the Digital Marketing Strategy executive education program, and teaches both graduate and executive education classes. His book *Digital Marketing: Strategy and Tactics*, the first textbook for digital marketing, was published in 2018 by Wessex Press, and is now in its second edition, with international editions now available as well.

Kagan previously was the founder and CEO of Pricing Engine, a digital marketing platform that enabled small businesses to benchmark, optimize, and expand their search and social advertising campaigns. He was part of the Entrepreneurs Roundtable Accelerator's (ERA) first cohort in New York City, and remains an active alumni mentor with both the regular and global programs. Kagan is also an award-winning mentor at other accelerators around the city, and is an entrepreneur in residence for the Founder Institute.

Kagan has been a speaker and corporate trainer in the digital media industry, where his clients include companies in content, services, and e-commerce, as well as traditional advertising agencies needing digital media expertise. Kagan previously worked at Sony Music Entertainment in the Global Digital Business, where he was the vice president of Global Account Management, working with large partners such as Nokia and Sony Ericsson.

Before this, he was vice president/director of Strategy and Customer Insight for Publicis Modem, a leading digital advertising agency, where he headed research and innovation out of the New York office.

Kagan lives in New York's East Village with his wife and children, and now walks his kids to school around the corner from where he used to produce indie rock concerts. Life's funny that way.

Introduction

Now more than ever, big companies realize they must continuously innovate to survive. It's famously been said that software is eating the world, and we see technology-native startups licking their lips, preparing to make a meal of enterprises that are slow to adopt new technologies and business models. From automotive to insurance to retail and everywhere in between, innovative startups are attacking slower-moving incumbents – and the stakes are nothing less than survival. To arm themselves in this competition, it's no surprise that big companies are fighting fire with fire. And the hottest weapon du jour in corporate innovation is the corporate accelerator.

Accelerators are on the rise, with now thousands of programs established around the world since Y Combinator started as the first modern accelerator in 2005, and more are popping up every day. In the past few years, the surge in accelerators run by large corporations is astounding. It seems that every corporate innovation team feels the need to have an accelerator as part of its innovation program.

However, while intentions are good, most corporate accelerators are not achieving the intended results. Sixty percent of corporate accelerators fail within two years, and partnerships with the participating companies are achieved less than 1% of the time.[1] Corporate accelerators are often seen as "innovation theater," one of several cliché and ineffective innovation initiatives that do not produce results and are a last resort for companies that are falling behind the curve.

The reasons for this are complicated. In the modern era, the pace of innovation has dramatically increased, resulting in traditional R&D programs being augmented by more nimble internal innovation initiatives such as venture studios, corporate venture capital (CVC), accelerators, and startup partnership programs. This is a critical development, as big companies no longer have time to wait for R&D labs to perfect and commercialize technology. They need to go to market earlier, move faster, and allow for quick failures. This is not easy for large, complex organizations to do. Big companies need a way to translate startup energy and speed into the established processes and assets of the corporation.

In an effort to adapt to these new market conditions, corporate accelerators have become a favorite tool for big corporations. The current version of these programs simply mimic successful independent accelerators that are effective in the startup and venture capital industry.

The intention is to give big companies an early view into emerging technologies and business models that could threaten their future, and to develop partnerships that form powerful alliances to turn this threat into opportunity while positively impacting corporate culture. On the flip side, for startups that participate, the potential partnerships with big companies are appealing because they allow for quick learning, an increase in credibility, and massive distribution channels.

This should be a win-win, but most of the time corporate accelerators do not live up to their potential. So why aren't they working? Let's look at a specific example.

A CASE STUDY ON CORPORATE INNOVATION

A didactic case study to demonstrate the complex dynamics of corporate innovation is that of Fabricated Company, Incorporated – or FabCo for short – a typical multinational public company that has stagnated and started down the path of corporate innovation. FabCo is starting to invest in a variety of innovation initiatives to breathe life back into the aging organization and keep it competitive by partnering with emerging technology-native up and comers. Through its 100-plus-year history, it has experienced both meteoric successes and near-company-killing failures based on its ability (or inability) to innovate and adapt.

It's worth summarizing the corporate story as a benchmark to guide us throughout this book.

From humble, entrepreneurial beginnings, FabCo started in 1912 as a manufacturer of components for the electric telegraph. When 21-year-old founder Federico "Freddie" Giovanni – an electrician and Italian immigrant living in Newark, New Jersey – lost his cousin Vincenzo during the sinking of the *Titanic* in April of that year, he was inspired to start a company that would have saved more lives in that disaster. At the time, wireless telegraphy was critical to enable effective communication between ships, and although it was extremely valuable in the rescue efforts of the *Titanic*, Freddie knew there was room for improvement that could have saved his precious cousin Vincenzo's life.

Based on his experience fixing electrical systems throughout New Jersey that expanded and contracted throughout the year in the cold winters and hot summers, Freddie patented a special polymer for electric telegraph wiring that dramatically increased transmission speeds and was more durable in harsh conditions. He quickly became a go-to component provider for the major telegraph, then telex, then typewriter companies around the world.

Over the years, with slow and methodical growth, Freddie led FabCo to become a major market player. At that time, the Roaring Twenties were in full swing and public markets were expanding faster than anyone had ever seen before. Freddie successfully took FabCo public on the New York Stock Exchange (NYSE) ringing the bell in March of 1929. Thirty-eight-year-old Freddie was at the top of the world, and this immigrant from working-class beginnings was now a very wealthy man with a thriving business. Coincidentally this month was also when his first and only son, Freddie Jr., was born. "Junior" was Freddie's pride and joy, and also his heir apparent to the business.

Then, only a few months later on Thursday, October 24, 1929 – now known as Black Thursday – the stock market started plummeting in a record crash, culminating a few days later on Black Tuesday, the worst day in stock market history. A tidal wave of panic consumed Wall Street, and the share price of many companies, including Freddie's, plummeted while consumer confidence was obliterated. This led to the Great Depression, the worst economic downturn in the history of the industrialized world, which lasted for nearly 10 years.

FabCo was one of the lucky ones that was able to salvage the business from the brink of destruction. Freddie slowly built the company back up from near ruin with a steady hand and reversion to fundamentals, reinvesting in his core products and services. During these dark times, Freddie was hesitant to take risks and invest in newer technologies. Throughout the 1940s FabCo slowly clawed its way back to stability, and in the 1950s even started growing revenues by single-digit percentages each year. During that time, Freddie had been grooming his son Freddie Jr., affectionately known as Junior, to take over the business. In 1964, at the age of 73, Freddie Sr. retired and Freddie Jr. became the new CEO.

Junior had worked at FabCo since graduating from Yale at 20 years old, with the exception of the 2 years he took off to attend Harvard Business School and a short stint working with his HBS professor Georges Doriot at American Research and Development Corporation (ARDC). He had big ideas and wasn't a fan of his father's old-school business traditions; he wanted to make his own name in the business world by transforming the stodgy telegraphy components business into an innovative company of the future.

By the time Junior took over the business at the age of 35, he was particularly excited about the nascent field of computing as the path forward for FabCo. He was an early follower of Alan Turing once he presented the idea of a universal machine capable of computing anything in 1936. He met with David Packard and Bill Hewlett in their Palo Alto garage in the 1940s and wanted to invest in their business with a new form of financing called "venture capital" that he learned from Professor Doriot at ARDC, the first-ever VC firm. But his father did not allow it. Junior followed closely when William Shockley and his research team at AT&T's R&D arm Bell Labs invented the transistor in 1947. The year he took over as CEO, he watched intently as Douglas Engelbart at Stanford Research Institute (SRI) presented a prototype for the graphical user interface (GUI), which made computing more accessible to the mass market.

Junior believed this was the future and wanted to reinvent FabCo as a modern computing company. He heavily invested in new products related to computing, built up expensive R&D labs and started slashing and burning the existing business related to telegraphy. He set up experimental secret divisions to create new products, which caused intense tension among the executive ranks.

While arguably ahead of his time, Junior struggled to make these initiatives work. Through a series of overambitious plans, huge R&D budgets, internal politics, executive attrition, slower than expected adoption of personal computing, and the depletion of necessary resources from the core "cash cow" businesses, Junior rapidly drove FabCo into the ground. The company was performing so poorly that they were about to be delisted from the NYSE and investors were lobbying intense pressure to break up the company. In 1971, on the same day as Alan Shugart and IBM announced the invention of the "memory disk" (better known today as the floppy disk), the board of directors forced Junior out. In a bold move, the board hired Louis Garrison, a senior partner from consulting firm McKinsey & Co. and outsider to the tech industry, as the CEO to manage this transition.

Instead of breaking up the company, Garrison renewed FabCo's focus on the customer, cut millions in annual costs, returned to the fundamental polymer and telegraphy (now telephony) business, shut down underperforming (and secret) departments, and established the "One FabCo" philosophy to restore the old corporate culture. By the mid-1980s FabCo was back to profitability and out of death's shadow, and even made it to the lower ranks of the Fortune 500.

In the meantime, the computing industry was starting to pick up, as predicted earlier by Junior. Many of FabCo's top researchers had fled to Xerox

PARC and continued refining the GUI, leading to technology that became the foundation of most computing systems today. Even Steve Jobs, who started Apple in 1976 with Steve Wozniak, cited FabCo's now-defunct work as an inspiration.

When Garrison retired in 1992, FabCo insider Pam Salisano took over as CEO, becoming only the fourth-ever female CEO of a Fortune 500 company, after Katherine Graham at the *Washington Post*, Marion Sandler at Golden West Financial, and Linda Wachner at Warnaco Group. A new breed of manager, she focused on both nurturing the core business and investing in the long-term future. This was done with the guidance of management consultants, who later wrote a book about different horizons based in part on Pam's philosophy. Pam was famously quoted as saying, "It's so easy to stick to things that made you profitable, but a core responsibility of leadership is understanding when it's time to change." Unfortunately, most people don't like change. Due to political discontent among her all-male executive team, Salisano was pushed out of the CEO role in 1996.

When her cutthroat deputy Ashwin Templeton took over as CEO, he doubled down on existing businesses, squeezed margins, and reduced R&D in favor of increased services offerings. This kept the company stable, but it faced more than a decade without meaningful growth and missed several disruptive technologies in its industry. FabCo also struggled with the cultural resistance to change and, because "no one got fired for using FabCo," their expensive sales force lost touch with their customers. People didn't really like working with or at FabCo anymore and attrition was high. By the late 2000s, FabCo's market share and profits were steeply declining and FabCo was on the brink of death once again.

Templeton retired in 2009 "to spend more time with his family" – rumor had it that he was forced to retire after a scandalous affair with a subordinate – and the former CFO, Kevin Pearson, took over. He spent the next decade buying growth through expensive mergers and acquisitions, but struggled to integrate the more entrepreneurial companies into FabCo's traditional corporate culture. Most of the original teams left after their earnouts and the businesses were taken over by seasoned FabCo executives. However, those managers were not equipped with the right skills to lead the more disruptive businesses, and most were shut down or spun off after a few years.

Pearson also started a corporate venture capital arm, now a major trend in corporate innovation fueled by the Silicon Valley companies. This was led by his head of corporate development and a team of all FabCo insiders, none of whom had startup or VC investing experience. They received great press for being "innovative," but ultimately most of the portfolio companies were writeoffs. When the head of corp dev retired leaving the team with no senior-level internal sponsor, they struggled to get new investments approved. In addition, Pearson rebooted the R&D initiative, building out eight award-winning research labs with more than 25,000 top researchers. This led to several hundred patents being filed each year, but only a handful translated into successful commercial product launches.

This brings us to the present day. Despite ticking all of the boxes on what a company is supposed to do to be innovative, FabCo is struggling to grow and is again fighting for its survival. Pearson retired in 2020, and the new CEO, Jordan Burns, has been tasked with reestablishing growth in the company. After a settling-in period, Burns took the bold move of hiring Ava Lopez, a former VC and Google executive, as chief innovation officer. One of the major initiatives Lopez has been asked to launch is a corporate accelerator.

Why Is This So Difficult?

Lopez has an exceedingly difficult task ahead of her. As with most companies, FabCo faces several hurdles to innovation.

First, as with most of their public-company peers, FabCo faces the challenge of balancing long-term investment with short-term profits beholden to a 90-day earnings cycle. In order to adapt and thrive in the face of disruptive innovation, business leaders must often risk hard-won career capital to ignore the pull of short-term management and commit to long-term risk-taking and investments in innovation.

Second, big companies tend to overly focus on serving the needs of existing customers versus thinking about, and investing in, future ones. This is the innovator's dilemma: what has led to the company's success thus far is preventing success in the future. To achieve growth in the face of more nimble upstart competitors, big companies must look to future customers and stay ahead of trends. As the oft-used Wayne Gretsky quote goes, you need to skate to where the puck is going, not to where it has been.

Finally, recruiting and retaining the right talent that deeply understands both the startup world and the inner workings of your big organization is exceedingly difficult. Most big companies have limited entrepreneurial talent – entrepreneurs like being entrepreneurs! The ones who do come into the business often don't stay long. The most talented innovation leaders thrive on a success-based upside and the corporate world is rarely structured to incentivize them properly. When institutional barriers lead to limited and slow success for innovation initiatives, along with a whole lot of frustrating politics and bureaucracy, people who have other career opportunities in the startup or VC world often take them.

This list should resonate with any manager as key challenges to innovation, likely alongside many others. These challenges will not go away, so it is critical for business leaders to understand what works, what doesn't work, and how to adapt to new market conditions. This is the task at hand.

What would you do in Lopez's shoes?

TRUTH IN (HISTORICAL) FICTION

The story of FabCo is, of course, fake. But the historical facts and context outlined here are real. We created this parable because it is inspired by the real stories of big companies, the start of Silicon Valley, and the current arena of corporate innovation. We've heard privately, and seen first-hand, so many horror stories from big companies that we can only share them if we protect the innocent (and sometimes the guilty) through a narrative that is based on real life but disguises the specific examples. Companies do not like to talk about their failures publicly, so the story of FabCo should give you unprecedented insight into the real challenges and opportunities along the corporate innovation journey.

Throughout this book we will take you through FabCo's quest to design and execute a successful corporate accelerator. Though the context is mostly North American due to your authors' personal experiences, we have included global context and case studies wherever possible. Either way, the insights and applications for corporate innovation should shine through, no matter where in the world you are.

Our allegorical hero Ava Lopez will face many challenges along the way, as will you and your organizations. We will share her story as a proxy alongside real case studies and lessons learned from the many corporate accelerators we've interviewed, profiled, and run ourselves.

CORPORATE ACCELERATORS AS A CANARY FOR BROADER INNOVATION

The purpose of this book is to focus on one form of corporate innovation: the corporate accelerator. When done right, the accelerator is a tool that can provide the perfect interface between corporate muscle and startup hustle. When done wrong, it's innovation theater.

As one piece of a large, complicated innovation puzzle, how you approach an accelerator program can be a barometer for a wider thesis on innovation. It is also a reflection of your company's brand and strategy in the market, and often serves as the first interaction (via participation or observation) with external innovators who are deciding whether they want to partner with you or compete against you.

The approach for this book is to give a framework for corporate innovation, then specific ways to apply this framework tactically to accelerators and other corporate innovation programs. We conducted in-depth interviews with leaders of top accelerators to identify and highlight best practices across fundamental areas such as funding, startup selection, performance metrics, and mentorship. We drew on personal experiences, as well as those from our peers and colleagues, to ensure that our guidelines are anchored in real-world experience.

The first half of this book sets the stage. Section 1 provides a crash course on corporate innovation and how accelerators fit in, with definitions, history, and context. If you are an experienced innovation executive you can skip this part or read through it as a refresher. Section 2 provides a framework for corporate accelerators and how to define your why, which drives all design decisions. Section 3 outlines the tough, but critical, work of getting your organization on board in the right way to set you up for success.

The second half of the book applies these concepts to reality in a "how-to," highlighting case studies from accelerator programs that have seen success in different areas, or those that have failed and learned lessons the hard way. Section 4 is everything before the program, Section 5 during the program, and Section 6 after the program. This will give you everything you need to design your own customized version of the successful corporate accelerator.

THE REWARD IS WORTH THE JOURNEY

When big companies and startups can work together effectively, magic happens. Corporates contribute to a startup's learning, credibility, and pipeline to help them scale rapidly. Startups bring the innovation, speed, and agility that corporates need to adapt and thrive.

Though startups and big companies often speak different languages, the corporate accelerator can act as a gateway between the two to translate and help them succeed together. It is our hope that building awareness of the techniques and practices of the world's top corporate accelerators can meaningfully impact the results of existing and future corporate accelerator programs.

Corporate innovation is never easy. We don't think anyone working in the space is afraid of a challenge or they would certainly be doing a different job. What helps make this challenge slightly easier is to see real results, which to date have been limited. By learning from the things that work and don't work, these results are not only possible, they will start to pay off in huge ways for the corporate teams who are able to execute successfully. This will also blaze a trail for others to do the same and encourage more calculated risk-taking.

We wish you good luck on your innovation journey . . . and it is just that, a journey. It certainly won't be easy, it definitely won't be fast, but in the end, it can make the difference between the long-term failure or survival and growth of your business. This book can be a traveler's guide of sorts to help you get to your destination faster and with fewer bumps in the road. The end result may not be what you intended, but with the right insight and tools to help you along the way, it may just be what you need.

To view all full color images found throughout the book, go to www.wiley .com\go\kagan-miller\DesigningtheSuccessfulCorporateAccelerator.

Designing the Successful Corporate Accelerator

CORPORATE INNOVATION IS HARD

CHAPTER **1**

ACCELERATORS AND CORPORATE INNOVATION

> The type of disruption most companies ... are facing right now is a once-in-every-few-centuries event. Disruption today is more than just changes in technology, or channel, or competitors – it's all of them, all at once.
>
> **STEVE BLANK**
> ENTREPRENEUR AND AUTHOR

Source: Harvard Business Review[1]

Innovation is a smoldering hot topic for executives in all industries, all across the globe. As with our allegorical team at FabCo, business leaders are increasingly concerned about the disruptive technologies and business models taking over their industries. In fact, the word disruption was mentioned more than 1,800 times each quarter in public company earnings calls in 2019, up from only ~300 times per quarter in 2009.[2]

According to a McKinsey survey, 80% of executives think their current business models are at risk to be disrupted in the near future, and 84% say that innovation is important to their growth strategy.[3] A similar survey by Accenture tells the same story: 84% of executives in the United States consider their future success to be "very" or "extremely" dependent on innovation.[4] A survey by KPMG showed that 88% of corporate executives thought that collaboration with startups was essential for their own innovation strategy.[5] There are a lot of surveys from consulting firms saying essentially the same thing: innovation is important for the future success of most companies, and partnering with startups is a critical component of that innovation plan.

Innovation is good for corporations in important ways – such as enabling faster growth, increasing stock prices, and even sheer survival. The *Forbes* list of the most innovative companies shows an innovation premium of 65–90% on the stock price of their top 10 innovators. This is billions of dollars of equity value attributed to innovation.[6]

On the flip side, companies that missed the innovation tidal wave in their industry have crashed and burned. For example, The Eastman Kodak Company dominated photography in the twentieth century and one of their engineers actually invented the first digital camera in 1975.[7] But executives did not see the full potential of this new technology, along with the new business model of online photo sharing, and this eventually led to the company's bankruptcy in 2012.[8] Many corporations live in fear of having their own "Kodak moment."

And there is real money to be made in helping corporations achieve their innovation goals. The "Innovation Management Market" is projected to grow from $422 million in 2017 to $1.5 billion by 2022, a 29% compound annual growth rate (CAGR).[9]

With all this talk about innovation, what's a corporate executive to do? Making innovation a part of a risk-averse corporation with legacy businesses requires hard work. Culture change over time requires unwavering management buy-in from the highest levels and the ability to overcome a lot of challenges along the way. There must be something quick and easy we can do to seem innovative, right?

Well, it's time to launch a corporate accelerator, of course! This is the newest and most exciting thing to ever hit the corporate world. And it checks all the boxes. Cool hoodie-wearing startup founders? Check! Trendy co-working spaces? Check! Guest speakers who are innovating innovation? Check! Disrupting disruption before it disrupts your business? Check! Lots of great marketing opportunities? Double check!

ONE TICKET TO THE INNOVATION THEATER, PLEASE

Are you ready to launch your corporate accelerator now? I hope not. If so, you're headed straight to the Innovation Theater. Unfortunately, too many corporate innovation programs feel like a lot of hype without much substance. They also lack a baseline understanding of what innovation programs, including corporate accelerators, are meant to achieve in the first place.

With the increasingly rapid pace of change coming from new technologies and business models, figuring out "innovation" has become an urgent priority for most businesses as they struggle to compete with new digital-native challengers who are dead set on taking their place. These disruptive newcomers can eat up market share quickly before the incumbent dinosaurs have time to mobilize their complicated corporate machines to compete.

To combat this threat of extinction, big companies have tried to copy startups by using the same tactics – hackathons, design thinking, lean startup methodology, agile development, and more – in their own organizations. The result is a variety of programs, including accelerators, that look innovative on the surface and generate a lot of activity, especially marketing, but rarely produce meaningful results.

This is innovation theater.[10]

For example, there is a professional services firm in Europe that launched a splashy accelerator program. They hired an interior designer from Google to create a gorgeous, super hip co-working space for the participating startups. The partners at the firm often wander downstairs to look at the companies and bask in the glow of their innovation, but there have been no partnerships or product integrations of significance. This has led to the program being known sarcastically as "The Zoo," where the startups are seen as curious things to look at, but not real partners. This did not win them any credibility from the gossipy startup or venture communities, or from their peers.

The worst thing about innovation theater is that, not only is it a waste of everyone's time and energy, it is almost always counterproductive. It might achieve some marketing wins at first, but this fades quickly. If a corporate accelerator program doesn't actually help the startups or the sponsoring big companies achieve their business goals, what's the point? Startups eventually get the message and stop taking you seriously, and once the word gets out it's difficult to change that perception, even if the program itself improves. It also often leads to high attrition rates on the accelerator team, as they are not able to achieve their own professional goals. (More on this, and how to prevent it, in Chapter 8.) Finally, and most destructive, is a sense that innovation isn't possible here and a reluctance to spend real time and energy on serious new initiatives.

Let us assuage your doubts: successful innovation is absolutely possible at every organization. A corporate accelerator can be part of a lasting, high-impact program that continuously pushes a company toward a better future – or it can be the first act of a bad performance of innovation theater. Corporate accelerators are a tool that big companies can use to foster innovation, but, like all tools, they need to be used properly to be effective. This book outlines the best practices and the pitfalls of corporate accelerators as a key element to enable meaningful and lasting innovation, giving corporate innovation leaders a better chance of success.

WHAT IS REAL INNOVATION?

Innovation is one of the most overused and misunderstood business buzzwords. So what does it actually mean?

There are at least 40 acknowledged definitions of the word *innovation*.[11] Merriam-Webster defines it as "the introduction of something new."[12] When put in a business context, noted management consultant and scholar Peter Drucker suggests that it is "change that creates a new dimension of performance."[13]

Both the concept of "something new" and "performance" are important here, and we think the goal of long-term growth should also be included. Therefore, we define *corporate innovation* as "the introduction of new technologies and business models that drive performance improvements and sustainable growth over the long term."

The word *innovate* comes from the Latin word *novus,* which means "new." It originally had negative connotations, signifying excessive novelty without purpose. For example, George Washington supposedly said on his deathbed, "beware of innovation in politics." However, in 1939 economist Joseph Schumpeter published an important study of business cycles, where he used the word *innovation* for the first time to mean bringing new products to market. This meaning of the word spread slowly in economics and business literature, gaining momentum in the 1990s, and becoming ubiquitous in the 2000s.[14]

How does this apply to big companies? Large corporations tend to be slow moving, process driven, and risk averse. This is by design and makes logical sense in many ways. They optimize for preventing failure and increasing margins incrementally, both of which are meaningful at scale.

But to innovate, you need to move fast, minimize processes, and take risks. Margins are less important than rapidly capturing market share.

The scale at which new initiatives need to succeed also makes innovation challenging for big companies. If a new startup gets to $10 million in revenue in three years, it's considered a massive win. But if a publicly traded Fortune 500 company creates a new business unit and doesn't achieve $150 million in revenue in three years, then it's likely not worth the company's time. It would not be considered a good use of shareholder money to invest its resources on such a small return on investment (ROI), especially if there is a high risk of failure.

Many corporations are forced to simply buy promising innovative companies in their industry – and pay a premium to do so – rather than nurture innovations internally. Big companies get criticized for being unable to innovate, but it's not always fair. They often have no acceptable way to unleash their innovations, compete with startups, and do experimental, creative, and risky projects that could prevent their future disruption.

But mighty oaks grow from small saplings. There is a pathway to achieve blockbuster results from corporate innovation programs, but the company must be willing to do what it takes. Just like many other business disciplines, innovation is a mix of art and science. There is a backbone of hard theory and research; then it's about hiring the right team and empowering them to execute, with a long-term commitment to see it through. Innovation is extremely hard to do well, and although there are some shining examples of success, the majority of big companies are still really bad at it. Most accelerators fail after only two years,[15] and most innovation programs do not live up to their potential.

This is what we hope to demystify with this book, with clear-cut, research-driven suggestions on how to not suck at accelerators. It's a guide to the background theory, the strategic planning, the tactical design, and the measurements of success. By having a framework and lessons learned from others in the market, innovation leaders (we suspect that's you!) can substantially increase their chances of success and create meaningful, lasting innovation for their companies and the world.

IS INNOVATION WORKING?

Many corporations already dedicate time, team, and capital to innovation in some combination of accelerators, corporate venture capital (CVC) programs, venture studios, and more. (These will be defined in more detail in Chapter 2.) According to a 2018 study by BCG, 19% of corporates were using at least one innovation lab or digital lab, 17% were using one or more accelerators, 17% were using one or more CVC units, 13% were using one or more partnership units, and 6% were using one or more incubators.[16]

CORPORATES CONTINUE TO BUILD MORE INNOVATION VEHICLES

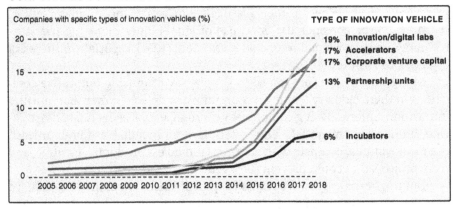

Source: Boston Consulting Group[17]

But are these initiatives working? The data suggests that they are not.

Deloitte's Doblin innovation consulting unit found that 96% of all new innovation initiatives do not make a return on investment.[18] And 95% of all product innovations fail, according to Clayton Christensen at Harvard Business School.[19]

Many innovation teams are launching programs in isolation with limited resources. They are not doing the up-front strategic planning process common with other new initiatives, such as benchmarking themselves against and learning from other programs in the market. As a personal example, when Jules was at IBM and asked to launch a new blockchain accelerator as a one-woman team, IBM already had at least a dozen other accelerators up and running around the world. Despite her reaching out proactively to these teams, there were no shared resources or structured lessons learned, and she ultimately had to build the program from scratch. This is within just one company, not even looking to the wider market. Why are we re-creating the wheel every time with corporate accelerators?

Measuring success is also a major challenge, and Chapter 12 is devoted entirely to key performance indicators (KPIs) and metrics. If you get this right, your program has a better chance of being supported by the parent company in the long term. Metrics are notoriously tricky to get right in corporate innovation, but what gets measured matters.

The innovation industry is still maturing. We have laid the groundwork and done a lot of experimentation, but are still unsophisticated compared to other business initiatives. However, there are some emerging success stories and indicators that we are moving in the right direction. As we enter the next phase of corporate innovation, where things actually work the way they're supposed to, this book should serve as a guide to do it right.

WHY INNOVATE?

The way businesses succeed and survive has changed. Corporations used to develop new products exclusively in their R&D labs, where scientists and researchers spent years, often decades, testing and perfecting new technologies or product offerings that may or may not ever be commercialized.

With the explosion of technology startups starting in the 1990s, a new model of innovation was created by smaller companies, who were more nimble and could take bigger risks. The pace of change became faster, and commercialization happened in real time with no R&D lab involved. New technologies and business models blazed a trail of disruptive destruction to entire industries who could not adapt fast enough. The corporate graveyards are full of former incumbents who were laid to rest by not taking these external innovators seriously.

Netflix was founded in 1997, and, in 2000, then-Blockbuster CEO John Antioco refused a $50 million offer from founder Reed Hastings to buy his company.[20] Netflix then went public in May 2002 and continued to grow. Yet, in 2008, Jim Keyes, the Blockbuster CEO at that time, still proclaimed that it was not "even on the radar screen in terms of competition." In 2010, Blockbuster declared bankruptcy and was delisted from the New York Stock Exchange. The last Blockbuster store on Earth – in Bend, Oregon – is a monument to this failure, and there is even a forthcoming documentary movie called *The Last Blockbuster* that will likely be watched on streaming services such as Netflix.[21] Meanwhile, Netflix was the best-performing stock in the S&P 500 from 2010 to 2019.[22]

Amazon was founded in 1994, and has left a wake of corporate destruction in its path, creating a sense of fear in many corporate executives of "getting Amazoned"[23] if the company decides to enter their space. Amazon devoured unsuspecting industries starting with bookstores, then quickly expanded to music, toys, and sports, causing major problems for companies including Barnes & Noble, Toys "R" Us, and Sports Authority. With Amazon Web Services (AWS), launched in 2006, it created the now market-leading cloud computing service and retains a nearly 50% market share,[24] threatening (though not destroying) incumbents including Microsoft and IBM.

Even as one of the largest companies in the world, achieving more than a trillion-dollar market cap in 2018, Amazon continues to innovate. With the acquisition of Whole Foods in 2017, it expanded its threat to the grocery industry, and with the 2019 acquisition of PillPack[25] it will compete with brick-and-mortar pharmacies. In it's 2018 earnings report,[26] Amazon quietly announced that it's Amazon Logistics business is competing with other shipping services such as UPS and FedEx. Immediately after this news, FedEx's senior vice president of integrated marketing, Patrick Fitzgerald, still said he's not worried: "We honestly don't see a world where Amazon would be a competitor to FedEx; there is no sensible way to compare them."[27] Amazon is even testing grab-and-go technology – where consumers simply take products in a physical retail store and walk out – with the express purpose of selling this as a service to brick and mortar retailers. After conquering digital, they're coming for physical retail. These would-be competitors still say they are not worried.

Companies that used to be mainstays of the corporate world have shrunk or disappeared, while a new breed of technology-native companies have emerged rapidly, seemingly out of nowhere, to displace the largest corporations in the world. The stakes couldn't be higher.

In fact, the average lifespan of companies on the S&P 500 Index has plummeted. In 1958 the average tenure of companies on the list was 61 years. By 2011 it had shrunk to 18 years, and is forecast to be only 12 years by 2027, according to data from consulting firms McKinsey[28] and Innosight.[29] In 2018, 23 companies were replaced, making it the fourth year in a row that more than 20 companies have dropped out of this index (28 in 2015 and 2016, and 26 in 2017). At the current churn rate, only about half of the current list of 500 companies on the S&P 500 will be there in 10 years.

AVERAGE COMPANY LIFESPAN ON S&P 500 INDEX (IN YEARS)

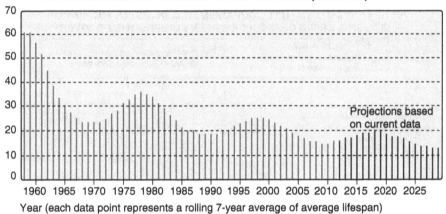

Year (each data point represents a rolling 7-year average of average lifespan)

Source: INNOSIGHT[30]

This rapidly changing market landscape is a barometer for a global trend that is not going away. Previously, a company at the top of their game had to do very little to stay there. Now, there are constantly disruptors who can move faster and take more risks to topple them and take their place. In order to remain competitive, companies can not afford to miss the opportunities presented by technological and market shifts. Big companies move slowly, but shifts in market adoption can happen swiftly. A company's leadership position, and maybe their company as a whole, will be gone before they have time to respond.

This is especially true in a time of crisis. At the time we wrote this book, the entire world was paused from the COVID-19 pandemic. Many businesses won't survive; many more will have a long path to recovery and will never be the same. This is a time to continue, and even push harder, on innovation investments. The COVID-19 crisis has mostly accelerated the technological changes and business trends that make innovation so important.

In past crises, companies that invested in innovation delivered superior growth and performance after the crises ended, compared to ones that were either not innovating to begin with or paused their innovation initiatives until there was more clarity. According to data from McKinsey,[31] organizations that maintained their innovation focus through the 2009 financial crisis, for example, emerged stronger, outperforming the market average by more than 30% and continuing to deliver accelerated growth over the subsequent three to five years.

HISTORY SUGGESTS THAT COMPANIES THAT INVEST IN INNOVATION THROUGH A CRISIS OUTPERFORM PEERS DURING THE RECOVERY

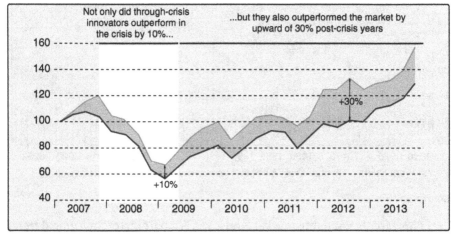

Source: McKinsey[32]

We will only know the long-term effects of the COVID crisis after many years. But one thing we do know is that businesses certainly cannot go back to how they were operating before. The global pandemic made it exceedingly clear that technology – in the form of digital transformation, enabling remote workforces, and increased automation – is needed in all businesses. There is no going back, and the pace of this change in the way of doing business is only increasing. The question is, can your company continue to innovate and keep up with these changes?

HOW DO CORPORATE ACCELERATORS FIT IN?

For corporations used to focusing on fine-tuning their massive operations and squeezing out efficiencies, it's neither possible nor practical to simply throw out what's working and embrace every shiny new object of innovation. Leadership can almost always see when a tide is turning in their industry, but often does not have the tools, processes, or talent to steer the ship in that direction without risking the core businesses. How can they bridge this gap?

The answer often lies with the one of the most promising, yet misunderstood tools of corporate innovation: the accelerator program.

Most executives understand that they can't possibly have all of the smartest people in the world at their own organization, and that the next truly disruptive idea is almost certain to come from outside their company. Accelerators provide the "innovation interface" and allow big companies to connect with and evaluate outside innovations coming from the startup world without having to change their entire organization immediately.

There are many types of innovation programs that bridge the external world of startups to the internal world of corporates operating at global scale. But the corporate accelerator remains a constant and is often one of the first forays into a more diversified corporate innovation program. However, what works in the startup world, with independent accelerators operating with a financially driven venture capitalist mindset, usually does not work in the corporate world. This is the first mistake made by corporate accelerator programs.

Many corporations have mimicked the models from independent accelerators, such as the popular Techstars and Y Combinator programs, by creating their own internal accelerators. Called "corporate accelerators," these programs are popular in large for-profit companies, many of which are publicly traded and need to be seen as innovative in the eyes of their shareholders. They provide some combination of office space, training, mentorship, product development, investment, and partnership paths for startups.

Independent accelerator programs focus on achieving financial returns through ownership in the participating startups. They make money when those shares in the company become liquid via an acquisition or initial public offering (IPO), and are motivated to help the startups succeed so they get a bigger financial outcome.

Corporate accelerators often do not have such clear-cut goals. The complex machinery of large corporations can pull these programs in many different directions, trying to please multiple stakeholders while satisfying none. Generally the goals are some version of market intelligence to prevent their own disruption and increased revenue for themselves. In the worst-case scenario, they only use the programs to boost their own PR agendas and to seem innovative (remember innovation theater?).

This is not necessarily a bad thing. In fact, self-preservation and profit are a fiduciary responsibility of public companies. Sure, some people within those companies are interested in helping startups for personal reasons, but big companies are not philanthropies and the potential financial reward from equity alone is likely not a big enough incentive.

As long as startups understand this, there are a lot of good things that can come of it. But never forget that the reason a corporation will launch an accelerator program is to benefit that corporation in some way. Unlike independent accelerator programs, who win big if the participating startups win big, corporate accelerators may not have the best interest of the startups as their main priority.

Despite this, the trend has caught on, and corporate accelerators have invested hundreds of millions of dollars in tens of thousands of startups.[33] However, we know that these programs tend to be short-lived, with 60% of accelerator programs failing after just two years.[34] Designing a corporate accelerator with the template that works for independent accelerators – where ROI is the focus and 5- to 10-year horizons can be the norm – instead of meeting uniquely corporate goals, can be a recipe for failure.

60% OF CORPORATE ACCELERATORS FAIL AFTER 2 YEARS

Corporate Accelerators Mortality Rate

This cohort just 2 years later

43

2016

1 —

26 Dead (60%)

Less activity (2%)

10 Same activity (23%)

6 More activity (14%)

Source: CBInsights[35]

It's like an innovation "cargo cult." Cargo cults are a metaphor for when we imitate behaviors without understanding how they work in the hope of achieving the same results.[36] They arose in the South Pacific as native islanders sought to mimic the behaviors and technologically-superior physical structures that brought rich cargoes and supplies to the soldiers stationed there during World War II. The GIs in the New Hebrides (now known as Vanuatu), part of the Melanesian islands off the northeast coast of Australia, found the natives re-creating their foreign planes, radios, roads, and landing strips from materials such as wood, straw, and sand. They practiced rituals and built these artifacts in the hopes that their wooden structures would rain down the same gifts of food and guns that they saw coming from the magic ships and planes sent by "Rusefel" (Roosevelt), the friendly king of America.[37]

Obviously the planes made from wood and straw did not yield bounties of food and supplies to the South Pacific islanders. But are the behaviors of corporate innovation executives mimicking the success of Y Combinator and others really so different? Just as islanders building wooden planes didn't result in their ability to fly, neither will simply copying nimble venture accelerators result in successful corporate innovation.

There are many challenges to corporate innovation, but there are also an impressive number of tools available for companies looking to be more innovative. In particular, partnering with startups in a structured program such as an accelerator helps companies stay up to date on transformational technologies that will drive the evolution and disruption of their industry. Corporate accelerators are one important piece of the complex innovation puzzle.

GOALS FOR THIS BOOK

In the following chapters, we will present a portfolio approach to corporate innovation and how accelerators fit into this. We'll share our thesis on corporate innovation and a framework for success. Then we will give you three models of accelerator programs, based on your desired outcome, which you can use and adapt to your own organization. Finally, we will go through the various tactical components of an accelerator program and share case studies of what works and what doesn't work.

Corporate accelerators are powerful tools that, when wielded correctly, can jumpstart your corporate innovation program, drive cultural change, open new revenue channels, and transform your business. But getting corporate accelerators right for any given organization can be extremely tricky, as evidenced by the sheer number of failures. To tackle this challenge, we spoke with dozens of leaders from across the world's top accelerators and innovation programs to identify and highlight best practices that you can use to inspire the success of your own program.

Consider this publication your personal handbook outlining the accelerator rules of the road, identifying meaningful best practices and tools to make your corporate accelerator program a success.

CHAPTER 2

A CRASH COURSE ON INNOVATION THEORY

What [Facebook] worries about the most is the lack of change, the lack of innovation, becoming the innovator's dilemma company that gets big and stops moving and stops staying ahead.

SHERYL SANDBERG
CHIEF OPERATING OFFICER, FACEBOOK

Source: Business Insider[1]

Accelerator programs should be one part of a thoughtful, holistic, and clearly articulated innovation strategy for your company. However, there is no need to start from scratch; there are decades worth of research and theories on the topic of corporate innovation that form the backbone of what most companies practice today.

We will refer to many of the classic innovation theories throughout the book, and, although some are still useful, many need a refresh. It's still important to know them, either to find one that resonates with your organization or to know why and how to deviate. As the Dali Lama stated, you have to "know the rules well so you can break them effectively."[2]

For those already familiar with innovation theory, feel free to skim or skip past this section. For anyone working in the innovation space, or wanting to dig deeper, it's a great idea to read the original texts. Until then, here's a blindingly fast crash course on the key theories that form the basis of corporate innovation today.

THE INNOVATOR'S DILEMMA

You can't talk about corporate innovation without someone mentioning "The Innovator's Dilemma." Prolific management theorist Clayton Christensen published the classic business book *The Innovator's Dilemma* in 1997 to explain the power of technological disruption. He was particularly interested in why market leaders often fail, arguing that often it isn't because executives made bad decisions, but because they made the type of good decisions that had allowed their companies to be successful for decades. This type of decision-making, however, does not work in the context of technological disruption.

The innovator's dilemma is the realization that "doing the right thing is the wrong thing" in the face of disruptive innovation.

Christensen distinguishes between two kinds of technological innovation. The first is sustaining technology, which enhances the performance of existing technologies, mostly through extended functionality or increased capacity. This is where the incumbents excel. They have built up the processes and resources to enable incremental improvements at scale, and they have the leadership style and talent needed to succeed here.

The second is disruptive technology, which radically changes a whole industry or creates an entirely new industry that didn't exist before. This is where incumbents struggle, because disruptive technology requires a completely different mental model, risk tolerance, margins, and talent. This is where most startups excel.

DISRUPTIVE VS. SUSTAINING TECHNOLOGIES

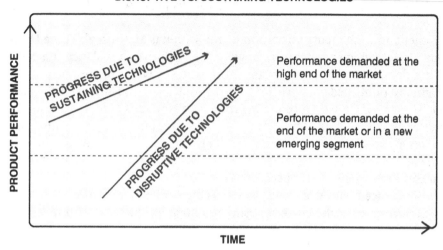

Source: HBS; MIT[3]

Christensen suggests that big companies should accept the limitations of their own processes and culture, because it's nearly impossible to succeed in developing both sustaining and disruptive technologies with the same strategy and talent pool. The solution he proposes is to create a separate entity or subsidiary that is allowed to operate outside the bounds of traditional requirements. This means different profit margins and new processes, and a team who understands how to manage for disruptive innovation.

Mistaking sustaining technology for disruptive technology is also a risk. At first, AT&T viewed mobile telephony as an extension of their existing technology, not a new market in its own right. Their famous R&D group Bell Labs had the smartest telecom people on the planet developing this technology, yet AT&T managed the mobile business the same way as their landline business. In the 1980s they worked with expert consultants to estimate that there would be 900,000 mobile subscribers by the turn of the century. In 1999, that's exactly how many subscribers were added – every three days.[4] AT&T's misassessment of the market opportunity allowed new players to quickly take market share and experiment with new business models for this highly disruptive technology. A decade after the incorrect decision to view mobile as a sustaining technology, AT&T had to acquire McCaw Cellular for $12.6 billion to recapture market share because they missed the opportunity to be an early leader.[5]

McKINSEY'S THREE HORIZONS OF INNOVATION

Another enduring theory on corporate innovation is McKinsey's Three Horizons Model, which creates a framework for executives to balance the competing demands of improving current businesses with creating new ones. Originally published in April 1999, three McKinsey consultants published *The Alchemy of Growth*[6] introducing the Three Horizons Model as a result of their work with clients. It provides a taxonomy for bucketing innovation initiatives in three categories or horizons. It also argues that higher risk innovation happens over the longer term and requires different management talent, strategy, tools, goals, and expectations.[7]

When faced with declining growth as big companies mature, maintaining performance in the current businesses must be balanced with investing in new growth opportunities that will pay off in the long term. Companies cannot focus on one or the other; they must do both.

THE THREE HORIZONS OF INNOVATION

Source: Skylance[8]

Horizon 1: Today

The first horizon, H1, is all about your core businesses right now. These are typically in mature areas that generate the majority of your profits and cash flow today. These are the cash cows, and "if it ain't broke, don't fix it."

Just figure out how to increase the profit from it! The timescale is short term, usually manifesting as new features or improvements that can be delivered in 3–12 months. An example is upgrading an existing product to a new version, or squeezing a few basis points out of costs. Existing corporate teams have the skills, knowledge, and resources to execute well here. This is unlikely to be an area appropriate for corporate accelerators or startup partnerships.

Horizon 2: Tomorrow

The second horizon, H2, focuses on riskier emerging technologies that are adjacent to your current business and can dramatically accelerate growth. This can be an extension of the company's existing business model and core capabilities to new customers, markets, or functionalities. The timescale is medium term, and product launches can typically be deployed in 24–36 months. Your existing team has some ability to execute here, but multidisciplinary teams from both inside and outside the organization can be extremely valuable. This is the ideal focus area for most corporate accelerators, because the combination of your existing talent, knowledge, and expertise paired with that of an aligned startup can expedite H2 success.

Horizon 3: Future

The third horizon, H3, focuses on disruptive innovation where new products and business models are created under conditions of extreme uncertainty and have the ability to radically transform your business. These are market creators, moonshots, and potential unicorn businesses that will be the seeds of your company's future. The focus is on disruptive opportunities, though this can often cannibalize existing businesses. Working on H3 projects will likely threaten or upset someone at your company who will be displaced if it is successful. This is a good thing! H3 time frames are typically 36–72 months out, though the time horizons will continue to compress as the pace of disruptive innovation becomes faster. This is a good area for accelerators, as long as the timeline expectations align. Accelerators here can be useful to gather market intelligence and keep your corporate finger on the pulse of future innovation, but are unlikely to result in partnerships (beyond research) or profits anytime soon.

The 70/20/10 Rule

The rule of thumb for a distribution of time and resources across the three horizons follows the 70/20/10 rule. That is, 70% of your time and resources on H1, 20% on H2, and 10% on H3. Different companies will adjust based on their desired innovation goals and resources, but this rarely means more than a 5% change one way or the other in each horizon.

Don't be surprised if your company discovers that resources, capabilities, and skills are way out of balance from the 70/20/10 rule. Most big companies focus primarily on H1, so innovation teams must fight to reallocate budgets and hire or partner to address H2 and H3. Also note that research and development (R&D) efforts are not sufficient for H3 since they usually do not focus on commercialization, which is critical for H3 efforts to achieve the intended revenue-generating opportunities of the future. Indeed, it is the very definition of H3 as being outside of the company's existing businesses that often makes these opportunities difficult to spot.

Comparing the Three Horizons

To remain competitive in the long run, a company should allocate innovation dollars and resources across all three horizons and manage each in tandem. Part of this requires understanding the very different success metrics, talent, and capability requirements for each horizon.

COMPARING THE THREE HORIZONS

	HORIZON 1	HORIZON 2	HORIZON 3
METRICS	Return on invested capital (ROIC)	Net present value (NPV)	Option value
PEOPLE	Business maintainers	Business builders	Champions and visionaries
CAPABILITIES	Fully assembled capability platform	Capabilities being acquired or developed	Capability requirements may be unclear

(PROFIT on vertical axis; TIME (YEARS) on horizontal axis)

TIME (YEARS)

Source: McKinsey[9]

Horizon 1 is measured by return on investment (ROI) and requires talent that excels in maintaining and optimizing current businesses, with a low degree of uncertainty and a resulting product with refined, complete capabilities. Your company has these people and they know exactly what to do.

Horizon 2 is measured by net present value (NPV) and requires talent that excels at building businesses, focusing on growth and operating with some level of uncertainty and comfort with a good but not perfect product. Your company may have some talent like this, and they need to be shielded from the same expectations required for running an H1 business. External entrepreneurial talent and partners can also be useful here.

Horizon 3 is measured by options value and requires talent who can be champions and visionaries, focusing on long-term opportunities, operating with high uncertainty and risk, and having almost no ability to produce a finished product in the near term. Your company is unlikely to have these people and it is your challenge to find them and motivate them properly.

Though many things have changed in the 20-plus years since the original Three Horizons Model was created, it is still a useful exercise that we encourage all innovation executives to complete. The framework continues to be helpful for balancing management priorities, especially in uncertain times.

LEAN STARTUP METHODOLOGY

The Lean Startup is a method for rapidly validating business models and shortening product development cycles. It turned the traditional process of launching new businesses and products on its head, and is now the de facto way of operating in startups and big companies alike. Many early-stage venture accelerator programs use this methodology as a core tenant of their curriculum.

Entrepreneur Steve Blank developed the idea starting in the 1990s, with additional concepts developed from Alex Osterwalder and others. Blank's *Four Steps to the Epiphany* introduced the customer discovery approach that would be the foundation of this new movement. Eric Ries worked with Blank to put this into practice at his startup IMVU, where Blank was an investor, and combined it with lean software development. Ries then popularized the method in his 2011 book *The Lean Startup*.[10]

Prior to this, business and product launches were conceived with detailed business plans, multi-year financial forecasts, and long product development cycles before anything was shared beyond the immediate team. This led to a high degree of failure, both for startups or new product launches within existing companies. After months or sometimes years of work, many new products were launched only to find out that customers did not need or want what they were selling.

The Lean Startup method favors real-time experimentation, early customer feedback, and iterative design to help new ventures reduce the risk of failure by launching products that customers actually want, far more quickly and cheaply than traditional methods. Concepts such as "minimum viable product" (MVP) – the most basic working version of a product that can be tested by customers – "pivot" – a shift in business strategy – and "product market fit"– when a product satisfies a strong market demand – are now standard language in the startup world and even becoming more popular in enterprises.[11]

The Lean Startup methodology consists of three main parts: (1) business model canvas, (2) customer development, and (3) agile.

Business Model Canvas

At the beginning, all new ventures are simply a series of untested hypotheses, or educated guesses. Instead of writing a lengthy business plan, the lean way is to summarize all hypotheses in a one-page template called a Business Model Canvas. This tool defines and documents a business concept, visualizing the important elements in a structured way.

The Business Model Canvas was initially proposed in 2004 by Alexander Osterwalder in his PhD thesis, then popularized for entrepreneurs in his 2010 book *Business Model Generation*.[12] It outlines the nine building blocks of the business model design in a one-page template.

The right side of the template focuses on the customer (external), whereas the left side of the canvas focuses on the business (internal), and the value proposition (a mix of both) in the middle. Together these elements provide a coherent view of the business hypotheses.

BUSINESS MODEL CANVAS

KEY PARTNERS	KEY ACTIVITIES	VALUE PROPOSITIONS	CUSTOMER RELATIONSHIPS	CUSTOMER SEGMENTS
• Who are our key partners? • Who are our key suppliers? • Which key resources are we acquiring from our partners? • Which key activities do partners perform?	• What key activities do our value propositions require? • Our distribution channels? • Customer relationships? • Revenue streams?	• What value do we deliver to the customer? • Which one of our customers' problems are we helping to solve? • What bundles of products and services are we offering to each segment? • Which customer needs are we satisfying? • What is the minimum viable product?	• How do we get, keep, and grow customers? • Which customer relationships have we established? • How are they integrated with the rest of our business model? • How costly are they?	• For whom are we creating value? • Who are our most important customers? • What are the customer archetypes?
	KEY RESOURCES • What key resources do our value propositions require? • Our distribution channels? • Customer relationships? • Revenue streams?		**CHANNELS** • Through which channels do our customer segments want to be reached? • How do other companies reach them now? • Which ones work best? • Which ones are most cost-efficient? • How are we integrating them with customer routines?	

COST STRUCTURE	REVENUE
• What are the most important costs inherent to our business model? • Which key resources are most expensive? • Which key activities are most expensive?	• For what value are our customers really willing to pay? • For what do they currently pay? • What is the revenue model? • What are the pricing tactics?

Source: Harvard Business Review[13]

The Business Model Canvas is popular with entrepreneurs and intrapreneurs because it forces a structured, yet simple, articulation of your hypotheses. It can help to quickly achieve focus and transparency by seeing everything in one place. Print it out or project it on a whiteboard and go to town!

Customer Development

A critical component of lean startup methodology involves early interaction with customers. It is based on Steve Blank's customer development methodology, which he started articulating in the mid-1990s. In *The Four Steps to the Epiphany* (2003),[14] Blank explains that startups are not just smaller versions of large companies and laid out the customer development process in detail.

After articulating the hypotheses, the lean startup focuses on immediately testing them in the market. It promotes getting out of the building to talk to prospective customers, partners, and others for feedback, then using this to refine the product or service by iterating on the MVP in quick development cycles, taking no more than one or two weeks for each discovery and iteration cycle. The emphasis is on nimbleness, speed, and rapid iteration.

CUSTOMER DISCOVERY PROCESS

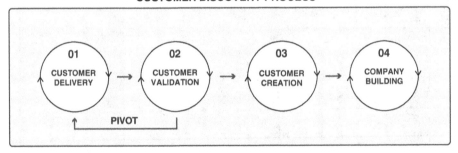

Source: Harvard Business Review[15]

Agile

Agile is a methodology of software development based on the idea of incremental delivery. It is circular and iterative, with loops of development intermixed with engaging customers for feedback.[16] It includes collaboration between self-organizing and cross-functional teams, allowing them to deliver value faster, with a higher quality, and a better response to change.

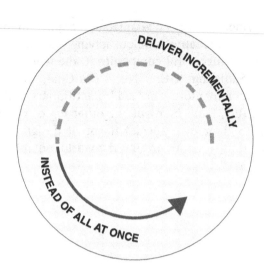

This has mostly replaced the waterfall methodology, which breaks down projects into sequential phases where progress flows downward (like a waterfall), delivering a product all at once near the end.

In 2001, 17 software development professionals created the *Manifesto for Agile Software Development,*[17] which outlines four core values and 12 principles for Agile. Though some of this has evolved since its creation, Agile as a mindset touting rapid, incremental delivery is still a key component of lean product development. It's about short cycles, rapid iteration, failing fast, getting immediate feedback, collaboration, and delivering business value to customers early. Scrum and Kanban are two of the most widely used Agile methodologies.[18] They are a set of engineering best practices intended to allow for rapid delivery of high-quality software, aligning product development with customer needs and company goals.

Agile is now the de facto method of product development in startups, though the newer practice of DevOps is starting to gain traction. In enterprises, it's a slow transition to Agile and many organizations still have not fully converted.

DESIGN THINKING

Design thinking is a user-centric approach to problem solving and innovation, based on the longstanding practice of designers to integrate the needs of people, technology, and business success. It encourages companies to focus on the people they're creating products for, which leads to better products, services, and internal processes. There is no single definition for design thinking, but the concept has been adapted and applied in many ways, with the underlying theme of creative problem solving that focuses on the user.

Some of the most successful companies in the world – Apple, Google, Airbnb, PepsiCo, Samsung, GE, Nike, Coca-Cola, Procter & Gamble, Fidelity, Intuit, and many more – are avid practitioners of design thinking. IBM, McKinsey, IDEO,[19] and many of the other big consulting firms have large practices with their own special flavor of design thinking. Design thinking is taught at universities around the world, notably including Stanford, Harvard, and MIT.

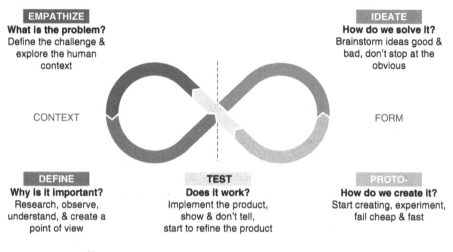

Source: Medium[20]

Design thinking has demonstrated impressive results over previous methods, and there is a lot of data to show this.[21] Organizations that follow design thinking practices see one-third higher revenues and 56% higher returns than those that don't,[22] and have outperformed the S&P 500 by more than 200% over the past 10 years.[23] They also cut initial design costs by 75%,[24] increasing profits by more than $1 million on average for major projects. And 71% of companies say design thinking has improved their working culture, with 69% saying it makes their innovation process more efficient.[25] Design thinking results in more satisfied and loyal customers, and 41% of companies who practice it report greater market share as an advantage of having advanced design practices.[26]

Though design thinking is not new – designers have been using human-centered practices for decades – it allows people who aren't trained as designers to apply creative tools to a specific problem.[27] It combines the human perspective with technological and economic realities.

OPEN INNOVATION

Corporate innovation tools tend to fall into one of two categories: internal innovation or open innovation.

Internal Innovation

Internal innovation is anything done within the walls of your own organization, by your own employees, that does not rely on third parties (e.g., startups). It includes things like R&D, skunkworks, and venture studios. It allows big companies who can afford significant headcount and investment to maintain control over the entire innovation process. This was the default model for most of the twentieth century and one that most big companies understand well.

Internal innovation enables trade secrets and patent protections – the twentieth century's intellectual property (IP) assets that allow big companies to exclusively profit from their expensive and time-consuming research processes. For example, IBM, a traditional technology giant, has issued several thousand more patents each year than any other company in the world for the past 26 years running.[28] The sheer number of patents is not just a source of corporate and national pride, but was once considered a leading indicator of future commercial success, making the assumption that these patents would lead to commercially viable products.

2019 TOP 10 US PATENT ASSIGNEES

COMPANY	NO. OF PATENTS (2019)	COUNTRY
IBM	9,262	United States
Samsung Electronics Co Ltd.	6,469	South Korea
Canon, Inc.	3,548	Japan
Microsoft	3,081	United States
Intel	3,020	United States
LG Electronics	2,805	South Korea
Apple	2,490	United States
Ford	2,468	United States
Amazon	2,427	United States
Huawei Technologies	2,418	China

Source: IFI; Nasdaq[29]

This hasn't necessarily come to fruition. Internal innovation is slow and is not always suited to the more rapid pace of technological change in the twenty-first century. There is also debate about the true value of patents and whether they achieve the promised lucrative commercial products to justify the investment, as well as creating potentially negative consequences such as stifling innovation, costly patent litigation, and the rise of patent trolls.

Open Innovation

Open innovation, on the other hand, assumes that not all innovative ideas come from within your own organization. It encourages looking outward to partner with smaller, more nimble companies on innovation to co-develop technologies, learn from each other, and share the risks and rewards. Big companies respond to external threats from more nimble competitors by partnering with them, which was a radical shift from prior behavior and is still a challenge for many corporate cultures.

Open innovation is slowly replacing or augmenting internal R&D budgets, because it reduces risk and increases the speed and number of innovation projects that big companies can bring to market. It can also include spinouts of things developed internally, which may thrive and scale better outside the confines of a large company. Open innovation creates a porous corporate border, with innovation flowing in and out of the organization.

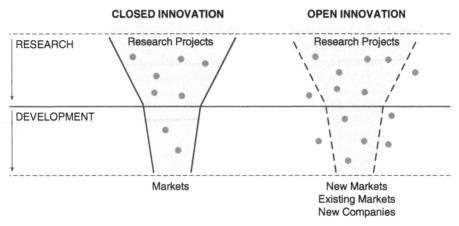

Source: Open Innovation: The New Imperative for Creating and Profiting from Technology[30]

Use of the term *open innovation* in this context was popularized by Henry Chesbrough, professor at the University of California Berkeley - Haas Business School. He defines open innovation as "the use of purposive inflows and outflows of knowledge to accelerate internal innovation, and expand the markets for external use of innovation, respectively."[31] His first book on the topic, *Open Innovation: The New Imperative for Creating and Profiting from Technology*, was published in 2003, and he has written many others since then.

Open innovation includes things like external partnerships with startups, corporate accelerators, corporate venture capital (CVC), and mergers and acquisitions (M&A). It often conflicts with the existing risk tolerance, desire for control, and cultural norms of most big companies. It also recognizes that innovation in areas such as process, software, algorithms, and business models often doesn't fit the mold of traditional patent-protectable scientific research. Or that even if you can protect the IP, you wouldn't want to because it impedes the market adoption and commercial success of that technology.

The epitome of open innovation is the open source movement, where software engineers from around the world contribute to a common code base. The collective efforts of so many diverse developers makes adding features and squashing bugs faster with higher quality results than would be possible in a single organization. Even though the code is open sourced, there are still commercially viable models to profit from the developments, including enterprise grade applications and consulting to implement and integrate open source code. Even the biggest, most traditional companies are adopting open source now. For example, in 2019 our R&D stalwart IBM acquired open source leader RedHat for $34 billion.[32]

Open innovation also has a profound effect on the culture and talent dynamics within a company. At first, many open innovation initiatives were led by R&D or "insider" innovation professionals. But they often do not have the skill set required for these projects and it led to a high failure rate, so now a successful open innovation program is usually some combination of internal and external talent. Open innovation programs attract and retain a more entrepreneurial, nimble, and market-driven set of managers and leaders inside your company,[33] which ultimately benefits your business in the long term.

THE CORPORATE INNOVATION TOOLBOX

There are several manifestations of these innovation theories that make up the tools in your corporate innovation toolbox. These are the vehicles for delivery of your innovation goals, and each one has different risks and rewards.

Internal Innovation

The following are programs that generally fall under internal innovation, or innovations done within the walls of your company.

R&D

Research and development (R&D) creates and tests new technologies in a research lab environment where engineers, scientists, and/or industrial designers attack scientific and technical problems, which may or may not lead to commercialization.[34] R&D tends to be slow, producing new products or services after several years or decades of research, and is not intended to yield short-term profit. Some of the greatest inventions of our time have been developed in R&D labs: Xerox's famous Palo Alto Research Center (PARC) invented Ethernet and the Graphical User Interface (first commercialized by Apple, not Xerox); Google X focuses on the biggest global problems or "moonshots" such as self-driving cars and insulin-detecting contact lenses; HP Labs created 3D printing and natural language detection; IBM Research created the floppy disk, the ATM, the smartphone, and the personal computer.

Intrapreneurship

This allows full-time employees to start and launch new products and services from within the company, with the hope of generating disruptive technologies from within through the people who know their business best: employees. The classic example is Google's "20% time" where they let employees commit 20% of their paid work time to personal projects. This resulted in many successful products, including Gmail, AdSense, and Google News. Google's intrapreneurship initiative was actually influenced by a program from the manufacturing company 3M, launched in 1948, which allowed employees to dedicate 15% of their paid hours to a project of personal interest.[35] Often it is not so formal, and intrepid employees simply propose new projects and run with them on an ad hoc basis. Though there are downsides to fostering entrepreneurship, such as a potential decrease in overall productivity, it can provide an outlet for entrepreneurial employees to drive change from the bottom up.

Skunkworks

An experimental laboratory or department of a company that develops new products or services, often in secret and with a high degree of autonomy, is commonly called skunkworks. The term was coined by Lockheed Martin,[36] which created an off-limits R&D team at their Burbank, California, facility to develop new jet fighters and spy planes. Skunkworks build small, empowered teams with streamlined processes and a culture that enables experimentation. This allows them to do things that haven't been done before and would be impossible in the normal corporate setting.[37] There is a separate management structure and budget, and it is often not meant to be permanent, so it will disband or reintegrate once the product or service is launched.

Venture Studios

Venture studios, sometimes called venture labs, are internal accelerators where a big company creates startups within its own walls. They use existing employees as the team, while getting strategic direction and capital from the parent company. Sometimes external entrepreneurs in residence (EIRs) are involved to supplement internal talent. If these internal startups are successful, they can be integrated into the parent company as a new business unit (BU) or part of an existing one, or be spun out of the company to an independent entity with the corporation retaining some minority equity ownership (which would then be part of an open innovation strategy). Venture studios allow a safe space for entrepreneurial employees who are intimately familiar with your business to rapidly launch new things and have a cushion for failure. For example, Fidelity Labs[38] has launched several commercially successful internal products, including a student debt reduction tool and a Medicare selection tool.

Open Innovation

When innovation efforts look outside the walls of the company for new ideas, they often borrow from or integrate with the startup world. Partly about innovation, partly about public relations and recruiting talent, these programs allow corporations to experiment faster, and at a higher volume than internal programs. The most common open innovation tools are:

Hackathons

A "sprint" event where developers, designers, project managers, and other entrepreneurial talent collaborate on product development in a short period of time. The teams come together quickly, usually over a weekend or a couple of days, to explore an idea and build a MVP, with prizes for the winner(s) at the end. Sometimes these are held on college campuses with the goal of helping company recruiters source better talent.

Pitch Competitions

These are one-time events hosted by the corporation where startups pitch their businesses to win exposure and possibly some sort of financial reward (e.g., a $10,000 cash prize). Often they are just marketing exercises and don't lead to real results for the corporation in terms of partnerships or product integrations. However, they can provide useful market intelligence and deal flow for an accelerator or investment pipeline, as well as positive employee engagement and branding.

EIR Program

Entrepreneur in residence (EIR) programs bring in seasoned entrepreneurs to help on internal corporate projects, including projects launched through a venture studio. This helps to augment your existing talent with experienced entrepreneurial leaders who don't necessarily want to be your full time employees.

Accelerator

Accelerators are time-bound programs for startups to rapidly iterate on a problem or partnership that is important for the corporate parent. This book is about corporate accelerators, and we will be diving deep into this topic throughout the book. When accelerators work well, they allow new ideas and products to be tested and adopted for a competitive advantage, without significant short-term disruption to the main lines of business or corporate culture.

Incubator

Sometimes used interchangeably with accelerators, incubators are a different model for partnering with startups that are less time-bound or programmatic (though they can also include speakers and mentors), and usually center on offering a physical space for startups to work. Incubators can be as simple as office space or mentorship programs, but can also be customized for more individual attention to each startup.

Corporate Venture Capital (CVC)

This is a program to make direct financial investments into startups in return for minority equity ownership. CVC must balance financial objectives with strategic goals, which is a complex challenge that makes this job incredibly difficult to do well. As a result, CVC doesn't have the best reputation and can be seen as "dumb money" led by unsophisticated corporate managers, rather than investment professionals. Due to the upside-limiting compensation of most CVC programs, it also has high attrition rates for the most talented team members as they move to traditional VC firms where they can capture carried interest compensation. However, this is starting to change, with well-respected CVC groups such as GV (formerly Google Ventures), Salesforce Ventures, Intel Capital, and a few others who have proven their mettle as talented investors. CVC works best when it offers startups a competitive advantage – such as market credibility, customer distribution channels, or product integration – to give them an "unfair" advantage in the market. CVC is a major part of the investment landscape, accounting for 23% of all VC dollars in 2019.[39]

Startup Partnerships Unit

There are many flavors of partnerships between big companies and start-ups, and these can happen within a structured innovation program like an accelerator or on a more ad hoc basis. Many companies have streamlined processes for onboarding startups as vendors or partners to avoid lengthy pro-curement processes, lightweight and templated legal agreements, and stan-dardized models for initial partnerships that work. This can include things like building custom products or integrations together, such as proof of con-cepts (POCs) or MVPs, or simply sales-focused, go-to-market partnerships.

Corporate M&A

A big company can also buy smaller companies outright rather than build similar innovations themselves. Mergers and acquisitions not only add prod-ucts or services to the purchasing company's repertoire, but also add entre-preneurial teams to their talent pool. An acquisition can even occur just for this talent, called an "acqui-hire." Though it can have long-term positive impacts on culture in the best of circumstances, too often the startup culture of the acquired company clashes with the big company culture of the new parent and there can be a rapid exodus of this talent. M&A works well when products fill a technical gap, enable rapid expansion (e.g., geographic), or can easily drop into existing sales channels.

USING ALL THE TOOLS: A PORTFOLIO APPROACH

The role of an innovation leader is to bring all of this together in a way that works for your particular company. Usually it involves a portfolio of the innovation initiatives outlined here. Innovation is risky and often doesn't work, but a small number of big wins can produce outsized returns overall. It requires taking risks – if you are not failing at some of your innovation initiatives, you're not taking big enough risks. This approach is very different from most corporate initiatives, where failure is not an option, and a cultural aversion to risk can get in the way of success in corporate innovation investments.

The only certainty in investing, especially in high-risk areas, is that it is impossible to consistently predict winners and losers. So, just like a financial investor, the best way to reduce risk is to diversify your portfolio. There are many possible tools in the corporate innovation toolbox, and often big companies will invest heavily in one activity, such as an accelerator. If it doesn't work in the short term, the company will shut the program down and declare that "innovation doesn't work here" or resign to only superficial marketing results. This puts enormous pressure on very–high risk activities to succeed, when they should be failing regularly. Rather than focusing on the ROI of any one initiative, a portfolio approach allows for experimentation and failure, so that when some initiatives succeed, the overall investment in your innovation portfolio yields a return and you can feel comfortable taking bigger risks.

"Don't just say I want an accelerator," says Jenny Fielding, managing director of Techstars–New York City and The Fund. "Say I want to infuse a culture of innovation at our organization and we're going to do a few different things. We're going to try an accelerator, we're going to start a small venture fund, we're going to do some intrapreneurship, or spin out some companies. Really just challenge yourself to try a few different types of programs."

What works at your particular company may surprise you, and having a mindset open to experimentation is key. "There is no blueprint," says Fielding. "Every company is going to react in a slightly different way, and you've got to figure out what works for your company. You may find that an accelerator is actually not the right thing, but wow, internal entrepreneurship is blossoming." You can do as much research as you want at the beginning, but you're not going to know what works at your organization until you try.

Innovation executives should look at accelerators as one part of the innovation portfolio. Use the innovation theories discussed in this chapter to articulate an innovation strategy aligned with your company's risk tolerance and resources. Then build a portfolio of innovation initiatives to achieve your goals, making sure to secure an adequate budget and the right team to execute successfully. Easy, right? Don't worry, we'll get into the nitty-gritty of how to do this for your corporate accelerator throughout the remainder of this book.

Just like any investment portfolio, this is not a stagnant exercise. It's important to constantly reevaluate and readjust. If the portfolio is not performing as expected, you can either adapt your strategy or manage timeline expectations. At a minimum, it is an opportunity to learn what works and what does not.

Remember that innovation initiatives often take several years to yield results, so beware of passing judgment on success or failure too early. It can take a few painful failures to get it right. It's also an unfortunate truth that the failures usually reveal themselves faster than the successes, which VCs call the J-Curve.

THE VENTURE CAPITAL J-CURVE

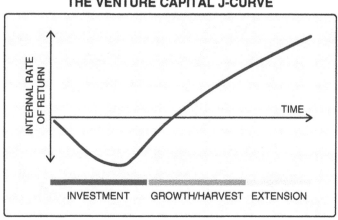

Source: Crunchbase[40]

Try to get buy-in for a longer-term commitment and give your team three to five years to refine the strategy, build a brand and credibility, and go through the ups and downs of managing an innovation portfolio. Then it can take another five-plus years to achieve the big results. Innovation takes time!

The portfolio approach is an easy way to think about investing in innovation; It's simply applying an existing financial investment portfolio methodology to corporate innovation. Investing in an innovation portfolio allows big companies to adapt to an evolving market and take risks in a manageable way. Accelerators have a better chance of succeeding in the context of a thoughtful and diversified innovation portfolio.

CHAPTER 3

A COMPLEX MACHINE
TO A SIMPLE MACHINE

In theory, theory and practice are the same.
In practice, they are not.

ALBERT EINSTEIN

Innovation theories and tools are great but mean nothing if you can't actually put them into practice. As Ava Lopez knows well from her days as a venture capitalist, execution is all that matters. Although it's always difficult to blaze a trail and do something new, for startups the limitations are around resources – mostly time and money. This is certainly challenging, but startups are nimble and can figure out how to operate within these constraints. In fact, limited resources are often what make startups think in innovative ways and beat competitors who have bigger budgets and larger teams.

Corporations are much more complex and are usually limited by factors such as culture, process, bureaucracy, talent, and competing internal priorities. FabCo is no exception. But the ability to implement innovation initiatives, such as a simple accelerator program, can seem achievable without too much friction. It's just a three-month program, right? Any executive with project management experience and a little knowledge about tech startups should be able to put this together with their eyes closed, right?

Not quite. The accelerator program itself is one thing, achieving the desired results is another. And why do one without the other? If your goal for an accelerator, for example, is partnership, there are a lot of institutionalized processes, risk-averse people, and misaligned incentives that can stand in the way of success. These are big, systemic issues and there's a lot that can go sideways.

Expectations around speed and process are common thorns. Startups have an urgency driven by their dwindling resources – time and money – and are incentivized to "move fast and break things." Corporations, on the other hand, are able to continue kicking the can down the road on innovation projects indefinitely. They are hesitant to launch anything less than a finished, polished product and have many gates in place to prevent going to market recklessly. The bigger the company, the more risk-averse and spider-webby the organization, and the bigger a challenge it is to partner with startups.

The purpose of this book is to help clarify the path to achieving results for both parties, or (sometimes just as important) when not to do things that are being set up to fail without the right structure and support.

Ava has read all of the innovation theory books and decides that the first step is to look inward and see where FabCo may have a competitive advantage when working with startups. She knows that, with a small team and limited budget, there's no way she can build an entire infrastructure of innovation on her own. To see if it's worth going down this accelerator path at all, Ava starts by reviewing the assets that FabCo already has at its fingertips. She's looking for anything within the existing organization that she may be able to leverage to provide real value to startups in an accelerator program.

LEAN STARTUP AT FAT ENTERPRISES

Innovation theories are just theories; the hard part is doing the work to implement them. This is particularly true within complicated corporate machines. Most innovation techniques – such as the lean startup methodology – were designed to create fast-growing tech startups from scratch. Applying these theories means trying to replicate the speed and tactics of a startup while having the scale, complexity, and existing baggage of a large enterprise.

Many hallmarks of innovation techniques – including rapid experimentation, iteration, user-centric design, and failing fast – don't come naturally to most big companies. Large enterprises have successful product lines and profits to protect and grow, and a small percentage increase in a major revenue source can often seem much more important than a small (at first) but promising new business. Entrenched processes and incentives that mainly reward short-term behavior make this even harder.

Many big company executives are aware of the popular innovation theories and practice some of them to a degree. But it is harder to achieve results when you have years, or decades, of institutional "fat" preventing the company from running lean and agile. This challenge requires entirely new organizational structures and employee skills that most companies simply do not have and are unwilling or unable to change. It takes time, resources, and long-term commitment.

Even well-known innovators eventually become complex corporate machines with an aversion to risk and increased processes over time, often for good reason. For example, as they grew, Facebook changed their iconic startup motto of "move fast and break things" to "move fast with stable infrastructure" and eventually just to "move fast" as they became a more complex organization and added internal controls over time. In 2017, CEO Mark Zuckerberg acknowledged that "we've come far from the cowboy days when Facebook was a small company . . . we're [still] like a startup with the resources of a big company, but we can't tolerate careless interns breaking the site and losing us millions of dollars a minute . . . [so] please for the love of god don't break anything."[1]

He refers to an incident where a Facebook intern was microdosing LSD at work and had a bad trip, causing an hours-long outage to one of the most popular websites in the world. The intern apparently took 10 times the suggested dose of acid and "began screaming about melting skulls and A/B testing before proceeding to drop all tables from a critical production database. He was quickly restrained by the on-call engineer from his team, though not before bringing down the main Facebook site." While the company said that no user data was lost, Facebook quickly put in additional process and controls to prevent its junior engineers from accessing important services that could single-handedly crash the site.[2] While controls such as these are obviously bred out of necessity, they can also stifle the ability to innovate and may constrain the culture needed to do so.

CORPORATIONS ARE COMPLEX MACHINES

Big, multinational companies are complex machines. There are many moving pieces, processes, and risk-prevention mechanisms put in place to make them work effectively over time and at scale. These serve a purpose: they create consistency at scale and reduce risk.

But while these processes help to create a well-oiled machine for core businesses, these are exactly the things that unintentionally serve as blockers to innovation and change. Innovation in some ways is completely at odds with the existing businesses. It requires trying new things, most of which are likely to fail, and some of which may actively cannibalize existing businesses or distract stakeholders from the successful systems.

When Jules was running two accelerators and a venture initiative at IBM, an acronym for International Business Machines, her partner would jokingly call it "Innovation Blocking Machine" when she would vent her frustration that every innovation initiative or startup partnership she tried to push through (which was her job) would be slowed or stopped by well-intentioned processes or risk-averse management who were not properly equipped or motivated to enable innovation. It was much easier for the entrenched executives, many of whom had been at IBM their entire career, to say no or let things get killed by cumbersome big company processes than to stick their neck out and do something outside normal protocol.

This is not necessarily the fault of the big companies or the individual executives. Corporations don't become mired in complexity and innovation-blockers on purpose. Like our FabCo example, every company was an entrepreneurial venture at birth. Then over time, by necessity, they put processes in place to ensure brand consistency, good decision-making, and survival. To give innovation initiatives a fighting chance of success, companies that have become the frogs in the boiling pot of water need to de-program themselves, or at least a protected portion of themselves, to allow innovation to take hold. This means that someone must take a risk, and most big companies punish rather than reward this type of risk-taking.

When done right, corporate accelerators can help to break these chains. They can allow the teams running them to be cross-functional and see the big picture in order to develop solutions that serve the entire company, rather than one area. They can spearhead partnerships that focus on longer-term success, and they can recognize patterns and gain market intelligence on the bleeding edges of technology.

Getting things done in corporate machines is also complex due to frequent leadership changes. The median tenure of an S&P 500 CEO is now five years, down from six years just four years ago.[3] This follows through to their management teams, where the average executive stays in a role less than three years before moving internally or leaving the company. Innovation initiatives rely heavily on senior executive sponsorship to operate in a different way with longer timelines than the rest of the company, and when these leaders leave their post, the new ones may not provide the same clearing and support as the previous leader, and the innovation initiative often crumbles as a result.

These are only some examples of the many internal mechanisms that have been built up by big companies to create a highly complex machine. While the actions are logical and may be good for these companies in many ways, they also make it extremely difficult to innovate.

PARTNERING WITH STARTUPS FOR A HYBRID MACHINE

This transition from an entrepreneurial venture to big company, then back to some version of a nimble innovator, is tough and not many big companies do it well. In fact, only 6% of executives are satisfied with their innovation performance,[4] and more than half (54%) of organizations with innovation programs have trouble bridging the gap between innovation strategy and the larger business strategy.[5]

One way to improve a big company's innovation efforts is for them to partner with smaller organizations that are innovative by nature: startups. Creating an environment, both programmatic and cultural, where startup and corporate cultures can work together effectively is key to driving long-term innovation efforts in large companies. Accelerators can create a shared space for joint innovation to take root and thrive.

Innovation does not only come from within your own company. There are more ideas, technologies, and talent outside any one company than inside it. Established companies must keep an eye out for disruption from startups in their industry, and either engage with these potential disruptors to succeed together or risk getting left behind. This is the core tenet of open innovation.

In the spirit of "keep your friends close and your enemies closer," incumbents can partner with disruptors before they are big enough to seriously challenge them. A small company doubling revenue every year might be a tenth of the size of one of your business units one year and not even a blip on your radar, but then they will be more than triple your size just five years later (assuming you have minimal growth), with the ability to pick off your customers rapidly when it is too late for you to adapt and compete.

Though often in the best interest of both parties, partnerships between startups and big companies can be more difficult than they first appear. It is like brokering a peace accord between two different countries where the people grew up in very different cultures, speak different languages, and one of them has been created with the single-minded goal of conquering the other one. Innovation teams must act as the translators between these two foreign entities, serving as the diplomats who facilitate their ability to work together well despite their differences. The best innovation translators have experience in and know how to navigate both countries.

While startups and corporations are very different, it is certainly possible to work together successfully, and accelerators are tailor-made to facilitate this. They offer a hybrid solution by providing a safe space to take risks, experiment and work on a potential partnership in a timebound, structured framework. If it works, then you move on to phase two. If not, no hard feelings and everyone walks away with their head held high.

As a practitioner of design thinking, Ava focuses on who she thinks is her main user of the accelerator: the participating startups. She hypothesizes that if the founders are happy after the program ends, they will speak positively about FabCo to other startups and she'll be able to continuously recruit better and better companies for future cohorts. If she has best-in-class startups in the accelerator, then FabCo executives are more likely to be excited about partnering with them. So, one of her first priorities is to figure out how to provide unique value to the startups during the accelerator and make sure they are happy.

However, Ava is overwhelmed by FabCo's complex corporate machine and is not sure how to navigate it. At first glance she sees FabCo as a series of business units that are difficult to mobilize and mostly uninterested in working with startups. She needs to have a clear plan to activate parts of the company effectively so that she can provide value to the startups. She must understand how the complex corporate machine works.

Luckily, Ava was a mechanical engineering major and philosophy minor at Stanford, so she remembers that when faced with a complicated piece of machinery, it helps to isolate and simplify it into its most basic units. She remembers Archimedes. Eureka!

GAIN LEVERAGE WITH SIMPLE MACHINES

The concept of simple machines is an ancient mechanical framework that is a useful inspiration to break down the complex corporate machine. By reducing a big company to its most basic parts, a clearer path emerges for startups to hook into the corporate machinery in the right way.

So what is a simple machine? Greek philosopher, mathematician, and engineer Archimedes originally suggested the concept of simple machines in the third century BC, and it was refined in the Renaissance by philosophers and scientists including Galileo Galilei and Leonardo da Vinci.

A simple machine is the simplest device that performs work.[6] It applies a single force to a single load to change the magnitude or direction of that force. It is the most basic mechanism for applying leverage, or mechanical advantage, to multiply force.

Each simple machine is a building block for more complex compound machines (e.g., car, bicycle). There are six classical simple machines: inclined plane, wedge, lever, screw, wheel and axle, and pulley.

1. Inclined Plane = Lifting or Lowering

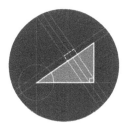

INCLINED PLANE

Also known as a ramp, an inclined plane is a flat supporting surface tilted at an angle, with one end higher than the other. It is used as an aid for raising or lowering a load as the amount of force required to move an object is reduced with an inclined plane: Moving an object up an inclined plane requires less force than lifting it straight up. For example, a ramp used to load goods into a truck or a person walking up a pedestrian ramp on a hill requires less work than a vertical lift or climb. The steeper the slope, or incline, the more force is required to push or pull something up the inclined plane.

2. Wedge = Splitting and Holding

WEDGE

A wedge is a moving version of an inclined plane that tapers from a wide end to a thin edge, whereby applying pressure to the wide end transfers energy to the pointy end and creates force in a sideways direction. This can be used to separate two objects or to hold an object in place. Although a short wedge with a wide angle may do a job faster, it requires more force than a long wedge with a narrow angle. An axe blade is an example of a wedge that splits an object, and a doorstop is an example of a wedge that holds an object in place.

3. Lever = Multiplying Force

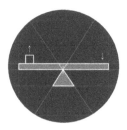

LEVER

A lever consists of a rigid plane that rotates or pivots at a fixed hinge, known as a fulcrum. This serves to multiply the force applied to one side to generate increased and oppositional force on the other. For example, a downward force exerted on one end of the lever can be transferred and increased in an upward direction at the other end, allowing a small force to lift a heavy weight. Examples are a seesaw, or the claw end of a hammer being used to pry nails out of wood.

4. Screw = Fastening

SCREW

A screw is an inclined wedge wrapped around a cylinder that converts rotational motion to linear motion. A small rotational force (torque), on the shaft can exert a large axial force on a load. The screw has grooves that bore through another object or medium when force is applied and is commonly used to hold objects together. For example, the screw top on a jar or the millions of screws that hold together your Ikea furniture.

5. Wheel and Axle = Rolling

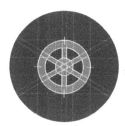

WHEEL & AXLE

The wheel and axle consist of a circular frame (wheel) that revolves around a smaller shaft or rod (axle). A hinge or bearing supports the axle, allowing rotation. It can multiply an applied force, as a small force applied to the periphery of the large wheel can move a much larger load attached to the axle. It is a version of the lever with force applied to the perimeter of the round wheel instead of a straight bar. Examples are gears or a wagon wheel. An important concept here is velocity, which is a measure of how fast and in what direction the force amplification occurs.

6. Pulley = Hoisting

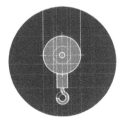

PULLEY

A pulley is a wheel and axle with a flexible rope, chain, cord, cable, or belt around the rim. It is used to change the direction of an applied force, which allows it to be effective in lifting heavy weights or pulling loads. The axle or shaft is designed to support movement and change of direction, or transfer of power between the shaft and cable or belt. A flagpole is one example of a pulley, and Archimedes used a pulley to drag a large boat by himself.

THE SIMPLE INNOVATION MACHINES (SIMs)

Ava feels a sense of relief as this concept of simple machines really helps her to break down the overwhelming corporate machine into manageable pieces that can support her innovation initiatives. She realizes that there is a set of simple innovation machines (SIMs) where FabCo excels and she can tap into these SIMs to provide value to startups in her accelerator program.

Just as these six classical simple machines can take a given level of input force and produce a greater level of output force, so do the most basic units of corporate machinery produce greater output for startup partnerships and corporate innovation than either partner could do on their own. Ava is starting to see the key categories of simple innovation machines that she can leverage within FabCo, and now her goal is to figure out which SIMs are best suited for the job at hand. This will help her to determine the right accelerator model (more on this in Chapter 5) to leverage FabCo's strengths and achieve her user-centric goal of making the participating startups happy.

She sees six key SIMs, aligned with the classical simple machines, as follows.

1. Inclined Plane = Brand

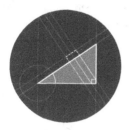

INCLINED PLANE

As inclined planes are used for reducing the force needed to raise a load, in corporate innovation brand is used to raise the profile and credibility of a product or company. A corporate brand has built the ramp of trust and customer awareness over the many years that it has existed, which makes it easier to launch new products and services. FabCo has been around for more than 100 years and is not going away any time soon; their customers know what they stand for. But startups are new and do not have the same track record, so Ava knows that potential customers and partners could be skeptical of the startup and wonder if it is serious or if it won't even be around in a few years.

With the brand of a large corporation like FabCo acting as a ramp, the startups in her accelerator can probably launch products or services faster and with more credibility than they could alone. It even works in reverse. Though FabCo has a strong brand overall, it is not known for its AI prowess, which is an area it wants to develop. Ava could potentially bring in some of the better-known startups that are leading AI-based innovations and this could help ramp up FabCo's brand around AI.

Brand is a powerful tool to make the uphill battle of launching new products and building credibility a slightly easier load to bear.

2. Wedge = Talent

WEDGE

As a wedge creates a reverberating force in a sideways direction, talent is the equivalent SIM that creates orthogonal impacts at a company. The people who build the products, services, and new businesses can make or break a new initiative. Top talent makes a massive difference in the fast-paced world of innovation.

Ava sees how FabCo could contribute to this wedge by leveraging internal experts, deep industry knowledge, R&D teams, and a thorough understanding of the customer in the telecommunications industry.

In contrast, FabCo has trouble hiring top engineering talent due to their compensation structure and just not being a "cool" place to work. Startups could provide them with a wedge of talent in areas where FabCo is not able to recruit, incentivize, or retain the best and brightest in the world. Startups are able to do this because incentives are aligned with equity: if the startup is successful, the people who own the company's equity share in that value creation.

The wedge of talent pushes the best people back and forth between the corporation and the startups to more easily lift the heavy, and risky, load of launching new things in uncertain conditions. The best teams almost always win.

3. Lever = Marketing

LEVER

As a lever multiplies the force applied to one side in order to generate increased and oppositional force on the other, marketing can enable a small effort to have a large impact. A marketing campaign can apply outsized force to a product or brand by amplifying the message. However, just like a lever, the thing being lifted needs to have the right substance. If something is being amplified, it must have a solid base and not be full of hot air.

Obviously FabCo will benefit from marketing messages about the startup partnerships because they will be sharing details about exciting innovation initiatives that FabCo is a part of. The startups will benefit from getting their name out there in the world to potential customers who may have never heard of them, but already know and respect FabCo.

The marketing lever can benefit both the startup and the corporation, and the fulcrum is the foundation of a well-established partnership.

4. Screw = Product

SCREW

As a screw is used to hold objects together, product integrations between a big company's existing product and a new startup product can benefit both parties. The rotational torque of an existing product can plow through a wall or piece of wood if it's the right shape and size, with the right amount of force.

Often a corporate product suite will have "a screw loose," or gaps that do not satisfy the full needs of their customer. But when paired with the right startup product that fills these gaps, it screws in perfectly and addresses customer needs better. The same is true for startups – they may be missing a few screws needed to make a full solution, and the alignment with an existing product can make it all work better.

For example, Ava realizes that FabCo products collect an enormous amount of data, but they do not have the analytics chops in their products to pull useful insights from this data. With a business intelligence startup that has better "big data" analytics functionality, FabCo can provide immediate additional value to their existing customers.

5. Wheel and Axle = Sales

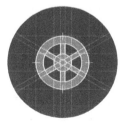

WHEEL & AXLE

Similar to a wheel and axle rotating together to multiply an applied force, sales can be more effective if done in partnership. The existing distribution channel and entrenched customer base of a large corporation can make it easy for a startup to roll in quickly with their own product.

On the flip side, a big company can "grease the wheel" of a sales channel that has slowed or stalled by injecting a startup partnership that reenergizes the customer relationship. The concept of velocity here, or how fast and in what direction the force amplification occurs, is also useful. Partnerships can start with a "slow roll" to test the distribution channel, then speed up when it is working.

Ava and her boss Jordan have been tasked with creating growth for FabCo. She realizes that if she can negotiate revenue-share agreements with the startups and drop their products into FabCo's existing (but stale) sales channels, they can quickly achieve some growth. In addition, it could reinvigorate the sales team and help them reconnect to their clients. She also knows the startups have limited sales resources, so having the FabCo sales team sell their product for them is going to be an easy way to make them happy.

6. Pulley = Knowledge

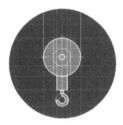

PULLEY

As a pulley changes the direction of an applied force to allow lifting heavy weights, knowledge can dramatically alter the direction of a startup's or a corporate's trajectory. This can be market intelligence, expertise in a particular area, or any other insights not widely available by which companies can make better decisions. For startups, the access to experts at the big company who know their industry inside and out or have a particular technical expertise can help them build a better product much faster. On the flip side, a big company can gain market intelligence about trends or the competitive landscape that are not accessible from public resources or having a researcher simply look into it.

When Ava looked at a competitive landscape for the 5G space, there were several startups marked as "stealth mode." By focusing on an accelerator in this area, she can get a better lay of the land by recruiting these companies or hearing about them from their closest competitors. In addition, the technical expertise of her 5G team was beyond compare, and they would be able to help the startups inform their product design in a way that would be very valuable. What a win-win!

SIMPLE INNOVATION MACHINE CHEAT SHEET

INCLINED PLANE	WEDGE	LEVER	SCREW	WHEEL & AXLE	PULLEY
BRAND	TALENT	MARKETING	PRODUCT	SALES	KNOWLEDGE

Play the SIM Card

The concept of simple innovation machines helps to isolate key areas where startups and big companies can exchange value, and if they use these tools wisely then it can lead to impressive results.

Ava knows that FabCo is better at some of these SIMs than others, and she still needs to get the right executives on board in each of these SIM areas to make it happen. But there is now an obvious value proposition in both directions for colleagues who runs these divisions. She can articulate her asks and explain "what's in it for them" much clearer now, and is optimistic that she can get them on board.

These six categories of SIMs are common in most companies, but every organization is different. Innovation leaders must understand the unique corporate machine that they operate within and figure out where to gain leverage through the most basic units where value is created.

GET WITH THE [ACCELERATOR] PROGRAM

CHAPTER 4

STARTUP ACCELERATORS

> The point of an accelerator is to teach you about companies and business, not about technology.
>
> **SAM ALTMAN**
> FORMER PRESIDENT, Y COMBINATOR

Welcome to the era of startup accelerators. The modern accelerator concept only began relatively recently, with the launch of Y Combinator in 2005 in Cambridge, Massachusetts, and has grown exponentially since then. The "corporate accelerator" came into existence shortly thereafter in 2010,[1] and a decade later there are hundreds of corporate accelerators, with more launching each year. A few corporate accelerators have seen noteworthy successes in some areas, but many of the programs are not producing meaningful returns for either the corporate or the startups involved.

It is very possible to achieve material results from corporate accelerators, and the examples and suggestions in this book should set innovation leaders on the right track. But in order to understand the corporate accelerator, you must first understand the startup accelerator more broadly.

WHAT IS A STARTUP ACCELERATOR?

A startup accelerator is a fixed-term, cohort-based program to help startups accelerate their development and growth. It includes some combination of mentorship, education, office space, networking, introductions, and more to support the growth of the business. An accelerator program typically culminates in a public pitch event or Demo Day.[2]

The acceleration industry is evolving rapidly, and the term *accelerator* is used to describe an increasingly diverse set of programs. Often, the lines that distinguish accelerators from similar programs, such as incubators and early-stage venture capital funds, are blurred. Though there is some variation, accelerators tend to share the following common traits:[3]

1. A competitive application process
2. Funding, in the form of a grant, equity investment and/or in-kind products and services
3. A focus on founding teams, not individual founders
4. Time-bound support, including programmatic events and intensive mentoring
5. Cohorts or classes of startups rather than rolling acceptance of individual companies

The goal of an accelerator is to condense the learnings and experiences of building a very particular type of business – a tech startup – into a shorter period of time than it would take otherwise. The accelerator model was originally meant to fast-track the beginning stages of a startup and train high-potential founders on how to launch and grow a new business. Before this, it was a rite of passage for entrepreneurs to learn the hard lessons of how to build and grow a startup on their own. The serial entrepreneur starting their second or third company found faster success and raised venture capital (VC) money more easily because they knew the inside tricks of the trade, and had the battle scars to prove it.

Accelerators were created to give first-time entrepreneurs a way to learn the ins and outs of building a startup even if they haven't actually done it themselves, enabling a startup education and hands-on training under the guidance of seasoned entrepreneurs. Though there is no replacement for real-world experience, accelerators help founders to prevent novice mistakes and learn from people who have done it before. As Paul Graham, founder of the first and arguably most successful startup accelerator Y Combinator, said when they launched in 2005, "Y Combinator is just accelerating a process that would have happened anyway."[4]

For example, an accelerator can condense at least one year's worth of learnings into a three-month period, at a critical time when speed is important. Accelerators are a crash course for tech entrepreneurs. They open doors and provide networking opportunities, which are critical for startups to succeed. Program participants gain access to peers and mentors who include successful entrepreneurs, program alumni, lawyers, venture capitalists, angel investors, and corporate executives.

Accelerators are not intended for all types of businesses, though recently the term and program have been applied more broadly. Accelerators are intended for a very specific type of business: the rapid-growth technology startup.

WHAT IS A STARTUP?

Accelerators are programs for startups. So what exactly is a startup? This may seem like something everyone knows, but many corporates actually have trouble with this definition and regularly work with so-called startups who are not actually the right kind of companies for their programs. There is a particular definition of a startup from the VC and Silicon Valley tech world, and corporate leaders not operating in the startup world every day may not be calibrated to the difference.

To most big company employees, all small companies could be seen as startups. Although they certainly might be entrepreneurial smaller companies, we'd wager that most of the "startups" a corporate executive meets are not really startups, they're small- and medium-sized businesses (SMBs). There is nothing wrong with SMBs, and they still may be good partners for a bigger company, but it's important to understand the difference. Although the outcomes needed for success for the corporate accelerator are not the same as an independent accelerator with investment return goals, the types of companies that provide the biggest successes are the same: tech startups.

This matters because there are wildly variable expectations for how startups operate, capitalize, and grow. Understanding the nuances is critical to designing your accelerator program, because if you expect startup-type returns and work with companies that are not actually startups, you will likely never achieve your innovation goals from an accelerator. However, with eyes wide open, you can design a program that attracts and supports the best startups in the world and avoids the mistakes of your less-educated peers.

To understand startups, there are three key questions to answer:

1. What is the difference between a startup and a small business?
2. What is an early-stage startup vs. a growth-stage startup?
3. How do you know what is a "good" startup?

Startups = Growth

There are seven key indicators of startups: rapid growth, large market, scalable technology product, employees as owners, operating at a loss, VC investment, and exit plans.

1. **Rapid Growth**

   First and foremost, startups are defined by rapid growth. The other six indicators all point back to this one. This is a "go big or go home" business, and if the company is not growing a minimum of 100% year over year, at least in the first few years, it's probably not a startup. Startups have world domination plans and need to become a market leader *fast,* not just one of many players in the space. Each additional dollar spent at a startup should grow it more than the previous dollar did. For example, if the first $10,000 spent brought in 10 customers, the second $10,000 should bring 50, the third should bring 500, and so on. Unit economics should improve as the company grows. So the name of the game is exponential scale combined with high speed. It's logarithmic, not linear growth.

2. **Large Market**

   The target market should facilitate this scale and the total addressable market (TAM) should be in the billions, not millions, so that startups can realistically achieve rapid growth over many years. The typical tech startup has financial projections that go from zero revenue to the "magic number" of $100 million revenue in just five years. In order to achieve this, the market size must be big enough to grow this fast before the bigger players have time to react.

3. **Scalable Technology Product**

Startups make technology products or leverage technology to produce scalable gains in traditional businesses. The reason for this goes back to – you guessed it – growth. A technology product can scale exponentially, whereas a services business cannot. Simply using technology (e.g., having a website or app) does not make it a technology business. The core product that a company sells should be a scalable technology, meaning it can sell more and spend less as it grows. Revenues grow but costs don't grow at the same rate. Software businesses are a great example of this, as most costs are in the development and maintenance of the software with minimal incremental costs as the sales ramp up. Labor-based services businesses generally are *not* high growth startups; as they grow, they need more people to service each customer. As a result, scalable technology companies operate with high gross margins – often 80% or higher.

4. **Employees as Owners**

Startups run extremely lean operations where everyone on the team is an owner. In a startup, the team is incentivized by equity ownership so that incentives are aligned for a single-minded focus on growth. Everyone owns a piece of the business, with founders typically having double-digit percentages each and employees all owning smaller pieces of the pie through an employee stock option plan (ESOP). When Google went public in 2004, more than 1,000 employees became millionaires due to their stock ownership.[5] As a result, the salaries are relatively low and employees work hard for the upside, not for a cushy salary. When they create value for the business, they create value for themselves, which encourages creativity and thinking like an owner, not an employee.

5. **Operating at a Loss**

The financial strategy to invest heavily into growth rather than achieve profitability early is classic startup strategy. Although a startup can aim to be profitable down the line and can adjust the breakeven point as needed, its shorter-term goal is a higher valuation and an eventual exit, both of which are mostly based on growth. If a company is leaving money in its bank account as profit or (gasp!) offering dividends, it is at the expense of reinvesting this into growth. As long as every dollar invested in the business yields more than a dollar in growth, it's better to continue to invest in scaling the business. This creates significantly more value for the founders, employees, and investors than running a profitable business.

6. VC Investment

Startups are frequently capitalized by venture capital (VC) investment. Although this is not necessarily required and every once in a while a high-growth startup bootstraps their way to unicorn status, VC investment is a well-worn proxy for identifying high quality rapid-growth startups. Startups are too risky for traditional means of financing such as bank loans, but they need cash – often lots of it – to finance their rapid growth. Startups usually don't have traditional assets like inventory, machinery, predictable contracts, or even a dependable book of business. They have a vision of growth and a maniacal focus on execution. This means they look to risk-tolerant investors with longer time horizons who expect that most of their investments will fail, but the ones that don't will be so successful it will make up for the failures. Venture capitalists invest in startups that they believe can produce a 10 times or greater return on their investment in a relatively short period of time (5–10 years) to compensate for the high risk. Venture capital is the fuel for startups to grow fast.

7. Exit Plans

Finally, startups drive toward achieving a very particular set of outcomes – generally either an acquisition or initial public offering (IPO) – within 5–10 years of launching the business. There are no public markets to trade startup shares – it's way too risky – and in order for the founders, teams, and investors to realize the value they create, the company must have an exit to cash out on their equity ownership. Taking VC money means that startups must at least aim for a clear path to exit in this relatively short time frame. If a founder wants to maintain ownership and control indefinitely and not sell their shares to the public markets or to another company, it's likely not a startup and should not take VC investment or join an accelerator program.

There are many examples of startups that have succeeded on this trajectory to become massively successful household names, and of course countless others that didn't make it and are forgotten. Two examples of the enormous value startups can create quickly for themselves and investors are Twitch and Slack. Twitch, a streaming platform for eSports (watching others play video games), was acquired by Amazon for $970 million in 2014 when the company was barely three years old and had only raised $35 million in VC funding.[6] Twitch shares owned by corporate partner Take Two Interactive, which held a 2.3% stake, yielded the corporation a $22 million gain.[7] Slack, an enterprise communication platform, raised $1.4 billion in VC money before going public in 2019 (nine years after being founded) and the IPO valued them at $23 billion.[8] VC fund Accel initially invested $2.5 million in the predecessor to Slack, Tiny Speck, and continued upping their investment over the years to about $200 million in total.[9] When Slack went public, Accel's 24% ownership was worth more than $4.6 billion.[10] These are examples of true tech startups that created billions of dollars of value in only a few years.

SMBs Are Everything Else

In contrast, SMBs are your traditional small- and mid-sized entrepreneurial ventures. Any private company that falls outside the seven characteristics of startups just described is most likely an SMB. If the company is not at least doubling revenue year on year, is mainly focused on services or a consumer product, has gross margins less than 50%, or the market size is less than $1 billion, it is probably an SMB. If the company does not motivate all of its founders and employees with equity-based compensation, it's likely an SMB. If a company is not gunning to become the dominant market leader in their space and disrupt the incumbents (you?), it's probably an SMB. If a company simply wants to be a healthy, profitable business while growing a few percentage points every year, it's probably an SMB.

Venture capitalists often disparagingly call these businesses "lifestyle" businesses, implying that the founders of these small businesses aren't working as hard. This is not necessarily true – entrepreneurship is difficult and life-consuming no matter the type of business. But it's okay to not be a venture-backed startup. In fact, the dirty secret in startups is that most founders are personally better off building SMBs or working in a corporate job than founding a tech startup. Although startups may seem like the best way to become a millionaire overnight, this almost never happens. In fact, most of the time a founder would make more money for themselves in 10 years working a corporate job (with salary and benefits!) or building a small business than attempting to get rich from a startup in the same amount of time.

As Ava Lopez knows from her experience in VC, accelerators are for startups, not SMBs. Accelerators are literally named for their ability to accelerate the trajectory of growth for innovative startups. However, not all of her colleagues at FabCo understand the difference, so she must spend time educating the stakeholders involved in the program, at a minimum those involved in the company selection process, to make sure she includes only companies in her program that have the seven characteristics of startups. She knows that there is simply no point in investing time and energy in a SMB that will never achieve the outsized results defined by rapid growth over a short period of time. She reminds herself to focus on startups, and to help her colleagues to understand the difference.

Maturity: Timing Is Everything

Corporates who want to partner with startups should also understand that there is a big difference in maturity between an early-stage startup and a growth-stage startup. Which stage you chose to be involved with will depend on your goals and your value proposition.

VC funding stages usually define startup stages. Early stage covers startups with no funding, or angel, pre-seed, seed, and/or Series A funding. They have minimal revenues, an early version of the product or sometimes just an idea, and a few million dollars in funding, if any. If their product is launched, they might have some early users or indication of traction, but nothing at scale. They have *a lot* of challenges and are fighting to survive every day. They are usually doing something ambitious, innovative, and exciting, but are mostly unproven.

Growth-stage startups are usually Series B–funded companies and beyond. They have likely achieved product market fit, are making money from their customers, and are growing quickly. They have a product that works well (though still continually improving), and substantial funding from VC investors, usually $10 to $100 million, though sometimes much more. Growth-stage companies have gotten their bearings and some indication from the market that they're on the right track. The focus is now on growth, as fast as possible and as big as possible.

Pre-IPO companies are another category to be aware of, as startups have remained private longer and many have become large corporations in their own right before an exit. There is some debate about when they stop becoming a startup and start becoming a big company themselves. Many companies (such as the earlier-mentioned Slack example), were multibillion-dollar companies before they went public. Though this is not clearly defined, once a company is earning more than $50 million in revenue annually, we'd argue they are no longer a startup and extremely unlikely to participate in an accelerator program. Growth companies at this stage will more naturally fit with partnership and corporate development teams than an accelerator model.

The stage of startup you work with depends on your goals. A corporate looking to gain market intelligence (pulley) and offer only limited marketing and mentorship support may want to work with early-stage startups who offer more experimental technologies that need to be piloted to be refined in the field. These early-stage startups may be attracted to the program from the brand lift (inclined plane) or marketing (lever) that are critical at the early-stage. By contrast, a corporate with an embedded base of customers and distribution channels in need of a jolt, paired with the ability to invest significant capital and team resources, may want to work with later-stage companies who have fully developed products that can be easily pushed out to its loyal following. These growth stage startups may be attracted to the sales pipeline and leverage from joint go-to-market efforts (wheel and axle), but will have more options in the market so corporates will need to demonstrate more actual value to outweigh the risks of aligning too closely with one bigger company.

Most traditional accelerators focus on early-stage startups, and corporate accelerators have followed this model (remember the cargo cult?). We will make the case in this book that partnership and/or increasing revenue are the most common goals for corporate accelerators, so the programs should consider working with growth-stage startups, who are better equipped to partner with large companies and achieve mutually beneficial and meaningful results.

A BRIEF HISTORY OF STARTUP ACCELERATORS

The accelerator concept emerged from a desire to improve the way businesses launch and grow. With an active community in Silicon Valley and beyond that developed hard-won wisdom on how to build successful tech startups throughout the 1990s and 2000s, there was opportunity to teach new entrepreneurs in the hopes of avoiding first-timer mistakes.

Accelerators also addressed a gap in the VC investment process, which hadn't evolved much itself. Instead of making bigger bets on a small number of companies, accelerators adopted more of a "spray and pray" mentality, doing a lot of small investments at a very early stage in batches or cohorts. This theoretically improves their chance of financial returns through a more diversified portfolio. They also offered hands-on support, training, and networking to give new ventures a better shot at success in a shorter period of time.[11] Accelerators were essentially created to provide help for early-stage startups at scale – from business formation and legal assistance to foundations of startup business training in everything from human resources and recruitment to venture finance. Helping a group of startups through these common challenges maximizes the value an experienced investor can contribute to their investments.

This model had humble beginnings in an unexpected place and continues to evolve in many ways. Big corporations have started adapting the model, and several VC funds have added more hands-on support in "platform" models at their funds to mimic accelerator benefits. One thing is for sure: the accelerator certainly isn't going away, and it will continue to play an important role in the startup ecosystem.

Chickens Before Unicorns

Though the modern accelerator started in 2005 with Y Combinator (more on this next), the groundwork for accelerators and incubators came from an unlikely source: an abandoned chicken hatchery in upstate New York.

Batavia is a town that sits between Buffalo and Rochester in northern New York State, only about an hour's drive from Niagara Falls. When farm machinery company Massey-Harris decided to close a 1,000,000-square-foot chicken harvesting factory there in 1957, thousands became unemployed. In that empty space, a local business family, the Mancusos, saw an opportunity for growth.

The Mancusos were motivated by both self-interest and town pride. They owned several local businesses – a hardware store, restaurant, theater, and car dealership – and were very interested in making sure the space was utilized. "Little Joe" Mancuso was put in charge of the factory, transitioning from the family's hardware store, and he initially tried to get another large manufacturer to lease the space. When that didn't work, he thought creatively and decided to rent the place out to a handful of smaller tenants in what he dubbed the "Batavia Industrial Center."

In a radical move for the time, Little Joe offered "unusual perks such as short-term leases, shared office supplies and equipment, business advice, and secretarial services. If one of his tenants needed a line of credit, Little Joe Mancuso would help arrange it with a local bank. If they needed 80,000 square feet of space in which to store baby chickens (true story), Joe Mancuso would hook you up."[12] At the time, this type of support was not offered in existing office space for small businesses. When Little Joe was giving a tour to a reporter, he famously said: "These guys are incubating chickens, I guess we're incubating businesses."

But the world's first business incubator cared less about disrupting the global economy than about resuscitating its local one. The intention was to help local people in Batavia create businesses and jobs, which it has now successfully done for more than 60 years. The Batavia Industrial Center still operates in the same location and under the same mandate of hatching local businesses, and has a thriving tenancy of businesses being incubated there.[13] Though most of these businesses would be considered SMBs, the concept of the business incubator or accelerator was laid in the Batavia chicken hatchery.

Y Combinator

In March of 2005, Paul Graham and Jessica Livingston hatched the modern tech startup accelerator. They believed that there could be 10 times more startups than there were at the time[14] and set out to create a "startup school" to support young entrepreneurs in starting new tech companies. They wanted to encourage would-be founders who may have been intimidated by the process or lacked critical resources to take the plunge into tech entrepreneurship.

With the help of Robert Tappan Morris and Trevor Blackwell, they started the Summer Founder's Program in Cambridge, Massachusetts, which was originally touted as an "experimental replacement for the conventional summer job."[15] They soon renamed it to "Y Combinator" after "one of the coolest ideas in computer science, a program that runs programs, acting as a metaphor for the accelerator, which is a company that helps start companies."[16] They were conducting two programs a year, one in Cambridge and one in the Silicon Valley city of Mountain View, California. Then, as of 2009, they moved exclusively to Silicon Valley.[17]

PG, as Paul Graham is fondly called, and his team also felt that the VC funding model was broken and preferred to make frequent, smaller investments, as opposed to fewer, larger investments. They provided small seed checks and support to cohorts that increased in size over the years. The first batch of Y Combinator consisted of eight companies,[18] including Reddit (now a unicorn), and has swelled to multiple classes per year with 240 startups participating in the most recent class at the time of this writing in 2020.[19] They currently invest $125,000 in return for 7% equity in the participating startups.[20]

The accelerator model they created seems to have worked. In aggregate, Y Combinator has now invested in more than 2,000 companies that have raised more than $25 billion and are valued at more than $100 billion. There are at least 18 unicorns – companies valued at over $1 billion – and more than 100 centaurs – companies valued at over $100 million. Successful alumni include a who's who of Silicon Valley success stories, such as Stripe, Airbnb, DoorDash, Reddit, Instacart, and Dropbox.

The Next Batch Hatches

This new accelerator model was meant to fast-track the beginning stages of a startup and train high-potential founders on how to launch and grow a new business better and faster than they could on their own. The accelerator model was meant to democratize this asymmetry of information and experience, giving first-time founders a better chance at success by learning from experienced mentors, founders, and investors to avoid the many pitfalls of building high-growth tech startups.

The early success of this model developed by Y Combinator was replicated quickly by other organizations. Just two years after Y Combination launched, Techstars (Boulder, CO) and SeedCamp (London, England) launched their first cohort in 2007. Dreamit (Philadelphia, PA) and AlphaLab (Pittsburgh) launched in 2008, Founder Institute (Palo Alto, CA) launched in 2009, and 500 Startups (Mountain View, CA) started in 2010.[21] Entrepreneurs Roundtable

Accelerator (ERA) launched in New York City in 2011, with their first class in a space behind a billboard in Times Square. (Note: Jeremy was part of that very first ERA class in New York City. Sadly, he did not build a unicorn.) The international startup community participates in many of these U.S. programs and also eventually built their own local versions. There are now more than 10,000 startup accelerator programs globally[22] and the number continues to grow every year.

Corporates Get in the Game

Corporates soon took notice of this new collaboration model, and, just five years after the emergence of Y Combinator, they began to experiment with their own accelerators. Some of the first were run by Citrix, Microsoft, and Telefónica.

As opposed to the independent accelerators like Y Combinator, which are driven entirely by the desire for financial return, corporate accelerators are driven mostly by strategic innovation goals. Working with startups was a new concept at the time, when most corporations focused exclusively on innovation coming from within their own companies, such as research and development (R&D) labs. As startups became real competitors to the incumbents, those organizations started taking startups seriously and needed a mechanism to learn from and partner with these new forms of potential competitors. Accelerators helped them experiment with startups in a low-risk, time-bound environment and many corporates dedicated full teams and annual budgets to build or partner with accelerator programs.

At first, they exactly followed the playbook of the independent accelerators: early-stage companies focused on initial product development and finding product-market fit. This gained them some market intelligence and lots of marketing content, but mostly didn't achieve the strategic results desired. As the industry evolves, corporate accelerators are starting to adapt the model in positive ways that are more appropriate for and aligned with strategic innovation goals.

Corporate accelerators have different goals and different success metrics than purely ROI-driven independent venture accelerators. They can provide informational benefits like insights into new technologies, trends, and innovations. Accelerator participants can launch cheap and rapid pilots to identify new areas of growth. They can also provide an outlet for internal innovation talent and a way to identify new recruits – innovators whose companies don't make it can often work on the next challenge and leverage their experiences within the corporate.[23]

These days, it seems as if nearly every major corporation has an accelerator or is about to launch one. They have expanded beyond tech companies into a wide variety of industries, from aerospace to food products to media. Often a big company will have multiple accelerators – at IBM there were already at least a dozen accelerators before Jules launched two new blockchain accelerators in 2019.

Some corporates run their own programs, while others outsource them to entities such as Techstars, Plug and Play, 500 Startups, R/GA Ventures, and BlueChilli to operate accelerators on behalf of organizations as diverse as NASA's Jet Propulsion Laboratory, the LA Dodgers, and the Coca-Cola Company (more on this outsourced model in Chapter 9).

Despite this diversity of program alternatives and a significant evolution of the accelerator industry, corporate accelerators are often misunderstood and mismanaged. They are mostly still seen as a marketing initiative rather than something that is meant to achieve meaningful business results. As one CB Insights report jokes, "nothing says you're serious about protecting your multibillion-dollar revenue like dropping $500,000 on 10 startups that your corporation isn't suited to work with."[24]

THE NEXT PHASE OF CORPORATE ACCELERATORS

The successful corporate accelerator is an entirely different animal than an independent accelerator. Current incarnations are mostly misaligned with both the market needs and the corporate needs, and this is the result of big companies trying to simply copy the venture accelerator model (remember our cargo cult?). This is problematic for many reasons.

While traditional accelerators primarily seek financial returns on equity investments, their corporate counterparts are focused on gaining access to new ideas and technologies that can be parlayed into competitive advantages, such as go-to-market partnerships and technology integrations. This lends itself to later-stage companies and a different format.

Both kinds of accelerators have a time-bound program and some combination of mentorship, education, office space, investment, and networking. However, corporations can add value that traditional accelerators cannot, such as partnerships, supply chain efficiencies, and sales distribution channels. For a startup, this can be very compelling. It can also be a massive risk if it doesn't work, preventing them from selling into or being acquired by a competitor.

We believe that the value corporate accelerators can add is immense – and mostly untapped. By altering the accelerator model in a few key ways, corporate accelerators can provide enormous benefits to both the big company and the participating startups. We will show you how to do this in the chapters that follow.

CHAPTER 5

ACCELERATOR ARCHETYPES

> **Good artists copy;**
> **great artists steal.**
>
> STEVE JOBS
> FOUNDER AND CEO, APPLE
> (QUOTING PABLO PICASSO)

The rise of the accelerator coincided with a broader trend of technology startups disrupting large but traditional industries with software, web-based solutions, mobile applications, and radical new business models. From Uber in transportation to Airbnb in hospitality, change became the constant. Big companies have jumped at the opportunity to get in on the startup action - in part to avoid being outmaneuvered by nimble new players, in part because their competitors are doing it, and in part for the sake of innovation.

73

Naturally, many big companies seized on the model of accelerators after seeing the value being generated by the successful independent accelerators. For corporations, however, replicating this model is not a simple road to success. An accelerator that works in Silicon Valley doesn't necessarily work within a large corporation. The reality bubbling below the marketing friendly surface of corporate accelerators today is that, while well intentioned, most of these programs are not effective in achieving the strategic goals of the company hosting them.

As we've stated repeatedly, corporate innovation is exceedingly difficult. Despite substantial investments of resources from many companies, innovation initiatives such as accelerators frequently fail. Even when they do see some success, it is difficult to sustain and accurately track performance.

To burn these numbers into your brain one more time, we know that 60% of corporate accelerators fail within two years. The average time a corporate executive stays in one role is less than three years, yet it takes an average of seven years for early stage companies from an accelerator cohort to achieve the level of success needed for a corporate partner to take notice. See a problem? There is usually not a seamless transition when executives leave, so innovation programs frequently fall apart or get shut down before they've even had a fighting chance to produce results.

So, instead of throwing up our hands, what can we do to fix it? The answer is simple. Just as every great artist and entrepreneur has done before, use what you already know works.

BENCHMARKING AND BEST PRACTICES

The accelerator model has been tried and tested hundreds of times by a diverse group of organizations in the corporate world and beyond. Making things up from scratch or simply copying a model that was built to achieve very different objectives is not the best path to achieve your own goals. Don't build a cargo cult. There are plenty of data, case studies, and war stories about what works and what doesn't work. Until now, the information hasn't been presented in a way that is useful for corporate innovation leaders, if it is shared at all.

This book was bred out of feeling the pain personally. When Jules was tasked with launching a blockchain accelerator at IBM, she looked for resources like this to help her make key decisions. For example, it would have been extremely useful to have benchmarks for budget and team, for average duration of the program, and for key performance indicators (KPIs). It would have been amazing to hear about the successes that resulted from certain decisions and why, and even more useful to hear about the failures and lessons learned.

However, this information was not readily available, even from the dozens of other accelerator leaders within her own company. No one was sharing information or data in a systematic way. People were happy to share one-on-one, and based on dozens of these conversations it became apparent that a consolidated resource was needed to support corporate innovation leaders who were launching or wanting to improve an accelerator program. Thus, this book was born.

Why wasn't there more information available on corporate accelerators? First, most of the accelerator managers were downright exhausted. The grind of launching and running an accelerator program with minimal budgets and scrappy team resources, which was the case most of the time, can be overwhelming and leave little time to connect with the wider community of practitioners. The folks in these roles were constantly spinning plates and just trying to make it work. They would often crash and burn after a few cohorts, leaving the job within a couple of cycles. There was no motivation or incentive to write down what they had learned and share with their colleagues, much less peers in other companies.

Also, there started to be an ecosystem of consultants offering corporate accelerators as a service (CAaaS). They have lots of great data and best practices, in particular on accelerators that mimic the traditional independent accelerator model, but it is in their best interest to keep it to themselves and only share with paying customers. There are also a handful of organizations such as the Global Accelerator Network (GAN), which was originally affiliated with Techstars, and the Global Accelerator Learning Initiative (GALI) that focus mainly on independent accelerators.

Finally, the dirty little secret is that most corporate accelerator managers are hopelessly frustrated by the fact that they are (for the most part) not achieving their goals. Of course, there are some benefits achieved from the programs they run, but once you get beneath the surface, many accelerator leaders will admit that the model isn't really working in the way they had hoped. This is not something most people want to share proactively or publicly. Hence our mythical example of FabCo and Ava Lopez was born as a way to share some of these stories and lessons learned while maintaining the confidentiality and privacy of accelerator practitioners. The struggle is real!

There is certainly reason for optimism; not everything in the corporate accelerator world is broken. There are some truly inspiring examples of successes and well-executed initiatives. Often a program might excel at one specific thing, even though there are still problems elsewhere, but that thing is notable and worth replicating. And of course a few programs are simply knocking it out of the park. If we can learn what works and what doesn't work, we can figure out how to assemble the things that do work into an even stronger program that has a shot at achieving ambitious innovation goals. Based on your authors' personal experiences, a deep analysis of existing research, and our own interviews with dozens of corporate accelerator leaders, we've synthesized everything we wish we had known here.

The first, and perhaps most important, revelation is that most accelerators are very similar. There is obviously some variation, but they tend to cluster around three key archetypes, or models, of accelerators that should be a foundation point for 80–90% of the programs out there. Once you select the one that works best for your purposes, the rest can be customized to your specific needs. This eliminates a huge amount of work if you have a template to get started.

Selecting the right accelerator archetype can still be challenging. In order to do this, you must really understand why you and your organization are doing an accelerator in the first place, and also secure the right resources and support to make your chosen accelerator model successful. We will discuss how to make these decisions in the following chapters. But once you do select an archetype, it provides a clear blueprint as a starting point and you can focus your limited resources on customizing the final 10–20% to your company's unique needs.

THE THREE TYPES OF CORPORATE ACCELERATORS

Based on our research, there are three main categories of corporate accelerators. Each has a different purpose, approach, benefits, and metrics for success.

The three archetypes of corporate accelerators are:

1. The venture accelerator
2. The ecosystem accelerator
3. The partnership accelerator

When they work, corporate accelerators in each of these categories can achieve impressive outcomes, including:

- New sources of revenue
- Operational efficiencies
- Information advantages and market intelligence
- Branding and reputational improvements
- A more entrepreneurial culture
- Financial returns from equity investments

Ava Lopez didn't realize there were different types of accelerators; the Techstars and Y Combinator model was all she had seen first hand. She actually breathed a sigh of relief after hearing this, as she was struggling to see how working with very early-stage startups would help her achieve the main goal that her CEO Jordan Burns had as the #1 priority: growth for FabCo within a couple of short years. She hoped that one of the other models might provide a faster path to success here, and even wondered if she could experiment with multiple types of accelerators. Let's go along this journey with her.

ARCHETYPE 1: THE VENTURE ACCELERATOR

Venture accelerators are a replica of the traditional, independent accelerator model spearheaded by Y Combinator. This is what most people think of when hearing the words startup accelerator. They are essentially early stage venture capital funds that run startup bootcamps with one or two cohorts per year to accelerate the learnings and performance of entrepreneurs at the very earliest phases of their businesses. Venture accelerators help early-stage startups to launch or improve their MVPs and achieve product market fit. They invest in the participating companies in a similar way as an early-stage VC would, with the goal of achieving financial returns through an exit. The difference is that they tend to invest a standard amount of capital for a flat percentage ownership of all companies participating in the program, usually investments of $50,000–$150,000 in return for 5–7% ownership.

The main goal of independent venture accelerators is financial returns from the equity investment. Their success is measured in the same way a VC fund is measured, including internal rate of return (IRR), distributed to paid in (DPI – returns that have been distributed, not just marked up), total value paid in (TVPI – a measure of cash-on-cash return) once there is liquidity, and net present value (NPV). In the short term, a proxy metric can also be follow-on VC funding raised by the alumni of the program. Alternately, significant revenue gains, key new customers or partners, and other benchmarks can be used as metrics, though they are extremely difficult to track after the companies have left the program and require intensive portfolio management (more on this in Chapter 16).

Corporate accelerators originally started as venture accelerators. Big companies applied the independent venture accelerator model to try and achieve strategic objectives. However, the bigger the parent company, the more challenging it is for them to partner effectively with early stage startups and many of these programs failed.

Another challenge is that the financial returns alone from a venture accelerator are usually not compelling enough for a large corporation. Let's take the example, using simplified numbers, of an independent accelerator that manages a $10 million fund for their program over five years. If the team makes one hundred $100,000 investments in the participating companies, with two cohorts of 10 companies each year, and yields a 10x return on the portfolio, resulting in $100 million in returns by year 10, it would be considered a massive success in the top decile of VC fund performance benchmarks. However, for a multibillion-dollar corporation, $100 million over 10 years barely moves the needle. In addition, the corporate accelerator teams are not (usually) compensated by equity upside so this type of result does not motivate the team in the same way it does for independent accelerator leaders. While corporations can benefit from investing in early-stage companies seeking disruption, just as venture accelerators do, a sophisticated corporate venture capital (CVC) arm is usually the best pathway to achieve this goal.

In addition, as venture accelerators work with early-stage startups, the time horizon to see financial returns is longer than most corporates are willing to wait, typically 5–10 years. Exits from initial public offerings (IPOs) and large acquisitions are celebrated but take time. Often this is many more years than a budget is allocated for an accelerator program, and without success stories in the short term, the value of the program is questioned by those who don't fully understand the startup world's time frame.

Corporate-Specific Metrics of Success

When investment returns aren't the only key metric of success, the venture accelerator model can still be useful in a corporate setting. A venture accelerator can be a great way to achieve other useful outcomes related to:

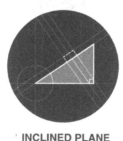

INCLINED PLANE

Brand

The simple innovation machine (SIM) of the inclined plane applies here as a brand lift. Accelerators heighten the parent company's reputation as an innovator (whether it is true or not).

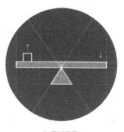

LEVER

Marketing

An enormous amount of positive content and increased awareness of innovation initiatives can result from the marketing of an accelerator program (lever SIM). There are ample opportunities to market the program itself, announcements from each individual company, and the splashy demo day for each cohort.

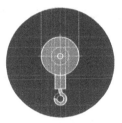

PULLEY

Knowledge

The pulley SIM of knowledge from an accelerator is useful in several ways, such as corporate employees getting smarter on market trends, new technologies, and disruptive business models. This applies initially to the core accelerator team, who should be methodically relaying back this intelligence to their senior stakeholders, and also to the mentors and other company employees who participate in the program in some way.

In addition, venture accelerators are one of the easiest to launch for corporations, as long as the budget is available. There are many experienced leaders who have run these programs before and can replicate the model quickly. If you don't have this experience internally, there are plenty of external options. Several of the traditional independent accelerators, including Techstars and 500 Startups, have developed consulting services to launch corporate accelerators as a service (CAaaS), leveraging their expertise in building independent venture accelerators. They know this model well, and can build a venture accelerator quickly and effectively on behalf of a corporate partner.

These benefits can be extremely valuable to large corporations, as long as they have expectations aligned with what a venture accelerator can realistically achieve. "A venture accelerator specifically allows you to create a pipeline of new and novel things," says Vijay Rajendran, head of corporate innovation and partnerships at 500 Startups. "When your goals are based on exploration, as opposed to application, then the traditional form of an accelerator for early stage seed companies is extremely valuable. What I see as a really important next stage, and evolution of accelerators, is application. That's where post-seed companies matter and more pilots and POCs are possible."

Venture accelerators can also work well if the main goal is VC-style financial returns, which may be the case occasionally. However, it may not be the best option for corporates who are looking for more substantive strategic returns in the short and medium term.

Examples of Corporate Venture Accelerators

A great example of a corporate venture accelerator is the Barclays Accelerator, which focuses on early-stage fintech startups, as you might expect from one of the largest banks in the world. It launched in 2014 and is managed by Techstars, with more than 140 portfolio companies across programs operating in New York, London, and Tel Aviv. They also offer cutting-edge co-working spaces, dubbed Rise, to host the Accelerator participants along with many other events for the ecosystem. The bank now takes an equity stake in the accelerator companies, though they didn't at first, and has launched Rise Growth Investments to provide investment capital of up to £10 million for each Barclays Accelerator program.[1]

Another example is IBM Alpha Zone in Israel. Launched in 2014, the program is well regarded for early stage startups locally, and many of its alumni have become very successful. However, IBM does not take equity or invest in the companies, and very few partnerships result due to the early stage of the companies participating. This venture-style accelerator program has been beneficial to IBM in terms of branding, marketing, and market intelligence, but not in strategic commercial or financial returns.

Finally, URBAN-X focuses on startups reimagining urban life and is also worth highlighting as a notable corporate venture accelerator. Built by the MINI (from the BMW Group) in partnership with Urban.Us, a VC fund that invests in startups that "upgrade cities for climate change,"[2] the program focuses broadly on technologies for cities. This includes real estate, mobility, urban infrastructure, construction, renewable energy, electric vehicles, water, waste, civic, and government technologies – and it often has a sustainability angle. The program provides 20 immersive weeks of customer development, product development, network-building, and expert guidance for startups – all in preparation for fundraising. They focus on a strong mentorship network of "experts in residence" who deeply understand design, development, regulated industries, and government procurement.[3] They invest at least $100,000 in every company in exchange for equity. It's notable in that it's sponsored by the MINI's strategy team – specifically the innovation and brand strategy practice – giving inspiration and market intelligence to the corporate parent, the BMW Group, who is tasked with building future products.

Snapshot of the Corporate Venture Accelerator

Objective: Financial returns as a VC-style investment, or more likely the strategic returns of market intelligence, branding, and marketing.

Company Profile: Early stage.

Program Structure: Cohort of ~10 companies, once or twice a year, with mentorship, networking, and curriculum as focus, and active engagement by the corporate marketing team.

Funding: Stipend or equity investment to participate, possible follow-on corporate venture capital (CVC) funding after the program, if equity it is usually a flat percentage for all participating companies.

Metrics of Success: Media mentions, trend reports derived from the market intelligence gathered, brand lift, financial returns (IRR, DPI, TVPI, NPV).

Other Noteworthy Activities: Marketing and branding are a critical piece of this for both the corporate and the startup, so plan to do lots of press releases, blog posts, and organize a splashy demo day.

Themes/Lessons: To quickly launch a venture accelerator, outsource the first few years to a CAaaS – hiring external partners to take on the risk and bring connections can expedite lessons learned and achieve results faster.

ARCHETYPE 2: THE ECOSYSTEM ACCELERATOR

The second model is an ecosystem accelerator, which is focused on user adoption of a particular product or service. It is highly focused on incentivizing usage and development on top of a particular technology or other product that the parent company offers, as well as creating an ecosystem of companies using this technology or product. Though they may give away access to the necessary technology or product at first, the goal is to drive revenue to the corporation once the startups scale and have to pay for it.

The ecosystem accelerator is also commonly used outside of the corporate world for economic development or cultivation of talent in a particular community, such as a city, region, or university. Generally, the motivation here is to create a bridge for ideas and talent to enter the startup world – for a university, for example, to move ideas from the laboratory to the commercialization stage.

The focus of ecosystem accelerators, in the corporate world or otherwise, is not on the success or failure of the startups themselves. It's about generating use of the product, service, or community that the ecosystem accelerator is promoting. Most of the time these programs do not take equity, but may offer grants, loans, or in-kind products and services to the participating startups.

Metrics for success here, naturally, have little to do with return on investment (ROI). Ecosystem success metrics are often the number of startups using the product or service, the volume of usage, or jobs created. These can be tracked by metrics such as API calls, software as a service (SaaS) fees, and overall revenue from the startups or their customers, which is an important outcome. The ecosystem model is useful for big companies who want to develop sales channels into or increase usage from startups, and generally support sales goals rather than innovation goals.

The ecosystem accelerator model is a great way to achieve outcomes relating to:

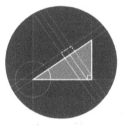

INCLINED PLANE

Brand

The inclined plane SIM of brand applies here as more companies using the product or service that is the focus of the ecosystem program helps to promote your brand to customers and channel partners.

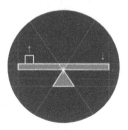

LEVER

Marketing

Marketing opportunities result from the typical accelerator activities around the program, each individual company, and the Demo Day. In addition, the participating companies are subtly marketing your products and services when they pitch it to their own customers, thereby amplifying your message with little to no marketing spend.

SCREW

Product

The participating companies are building on top of the corporate's product or service, thereby demonstrating its value and showcasing capabilities (tapping into the screw SIM). Some of the startups may also make the product stronger by filling gaps in the existing product or service.

WHEEL & AXLE

Sales

Revenue (the wheel & axle SIM) is generated from the participating startups once their credits or time limit for complimentary products has expired, usually as they are growing themselves and become reliant on the product for their business. This leads to direct revenue from the startup, as well as possibly secondary revenue from their customers. In addition, the corporate sales channels may also be activated and recharged to resell some of the products from the participating startups as a channel partner, which leads to increased usage of their own product.

Examples of Ecosystem Accelerators

Verizon's 5G First Responder Lab[4] is an ecosystem accelerator in Washington, D.C., focusing on public safety use cases for 5G networks, including weapon detection, geo-intelligence, autonomous security, virtual reality training, and situational awareness. The participating companies spend three months in the program and receive access to Verizon's 5G network and expert consultants. As a result, Verizon will make the products available to public safety agencies across the United States. The goal for Verizon is to increase usage of their 5G network and revenue from their consultants selling into the public agencies.

Another example is Google's Indie Games Accelerator that recruits game developers from emerging markets who are building games to launch in their Google Play app marketplace.[5] As a part of their larger Launchpad Accelerator initiative, benefits to the startup include a Google Pixel phone plus $20,000 in Google Cloud Platform and Firebase (their mobile app development platform) credits, with training and support.[6] This is a savvy way to encourage emerging creators to build in the Google environment.

Finally, the Amazon Alexa Accelerator, founded in 2017, is focused on having startups develop products on top of the Alexa AI technology and have them distributed through the Alexa device. They partner with Techstars to run the program, and it is part of the Alexa Fund, Amazon's $200 million venture capital arm for voice tech startups. In 2019 they revamped the program to move away from-early stage companies and launched Alexa Next Stage, an accelerator for later-stage companies that are more ready to develop on the Alexa product.[7]

Snapshot of the Corporate Ecosystem Accelerator

Objective: To enable increased usage of the corporate's product or service.

Company Profile: Mainly early stage, but can be growth stage.

Program Structure: Cohort of ~10 companies, once or twice a year, with curriculum and workshops focused on the product or service that is the foundation of the ecosystem.

Funding: Stipend to participate, in-kind products or services to enable usage of the particular ecosystem.

Metrics of Success: API calls, SaaS fees, revenue from the ecosystem-focused product or service.

Other Noteworthy Activities: Marketing and branding are a critical piece of this for both the corporate and the startup. So plan to do lots of press releases, blog posts, and a splashy demo day.

Themes/Lessons: This should be closely aligned with sales and channel partner initiatives, not necessarily innovation.

ARCHETYPE 3: PARTNERSHIP ACCELERATOR

The partnership accelerator is singularly focused on building commercial partnerships between the corporate and the participating startups. The accelerator serves as a structured vetting process to ensure there is alignment and mutual benefit between both parties, so that a subset of startups will result in a partnership at the end of the program. It is a convenient testing ground to build partnerships with flexibility and minimal commitment (at first).

As the goal is partnership in the short-term, the participants in a partnership accelerator are mostly growth stage startups. Early-stage companies are struggling to stay alive, launch their first product, and figure out the right way to attack the market, and are usually not equipped with the team resources or maturity to manage a partnership with a much larger entity. Growth-stage startups are still chaotic, but should have a clear direction, a larger team with dedicated resources, and enough patience to work through long partnership sales cycles.

As these are later-stage companies, the financial model of a venture accelerator that has a small amount of investment for a flat percentage of equity ownership also does not work. These companies have likely already raised significant VC money at much higher valuations than early-stage startups, so are usually unwilling to give up big chunks of equity for minimal capital. Investment may be part of the program but it is not necessary. If it is involved, it should either be a grant (no equity) to facilitate the costs of the program and of developing a partnership, or a much bigger (multimillion-dollar) investment that is at a fair market valuation. The investment is almost inconsequential, because the name of the game is sales for both the startup and the corporate parent.

In some cases, the accelerator can also include startups that the big company can use as a customer to reduce their own costs or improve operational efficiencies. Ideally, if the startup offers a product that the big company can use in any way, it is a stronger validation in the market and highly recommended for all partnerships where this is the case. Some accelerators even carve out a budget line to pay for the use of the startups' products and this is a recommended best practice. It reflects poorly on both the corporate and the startup if the bigger company tries to get a product for free from a much smaller company.

The partnership accelerator is the model we believe can have the highest value in achieving strategic corporate innovation goals, especially around driving long-term revenue, and most corporate accelerators should start with this model instead of a venture accelerator. A key data point for this is the sheer number of corporate accelerators that started with a venture accelerator model for early-stage startups, then after several cohorts did not produce the desired results, moved to a partnership accelerator model with growth-stage startups. It can leverage more of the simple innovation machines than the other models, thus tapping into more of your strengths as an organization.

The partnership accelerator model can also be a great way to achieve outcomes relating to:

INCLINED PLANE

Brand

The simple innovation machine of the inclined plane applies here as a brand lift. Accelerators heighten the parent company's reputation as an innovator that is willing and able to partner with emerging leaders, and not just marketing the innovation theater. Positive results from substantive partnerships go a long way to build the brand in an authentic way.

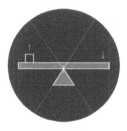

LEVER

Marketing

Positive, ongoing marketing content resulting from successful partnerships is the gift that keeps giving, as startups will proudly market the partnership both publicly and one-on-one with their customers. There are ample other opportunities to market the program as well, including each individual company's progress, and the demo day for each cohort.

SCREW

Product

A go-to-market partnership typically involves some sort of product integration or product alignment to co-sell, so the screw SIM is an important part of making technology-focused partnerships work.

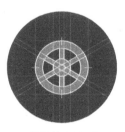

WHEEL & AXLE

Sales

The sales channels of both the parent company and the startup, which are usually different by their nature, are activated to the benefit of both parties. The wheel and axle SIM from partnership accelerators can be the most noteworthy success story of any innovation program. When this works, everyone makes more money.

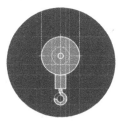

PULLEY

Knowledge

When a partnership works, the companies share information and work together effectively at a global scale. The impact of the pulley SIM is better decision-making and a strong foundation of trust between both parties.

Examples of Partnership Accelerators

The Disney Accelerator is an impressive success story of a partnership accelerator. Based in Los Angeles and founded in 2014, its primary focus is on entertainment, specifically tech-based new media. Originally managed by Techstars as a venture accelerator, it quickly moved to run the program in-house with a focus on later-stage growth companies and a clear path to partnership. A notable success is with one of the participating startups from the 2017 cohort, Epic Games, the creator of the Unreal Engine and Fortnite, which at the time of this book's publication in 2020 was a unicorn valued at more than $17 billion. The accelerator led Epic to partner with Disney on an LED stage production technology as part of The Mandalorian series, and Disney also used their real-time rendering capabilities to create an interactive ride at multiple Disneyland theme parks.[8]

Another good example is the Chobani Accelerator, which was started personally by the Greek yogurt company's founder Hamdi Ulukaya, and he still selects all of the final participants in the program. The focus is on supporting purpose-driven food and beverage product companies, in line with Chobani's values and growth plans. They look for companies who are "ready to go and grow," meaning they must have a product inmarket and some customer traction, up to about $5 million maximum in revenue. With their SoHo office in New York City as a home base, rather than having a traditional on-site requirement for three months, the program takes place during only one week for each of the three months on-site. It also includes visits to the Chobani manufacturing facilities, trips to retailers, and trade shows with the support of the Chobani team. They do not take equity and provide a stipend for founder travel and other costs.

Finally, SAP.io Foundry is another successful example of a partnership accelerator. It gives startups that could be partners with SAP or their customers a clear path to partnership and a way to develop a go-to-market plan during the program. They focus on B2B software startups and, with seed to Series B–stage companies, somewhat bridge the early stage–and growth stage–startup landscape. They do not take equity and focus the program on learning how to navigate SAP, integrating with SAP solutions, and collaborating with the SAP sales team and customers. They have nine global foundries around the world accelerating 18 cohorts of startups every year.[9] Although it took a year or two to get its bearings, the Foundries are now producing many successful partnerships for the corporation and SAP continues to replicate the accelerator program in different hotspots around the world.

Snapshot of the Corporate Partnership Accelerator

Objective: The key objective here is sales, and sometimes use of the startups product for operational efficiency. Most of the time it should result in go-to-market partnerships for a subset of the participating startups.

Company Profile: Growth stage – must have a product in market, some paying customers, and be ready for partnership with a large corporate (enough scale, maturity, focus, resources to execute).

Program Structure: Engagement on a more customized basis to support the partnership, focus on streamlining procurement and partnership process.

Funding: In-kind products or services to get the partnership up and running; possible stipend to support partnership costs; often follow-on

CVC funding if led by another VC to capture the upside that the partnership is creating.

Metrics of Success: Completed commercial agreements, successful integration with sales channels; revenue generation as a result of partnership.

Other Noteworthy Activities: Must have engagement from the corporate sellers, the business units (BUs) who own the corporate sales process, and usually procurement and legal.

COMPARISON OF THE THREE ACCELERATOR ARCHETYPES

	01 VENTURE ACCELERATOR	02 ECOSYSTEM ACCELERATOR	03 PARTNERSHIP ACCELERATOR
OBJECTIVE	Market intelligence, branding, investment returns	Product development, which can be joint development or use of a particular tech product or protocol (ecosystem)	Focus on partnerships, product integration, sales, and go-to-market
COMPANY PROFILE	Early stage	Early or growth stage	Growth stage
PROGRAM STRUCTURE	Mentorship, networking, or curriculum	Workshop and product development focus, curriculum about product, development focus	Customized, focus on vetting and establishing partnership
FUNDING	Grant, investment in all cohorts for flat equity $, follow-on funding at market valuation	Grant, follow-on funding, in-kind products and services	Grant, larger equity investment at market valuation if partnership materializes
METRICS OF SUCCESS	Press mentions, brand increase, funding for startups	POC, MVP, product integration or launch of product, transaction volume, SaaS fees, companies using your product	Partnership-linked revenue, POC, MVP

MULTIPLE MODELS FOR DIFFERENT GOALS

Sometimes one accelerator may not meet all of your innovation goals, in which case it is possible to launch multiple accelerators with different goals and strategies. This is becoming more common, especially as accelerator leaders realize both the benefits and the limitations of a pure venture accelerator. When shorter-term results are desired, an ecosystem or partnership accelerator can be launched in tandem to the venture accelerator, and there are efficiencies and synchronicities that come from operating multiple models.

For example, London-based law firm Mishcon de Reya's MDR LAB started in 2017, and after learning a lot from three annual cohorts of a venture accelerator and a short pandemic-induced pause, they came back at the end of 2020 with three separate programs.[10] These include:

1. **Launch** – A venture accelerator where idea-stage startups go through a venture-building curriculum in collaboration with CAaaS partner Founders Factory. Mishcon helps to validate the ideas and business models, and also provides a stipend to founders for the first couple of months along with pre-seed funding. This is also open to staff at Mishcon who want to explore ideas without having to leave the firm, bridging into the internal innovation model of the venture studio.

2. **Improve** – An ecosystem-ish accelerator that focuses on product development in the legal ecosystem. This does not have cohorts and the 12-week program can be activated at any time during the year. Entrepreneurs work directly with potential customers, including Mishcon, to pilot and improve products and to understand where lawyers – and their clients – would benefit from new technologies.

3. **Sell** – A partnership accelerator for startups with a product in-market with some traction that is looking to build revenue and sell to Mishcon. The two-week program starts with a tailored software POC tested inside the firm.

Dan Sinclair, head of MDR LAB, provided insight on why they moved to this diversified model: "With only one program we weren't responsive enough because we were only running it one time a year, and it was a fixed start and stop. And that just clearly doesn't work given the sort of speed and velocity that technology is moving at the moment. So one of the key things we wanted to achieve was a more dynamic and fluid delivery model."

This is an excellent example of a diversified accelerator portfolio that tackles several different objectives and a company that is experimenting, iterating, and learning. This is what a thoughtful innovation program focused on accelerators looks like.

OTHER MODELS

Although there are some variations and outliers, these are the three main models of corporate accelerators that make up most programs today. There are a few other models that arise every once in a while that are worth noting as well, but are not as common.

One is the for-profit independent accelerator, which is usually focused on education for founders. For a small fee (essentially a tuition), cohorts of startup founders receive similar training and structure as other types of accelerators – lean startup methodology training, peer support, mentor networks, and demo days – but the curriculum is the point. It's pay for access. This does have the nominal benefit of avoiding dilution for the founders because the accelerators often do not have to give up equity (though it may include a small warrant amount).

In addition, there is a more customized partnership accelerator model for startups that goes beyond partnering with just one corporate. For example, the French telecom company Orange[11] launched OrangeFab in Silicon Valley initially as a venture accelerator model. When this did not achieve the desired results, they re-launched it as a partnership program that selects the best Silicon Valley startups and navigates partnerships with a roster of Europe-based customers of Orange. It's slightly different than a partnership accelerator in the sense that it focuses on addressing the needs of their customers and deepening those relationships, rather than partnerships with Orange directly.

Finally, a nonprofit accelerator model can be launched as part of a corporation's philanthropic foundation, the personal initiative of an executive, or part of a corporate social responsibility (CSR) program. The goal of these programs is to give back to the community or the environment, and it is not necessarily intended to generate strategic returns. It's usually housed in a foundation or separate entity set up for this purpose, and sometimes is the pet project of a CEO or founder. One example is Harmony Labs, a nonprofit accelerator affiliated with BuzzFeed, which has since been expanded to include funding from MTV, the Ford Foundation, the Bill & Melinda Gates Foundation (Microsoft), Google, the Dalio Foundation (Bridgewater), and several more. It is focused on decoding the media's social effects to put their power to good use.[12] They recruit companies that help advance their mission to understand media and support healthy, democratic culture and healthy, happy people. They operate similarly to a traditional venture accelerator, but with a nonprofit mindset that seeks mission-driven results. The Mozilla Foundation recently launched something similar to "fix the internet."

SELECTING THE RIGHT ACCELERATOR MODEL

Ava Lopez sees potential in all three accelerator archetypes for FabCo and starts putting together a hypothesis on which model might be best for the company to achieve its goals. She wants to make sure that the accelerator takes advantage of FabCo's strengths, particularly its unique simple innovation machines.

She immediately thinks about their multibillion-dollar investment in 5G infrastructure. There is heavy competition in this space and lots of concern from senior executives about how to get customers using the products, as well as a big fear about the quality of the product. She thinks an ecosystem accelerator might bring in startups that could prove out specific use cases for the 5G tech that have, to date, only been hypothetical.

She also knows that FabCo's head of corporate development has been looking to acquire startups in the blockchain space to bring in talent and technology there, but does not fully understand the technology himself so wants to make sure there is a partnership in place first. This seems perfect for a partnership accelerator focused on blockchain.

Ava's wheels are spinning as she brainstorms a dozen possible accelerators based on these three archetypes. Somehow launching a new accelerator, maybe even more than one, doesn't seem so overwhelming any more!

With basic templates for the three main corporate accelerator archetypes it seems as if, while the execution of the program will still be intensive and time consuming, it will follow a basic blueprint. The most important thing Ava needs to get right is aligning the accelerator with the strategic goals that FabCo is trying to achieve. Since she is relatively new to the company, she decides to map out what she thinks are the objectives, along with proposed accelerator solutions, then validate them with her executive team.

CHAPTER 6

KNOW YOUR WHY

Very few people or companies can clearly articulate WHY they do WHAT they do. By WHY I mean your purpose, cause or belief – WHY does your company exist? WHY do you get out of bed every morning? And WHY should anyone care?

SIMON SINEK
AUTHOR, *START WITH WHY*

Source: Simon Sinek[1]

An important place to start your accelerator journey is understanding the reason for launching an accelerator program at all. Often an accelerator manager is simply tasked with creating or managing the program, without a full understanding of what the parent company is trying to achieve. This is a one-way ticket to failure.

In order to select the right model of accelerator that achieves your desired outcomes, knowing the why is critical. A corporate executive should already know the overall business goals of the company as a whole, likely based on an annual strategic planning process. How are the innovation goals aligned? The more in sync the innovation and accelerator goals are with the annual and multi-year strategic plans, the more likely the program is to succeed.

The prominence of the goals within the wider business should align with your available budget and resources. For example, if innovation is one of the top three stated corporate goals, but you do not have capital or adequate resources allocated to run your accelerator program, then there is an obvious disconnect. For something more tangential like growth or something related to product improvements, this can influence the way you build the accelerator to support this goal. Try to make the accelerator a meaningful part of the parent company's overall strategic goals.

If your company does not actively set short-term and long-term business goals and share with the entire company, or if the innovation team is not actively engaged in this process, then integrating innovation goals with some version of the overall company's strategic plan should be an immediate priority.

MOTIVATIONS FOR LAUNCHING AN ACCELERATOR

The biggest mistake we see from corporate accelerator programs is not having a clear understanding of why they are doing an accelerator in the first place. This seems basic, but it is shocking how often this step gets skipped.

Often the person selected to lead the accelerator isn't the one who proposed it or got it approved in the first place. The accelerator manager will articulate their own thoughts on why the company is doing the program, but often they are making their best guess with limited information and do not actually know why the senior leaders approved the program or what they hope to get out of it. Often the answer is something like "innovation" and we don't exactly know what that means.

It is critical to ask the key stakeholders why they are excited about an accelerator program. And don't stop by asking why only once – use the Theory of Three Whys, popularized by Richard Semler, CEO of Semco Partners in Brazil, in his TED Talk in 2015 about practices he's been using in his company and his life for 30 years. One of his main practices is simply asking three "Whys?" in a row to get to the core of the issue. The first "Why?" always returns a good, polished answer. Then the second "Why?" gets a bit more difficult and starts uncovering a deeper truth. By the third "Why?," you either get to the real reason or realize that, in fact, you really don't know why you're doing it at all.[2] This simple practice is extraordinarily powerful.

Then, like all good strategies, an innovation strategy for a corporate accelerator should clearly articulate the specific pieces of the program that address your why(s). This requires going beyond all-too-common generalities, such as "we must innovate to grow," "we innovate to create value," or "we innovate to stay ahead of competitors." Those are not achievable goals; they are too vague and it's impossible to know if the goals are achieved or not. Be specific with your goals.

A good example of a clearly articulated and thoughtful why, or actually several whys, is MDR LAB. Mischon de Reya LLP is a London-based law firm with a global reach. Founded in 1937, it has about 900 employees and specializes in practice areas such as corporate law, dispute resolution, employment law, intellectual property, and real estate. In 2015, after investing in an analysis and report to outline their 10-year vision, one of the big thematic pieces was around the importance of technology to their clients. They realized that technology would inevitably play a more prominent role in the business world and they needed to understand and use it themselves in their legal work. As a result, they started MDR LAB as an accelerator program for early stage legal tech companies, prioritizing technologies that they could use as a law practice to serve their clients better.

Nick West, the firm's chief strategy officer, describes the main whys, with clear prioritization, of MDR LAB: "There's no question that we are doing an accelerator for three reasons. First is to change the culture of our organization, to get more people here interested in technology. Second is to find technologies that we can use, that are better than the tools we use today, possibly so we can use them earlier than the rest of the market and gain an advantage. If we find a tool that we think is great, we're willing to accept that it might be in the early releases, it might not be perfect yet, but if we believe it is good enough then we'll get a temporary advantage. And third, there might be the potential for investment returns. MDR LAB is focused on finding technology that would give us an advantage first, then for a possible financial return as an investor." This statement demonstrates a clear understanding of why they are doing a corporate accelerator program. If you do not have a similar why statement, you are likely setting your program up to fail and it would be better not to do the program at all.

Always start by asking 'Why?' . . . then ask it two more times until you fully understand the motivations for any innovation initiative.

Why the Why Is Important

The why drives all other decisions, and if this is not understood from the outset, then the program is unlikely to succeed. If you don't know what you're trying to do and why, unless you have total dumb luck, you're probably not going to do it.

An important part of this process is honesty, with yourself and the organization. If marketing is a key goal because the company needs a brand lift, then don't be ashamed of this or cover it under the guise of something else. It's okay to have marketing and branding as an objective, and you can design an effective program around this to achieve marketing goals. It is also much better to acknowledge this up front and manage expectations with the startups. Co-marketing opportunities are extremely valuable for startups and they often jump at these opportunities. However, it will be disappointing and damage your brand in the market if you say that the goal is partnership, but these never happen and marketing is the only outcome. A startup may be happy with only a marketing outcome, but not if they expected a partnership.

Jenny Fielding, managing director at Techstars–New York City and The Fund, emphasizes this point. "The thing that's interesting about the corporate partners I've worked with is that they all seem to want something different. For some it's a marketing exercise and they need to check a box for an executive and that can be okay. An accelerator can be a marketing exercise or a preliminary innovation exercise where you're exploring lots of different things. Then there are situations where they've ring-fenced a pool of capital and have a full group built around it, which can lead to something more game changing for the business unit that substantively moves the company forward from an innovation point of view," says Fielding. "I think it's just about being really clear about your objectives."

Ava Lopez scheduled a series of one-on-one conversations with multiple people at FabCo who she knew would be key stakeholders in the accelerator. She wanted to deeply understand their motivations and see if they were aligned. She also wanted to vet her hypothesis that a partnership accelerator, and maybe also an ecosystem accelerator, were better models to achieve FabCo's goals than the venture accelerator they seemed to have in mind.

Ava had three simple questions to each of them:

1. In your view, why are we launching a corporate accelerator? (She then followed up with two more whys to dig deeper.)
2. Assuming the accelerator is a massive success, what specific things would you be excited and proud to see that we have achieved?
3. In what time frame do you think is reasonable for these results to be achieved?

The conversations she had were astounding, and not what she expected at all. For example, the head of corporate development, who was partially funding her budget and also ran the CVC arm, shared with her after three whys that he was about to retire and wanted to "leave a legacy." What he meant by this was a desire to see significant wins before he left (in two to three years) in terms of sales and successful partnerships with name-brand Silicon Valley startups that he could tell his grandkids about.

Also the chief marketing officer had some choice words about being forced to spend his team's time and energy promoting these "superficial agreements with tiny little companies that will never amount to anything and are a pet project of the CEO." He thought the company should work with much later stage startups that had some brand-name recognition. He thought it harmed FabCo if there was no real substance behind the announcements, and wanted to see real revenue being earned or the partnership working in a big way before the company promoted it.

Perhaps the most surprising conversation was with the CEO, Jordan Burns, who had been explicit about starting this accelerator to achieve growth. Ava thought this was going to be a quick conversation, but what Jordan seemed to actually want when she got down to it was being able to respond to the investor questions about growth on the quarterly earnings calls to show they were doing something "innovative," but didn't actually expect much in terms of actual results.

Ava realized she had her work cut out for her! And, most of all, she was really glad she asked. Otherwise she would've spent the next several months building something that would not have made any of her stakeholders happy.

I Got 99 Problems and the User Is All of Them

As you would advise a startup in your accelerator, when starting something new it is important to first understand your user and the problem you are solving for them. This holds true for an accelerator too! This is a great opportunity to use the Business Model Canvas in the Lean Startup methodology on yourself.

In particular, you need to know your users. Design thinking is another useful tool here. Your users are certainly the startups participating in the program, but also your key stakeholders. For example, when Jules was tasked with launching a blockchain accelerator program for IBM in partnership with Columbia University, it was clear that the two entities had different goals. Columbia wanted to cultivate strong entrepreneurs from their student and alumni community, while IBM wanted to sell more

IBM products to startups and develop profitable go-to-market partnerships. Rather than meet in the middle and satisfy no one, she launched a venture accelerator that catered to the desires of Columbia to train the student and alumni entrepreneur community, and a second partnership accelerator to focus on curating partnerships with growth stage entrepreneurs for IBM.

It is good practice to select one key internal and one key external user and map out their needs, for example your chief innovation officer or CEO as the internal user and the participating startup or your typical customer as the external user. Then, be very clear about what problem you are solving for each of these users with your program. How will the program create value for each user? How does this map to the type of accelerator you will create?

INNOVATION = PROFIT

Our definition of innovation from the very beginning of the book is "the introduction of new technologies and business models that drive performance improvements and sustainable growth over the long term."

For corporates, the ultimate result of innovation is all about financial growth and profit. Remember, these are for-profit companies that have a fiduciary responsibility to use shareholder capital effectively to increase the value of their shares, whether it is a private or public company. This is not a charity and its primary responsibility is to act in its own self interest, not in the interest of the participating startups. Although there is certainly mutual benefit if the accelerator is done right, any innovation program, including a corporate accelerator, is intended to benefit the parent corporation financially and strategically.

New initiatives, especially for public companies using shareholder money, are about doing things that impact the bottom line, either reducing costs or increasing revenue, which in turn will increase the value of the parent company. With all the hype about innovation, it is sometimes seen as equivalent to corporate social responsibility to do good and give back. This is not the case. Unless your accelerator results in a meaningful impact on profit, it is unlikely to be supported long term.

There is a lot of discussion, particularly in corporate venture capital (CVC), about financial versus strategic returns. Financial returns mean the value of the equity you own at the point at which it is liquidated. Strategic returns are a bit more amorphous and require that the investment or partnership has a strategic benefit to your company. This can mean many different things, and the discipline of identifying and tracking strategic metrics is still nascent.

However, at a basic level, it's all ultimately financial. Strategic value is about making money for the parent company, plain and simple. Direct strategic returns are revenue resulting from sales, usually best enabled by an ecosystem or partnership accelerator. For indirect strategic returns, the value of brand, marketing, and market intelligence is not necessarily immediate, but it creates financial value in the long term. This can be achieved by a venture accelerator.

STRATEGIC VS. FINANCIAL RETURNS

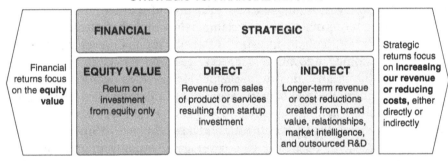

Financial returns focus on the **equity value**	**FINANCIAL**	**STRATEGIC**		Strategic returns focus on **increasing our revenue or reducing costs,** either directly or indirectly
	EQUITY VALUE	**DIRECT**	**INDIRECT**	
	Return on investment from equity only	Revenue from sales of product or services resulting from startup investment	Longer-term revenue or cost reductions created from brand value, relationships, market intelligence, and outsourced R&D	

It's important not to forget that, although there may be other fantastic reasons to innovate, if it's not adding revenue or decreasing costs to the parent company in the long term, it will be difficult to garner long-term commitment from the parent company. Results will speak for themselves!

COMMON WHYS FOR CORPORATE INNOVATION

There are a few common reasons that corporations choose to launch innovation programs, and you need to understand which apply to your company before launching an accelerator. These align mostly with the simple innovation machines (SIMs) outlined earlier, and here is a quick view of how you might start thinking about implementing each of them.

Reputation, Brand, and Marketing

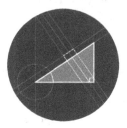

INCLINED PLANE

The impact of corporate accelerator programs on the corporation from a reputation and brand perspective - our inclined plane SIM - is the most challenging area to measure impact. The lever SIM of marketing is a bit more quantifiable in terms of activity, for example the number of media mentions, but is still very difficult to measure. After all, big mature companies are notorious for doing "innovation by press release" for the quick fix of a headline or a profile in an industry magazine. However, to dismiss the impact here would ignore the real benefits experienced by companies that commit to and maintain true innovation through a successful corporate accelerator program. When marketing is authentic and has substance behind it, it works.

The impact from positive media coverage of innovation and corporate accelerator programs can be meaningful. Customers may begin to notice and choose to do business with the company because it is perceived as more innovative, and may even ask for this information in request for proposals (RFPs). The investor community can also translate this into a positive impact on a public company's stock price. And critically in key industries where the battle for technical talent is a struggle, companies may find it easier to recruit and retain the scientists, engineers, entrepreneurs, and other talent they need to drive future growth.

The marketing activity starts, appropriately, at the beginning: with the announcement and kickoff of the accelerator program. Favorable press for launching an accelerator program is the first step to being perceived as an industry innovator and leader. But if that's where it ends, well, you may be at the innovation theater.

A good corporate accelerator program provides a drumbeat of press coverage over the course of many months. The launch press can serve to attract promising prospects to the program for the initial cohort of companies in the accelerator. Then once the cohort kicks off, there are ample opportunities to highlight the participating companies as a whole and individually. Demo Day is a splashy, marketing friendly event, with the companies announcing investments, new customers, or newly inked partnerships with your company.

As time passes and alumni begin to expand and grow, there are many other opportunities for continuing to promote successes. In particular, as a successful partnership accelerator program matures over several cohorts, the number of resulting partnerships with accelerator graduates should grow. The success stories can be told with meaningful results, and linked back to your early work with them that started with the accelerator program. This is the true payoff longer term, when the media covers substantive successes that resulted from your innovation programs.

All three accelerator archetypes can support reputation, brand, and marketing goals. The venture accelerator in particular is geared specifically for this purpose, though we would argue that partnership accelerators are more effective in that the resulting partnership successes provide better opportunities to credibly demonstrate innovation results.

Culture and Talent

WEDGE

One important benefit of a corporate accelerator is the impact on the parent company's culture and interaction with new talent (the wedge SIM). When employees are able to engage with high-quality, rapid-growth startups, it can be a massive jolt of energy to infuse your culture with more entrepreneurialism. Each employee who interacts with the startup as a mentor, partner, or even just an observer often comes away inspired to bring in some of that entrepreneurial spirit into their own jobs.

Employees and recruits might not be the area of focus of a corporate accelerator, but for many of the most innovative employees at your company, a corporate accelerator program allows them to get inspired by outside innovators. Make sure to pull in high performers as mentors for the startups. Keeping talented employees engaged and inspired to innovate themselves can show up in reduced attrition, more engaged employees, and more intrapreneurial efforts.

Recruiting is also impacted by the existence of a real commitment to the innovation ecosystem, in particular with millennials and younger employees who tend to care about this deeply. Make sure to highlight innovation programs to prospective employees during the recruiting process and find ways for them to get involved, or at the very least invite them to the demo day.

While all three accelerator archetypes can be helpful here, the important piece of the program to activate talent goals is a robust mentorship program. These are most prominent in venture and partnership accelerators.

Sales

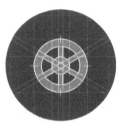

WHEEL & AXLE

One of the best ways to create long-term support for corporate accelerators is to generate sales for the corporation, our trusty wheel & axle SIM. When a corporate and a top-tier startup can sell together effectively, it is a win-win. Startups want to tap into corporate customers and their distribution channels, and corporates need fresh, new things to sell to their customers. If this achieves scale for the startup quickly, it is often more important and well received than investment dollars. For corporate partners, this can spur rapid growth, and these companies can also be potential acquisition candidates in the future.

When sales is an important why, it's critical to identify the time horizon expected. If it's less than four years, which is usually the case, then the accelerator is best suited to work with growth-stage companies through either a partnership or ecosystem accelerator.

Market Intelligence

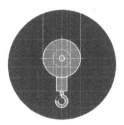

PULLEY

Accelerators can bring unparalleled insight into trends, technologies, and potential future competitors early on (our pulley SIM of knowledge). This allows your best people to do their job even better by making smarter decisions, and is a source of primary information not available via subscription or gathered by paid researchers. This is also not available to your competitors. Many corporations see startup programs as canaries in the coal mine, a leading indicator of where future opportunities and threats are coming from.

When this is an important goal for a corporation, a dedicated resource (part time is fine) should be responsible for summarizing market trends garnered from the accelerator program and reporting back to key stakeholders. This can come from a variety of sources. First, the high volume of deal flow – the applicant pool who applied to the corporate accelerator – can yield instant insights about market trends. In addition, the ongoing information from portfolio companies is worth tracking after the program. Their successes, failures, and growth can provide incredible on-the-ground proof points of customer perceptions and purchases in the real-world market. This requires active portfolio management and maintaining strong relationships with the startups after the program ends (as discussed in Chapter 16).

The best accelerator type for garnering market intelligence is a venture accelerator, as the earlier-stage companies are on the bleeding edge of technology trends.

Equity Returns

Though often not the primary reason for corporate accelerator and CVC programs, the adage goes "losing money is never strategic." Corporates may require a hurdle rate for all investments, often somewhere between 10% and 15% IRR. When investing in the accelerator participants for equity, these returns can eventually help achieve the financial hurdles needed for continued support over the long term. This is similar to CVC and should be managed as such. If equity returns are a goal, a venture accelerator is a good fit.

FOMO Isn't a Good Why

It's worth mentioning that there are also a lot of bad reasons for doing accelerators. Fear of missing out (FOMO) is a common driver, whether executives acknowledge it or not. When peers are bragging in the media about their own accelerators and big companies feel the pressure from startups taking some of their business, hastily launching an accelerator can be a problematic mandate.

Bedy Yang, managing partner at 500 Startups, articulates this well: "Corporations often come from a place of fear of being disrupted. When you say, 'I think the entire world is gravitating toward startups,' it's because startups actually mean innovation . . . I think a lot of the large corporates now are afraid. They might be afraid of the Amazon effect, or the Uber or Netflix effect, or whatever comes next. All of a sudden they're saying, 'for the sake of our future, we have to somehow collaborate with the startups.' So, very often they come from a place of fear, of wanting to hedge against it. And that's how they start that relationship."[3]

While fear might be a real and valid concern, before launching an accelerator make sure there is a real motivation from the executives that will sustain the program in the long term, such as one of the core SIMs. If there is not a solid foundation for why an accelerator is launched, it is not being set up for a path to success.

Taking the Why to How

Once the why is clearly articulated, then the challenge is how to translate this into an accelerator program that achieves those objectives. One way is to think carefully about the theme and mission of the program.

"Having a clear mission and focus has really helped us at URBAN-X," says Miriam Roure, program director and principal at BMW MINI's URBAN-X accelerator. URBAN-X is a venture accelerator for early stage startups that reimagines city life, including verticals ranging from transportation to real estate and construction, energy, and water to govtech. "For

BMW Group or MINI, we could have been an accelerator just focused on mobility, and at a first glance, there might have been more synergies with the core company. But those synergies and partnerships don't usually come until the companies are more mature, so for the stage at which we invest, focusing on building more sustainable cities has proven to be a very productive thesis. This thesis has opened the door for the BMW Group to be part of the conversation of what is the future of cities and sustainability, which has tremendous value. It's a more substantial mission and story, and we are passionate about it."

Aligning Corporate and Startup Whys

Corporate accelerators and startups often have divergent interests. For corporates, especially if they are publicly listed, shareholders expect incremental profits, executives expect consistent growth, and internal teams stick with what's proven. Startups are formed to disrupt entire industries and join corporate accelerators to gain access to funding, customers, specific expertise, office space, and mentorship. For corporate accelerators to succeed, it is important that the whys for both parties are clear and aligned.

Make sure you ask the question: Why would a top startup want to be in this accelerator? The name of the game in the startup world is to work with that 0.1% top performer. These are the startupss that are more likely to achieve scale quickly, which make it more likely that the corporate will achieve outsized results. Remember to always be thinking about why the best startups in the world would consider joining a corporate accelerator rather than a high-profile traditional accelerator such as Y Combinator or Techstars, if they join an accelerator at all.

Overall, a little bit of work at the beginning to understand your company's why for launching an accelerator, and also the startup's why for joining the program, can set the stage for a successful accelerator where both parties achieve meaningful results. This is the whole point of corporate accelerators.

BUY IN OR WALK AWAY

CHAPTER 7

STAKEHOLDER ENGAGEMENT

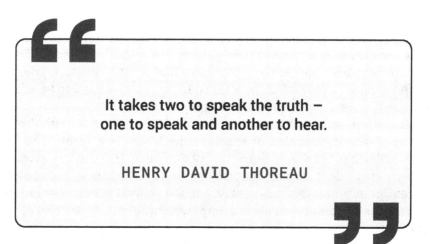

It takes two to speak the truth – one to speak and another to hear.

HENRY DAVID THOREAU

For any major initiative in a large organization, getting support from stakeholders is a critical step in ensuring that your project can go forward, have an impact, and continue to exist in the long term. Without stakeholder support, financial and human resources will eventually become scarce. Other projects with their own backers and competing visions take priority, and politics may create active opposition to your initiative. The need for stakeholder support for innovation projects – with their uncertain outcomes, longer time frames, and propensity to challenge the current established products and structures – is even more critical.

111

Stakeholder engagement is not important for corporate accelerator leaders; it's essential. You can have the most amazing program and the best startups participating, but if you have not taken the time to ensure the appropriate internal stakeholders are fully engaged and supportive along the way, the program itself may not receive continued support. Innovation programs take time and they are easily put on the chopping block when budgets are cut. Stakeholder engagement helps prevent, or at least minimize the possibility of, this happening. Stakeholder engagement can be a lot of work, but is well worth it in the end.

WHO IS A STAKEHOLDER?

A stakeholder is anyone who believes he or she has influence on, or is influenced by, the outcome of your project. The definition from the Project Management Institute (PMI) is "a stakeholder is an individual, group, or organization who may affect, be affected by, or perceive itself to be affected by a decision, activity, or outcome of a project."

By definition, stakeholders have a stake in the initiative, with the possibility of gaining benefits or experiencing losses as a result. The term stakeholder has been used since the 1930s, when Harvard law professor E. Merrick Dodd outlined four major groups of business stakeholders: shareowners, employees, customers, and the general public.[1] For our purposes, stakeholders are people or groups who influence the success of your accelerator.

There will obviously be external stakeholders, including (but not limited to) the startups in your cohort, VC investors, your customers, and your shareholders. But we will focus here on the internal stakeholders, which can be very complicated and challenging to manage well.

The perception of influence is important and goes both ways. You may have someone who wants to be highly engaged and take up a ton of time, but doesn't have any actual influence (e.g., a nosy mid-level manager). You may also have people who do not think they are stakeholders and do not want to be involved, but actually have a meaningful impact on the program (e.g., business unit leaders). There are also an array of key operational personnel, such as legal and human resources, who are needed to smoothly facilitate partnerships or unlock the benefits offered in the program. For example, if you offer co-working space on site for your accelerator teams, you'll need approval from facilities.

Knowing who your internal stakeholders are and managing them actively is an essential task for accelerator leaders. In order to do this well, you need to develop a clear understanding of the organization you operate in, as well as the different types of stakeholders you have within your company.

STAKEHOLDER SUPPORT IS CRITICAL

No one likes corporate politics, but getting the right internal support for your corporate accelerator is an important factor in its long-term success. The right advocates can make the difference between transformative innovation and a distraction. Stakeholder engagement is sometimes ignored because it is a complicated and time-consuming process of collaboration, communication, and consensus building. Fortunately, there are some practical ways to do it well, which starts with simply knowing who your stakeholders are and creating a plan to communicate with them effectively.

Broader stakeholder engagement differs from direct governance, though it is related. Governance relies on a particular group who directly influence decisions and are responsible for the outcome. These are very important stakeholders and we will discuss their role later in this chapter.

The business case for stakeholder engagement is simple: good stakeholder engagement leads to better performance. Companies that govern innovation thoroughly and systematically demonstrated double the revenue growth compared to those following a haphazard approach.[2] Good engagement also has meaningful long-term rewards – you can fine-tune your program over time by learning from the constant flow of information to and from your stakeholders, which gives you a better understanding of what works best in your particular organization.

A good basic process to follow includes stakeholder mapping and segmentation, then plotting an engagement plan based on influence and interest.

STAKEHOLDER MAPPING: WHO DO WE NEED TO ENGAGE?

There are many types of stakeholders, so the first activity is to list them all. There are usually many more than you think at first. Write down anyone within your company who has influence or is influenced by your accelerator program. Be sure to include people who believe they have influence or are influenced, even if you may not think their belief is accurate. We have outlined common accelerator stakeholders – if you are experienced with sales or business development you may notice similarities. In a lot of ways, stakeholder management is an internal sales process, and viewing it as such will help you to categorize, cluster, and implement an effective engagement plan.

Common Stakeholders by Role

C-level Sponsor

Who is the most senior sponsor of your program? For all corporate accelerator programs, you absolutely need a C-level sponsor. Innovation programs of any kind are difficult, and can take years to see tangible results. If the initiative is not supported at the highest level, it will be difficult to get the right internal support you need, or to maintain the long-term perspective (and funding) you need to see it through. Most programs we've seen and studied have failed without a C-level sponsor. Ideally, a corporate accelerator should be sponsored by the CEO, who can ensure that your program is seen as strategically important, give your program credibility, and help remove any blockers to success. If this is not the case, a C-level sponsor that has influence and credibility within the organization is important.

You won't likely get too much time with your C-level sponsor, but build a personal relationship whenever you can. Regular, brief meetings quarterly are best practice; the senior supporters should be aware of the progress and challenges so they know how to help, but do not want to get bogged down in the details. You can also passively push them regular updates with an email or summary report, so they can refer back to the updates when needed and can step in to remove blockers, which is the best use of their time.

Innovation Executive Sponsor

Most corporations have someone focused on innovation within the company, with varying levels of authority and influence. Whether the program is housed under them or nowhere nearby, make sure those senior executives are actively supporting you and your accelerator program. Accelerators are a foundational innovation program, so it's their job to be involved!

Business Unit Leader

Who is the main user or partner for the startups in your accelerator program? Typically this is one of the business units. The BU leader is the one who will ultimately own the P&L if a partnership is successful. Even though you might have managers in the BU supporting the program, it is important to get the main BU leader engaged. The accelerator or innovation team cannot, and should not, own the entire relationship with the startups after the accelerator program is complete. The accelerator is a funnel for finding and vetting top startups that might be a good fit for your company's innovation goals. Once you have startups that are vetted through your accelerator and starting down the path of partnership, they should be integrated into the corresponding business unit and spread their wings from there. Business unit leaders may not be involved in the accelerator directly but their engagement is critical. They can share information on where they have gaps that innovation partners could fill, and clear the path to a pilot or partnership. The earlier you get their buy-in, the better.

Program Sponsor

If you are in a large company, there may be several layers of management between the person running the accelerator and the program sponsor. Who is the person within the company that asked for the accelerator and will ultimately be responsible if it succeeds or fails? This may be the BU leader or innovation executive, but we've seen a wide variety of program sponsors from around the company. The program sponsor is invested in seeing the program succeed, since it also reflects on them personally and professionally.

Financial Owner

Who writes the checks for your program? This is the economic buyer, and they must justify the annual expense of your program each budget cycle. This is often someone in a finance or corporate development team who approves annual budgets. When the program sponsor got the budget approved, who signed off on it? This person may be very far removed from the program and might not care much about innovation. They care about numbers and results. Especially if it is a public company, they want to ensure that the program is a good use of shareholder's capital. This person will like to see quantitative results, with things like return on investment (ROI), revenues, or reduction in costs directly resulting from the accelerator. Setting the right metrics for success early on – tied to the company's wider goals and metrics – and sharing regular updates can help keep this stakeholder supportive of you and your program.

Accelerator Program Manager

Who runs the day-to-day accelerator program? This is the person hustling nonstop to do the millions of things needed to make an accelerator run smoothly. They are entrepreneurial, roll-up-your-sleeves people who do the recruiting, plan the curriculum, organize the in-person meetings, build a brand, engage the ecosystem, and attend to endless tiny details of the accelerator operations. It's important to acknowledge the enormous amount of work that this person or team must pull together in a short period of time. Many accelerator managers get burned out, especially if they aren't able to take time off after the Demo Day to decompress and recover. This person needs support, empathy, and time for an "off" switch after the chaos of the program is completed so they can come back refreshed and do it all over again.

Startup Sponsor

It is a best practice to have each startup you select for the program paired with the person who will be their sponsor within your company. This often means their potential customer within your company, or the person who will be necessary to integrate them with your product or service offering. That person will "own" the relationship with the startup after the accelerator program, and it is best to get them engaged as early as possible – ideally before the company is selected so they are bought in and feel ownership of the startup's success.

Expert

Who are your most important carriers of relevant expertise in the company? These can be your speakers for the curriculum, your expert mentors, or just people you can learn from directly to help set you up for success. They can have technical expertise, or expertise about your company, such as knowing how to get things done within the corporate machine. Especially if you have a vertical focus for your accelerator, these are the people working in that vertical every single day. Company experts may be the most knowledgeable in their industry and can provide a unique advantage to a corporate accelerator. This works both ways, as their exposure to the innovators in their field can provide them key insights into emerging new trends and new ways of thinking.

Mentor

Most accelerator programs have mentors who are either matched directly with each startup, or act as a pool of resources for the startups to tap into if/ when needed. For corporate accelerators, this is usually a mix of external experts (e.g., VCs, marketing specialists, technical specialists) and internal resources from your company. It could be the experts, sponsors, or other stakeholders, but sometimes it's just employees who are attracted to the startup world and have a particular skill to offer. This person spends a couple of hours a week maximum with the startups to share their expertise and help the company wherever needed. They can often become information conduits to other parts of the organization through informal structures – evangelists sharing your accelerator brand and ideas within the wider corporate culture.

Volunteer

Many accelerators will attract volunteers from within the company who do something entirely different in their day job but are excited about the program and want to volunteer some of their time. Often these are young, ambitious, enthusiastic, entrepreneurial people early in their career who are eager to learn and may want to start their own company one day. While they might not have enough skills or influence to be working directly with the startups, there is an endless amount of activity that can be done at accelerators and you can put them to work. If the management cost doesn't outweigh the benefit, it can be a win-win to give you more resources while providing an exciting learning opportunity and cultural influence for emerging leaders at your company. Filter for the ones who are doers and can actively "get it done" without much supervision or time on your part. Also make sure these individuals have approval from their manager to volunteer – it's best to specify time estimates and activities as concretely as possible to ensure that they don't get in trouble. Try to give them specific tasks that they can do independently and on their own time, so they can figure out how to manage the work within their day job. Also make sure to give them the thanks and appreciation they deserve by doing something special for them, either celebrating them or spending time with them as a mentor or coach.

There are many other possible stakeholders that may have influence, or be influenced by, your accelerator program. These can include, but are certainly not limited to:

- Corporate venture capital teams – They have capital to invest in the startups after your program ends and are already engaging the startup world so they can help build a competitive pipeline of applicants.
- The IT department or chief information officer's team – If there is a need for product integration, technical vetting, or security checks.
- Procurement – Most big companies have cumbersome vendor onboarding processes, and you will need their support to expedite and simplify.
- Legal team – To review partnership contracts, investment documents, and so forth.
- Marketing team – To promote the program and the participating startups.
- Sellers – If there is a go-to-market partnership, who will be working with the startup to sell together? Is there a competing product in their portfolio?
- Corporate development/M&A team – If they are interested in making acquisitions, they might want to develop early relationships with your startups.

There are likely many more, so make sure to understand the stakeholders in your own organization.

STAKEHOLDERS AND GOVERNANCE

A particular and important subset of stakeholders are those involved in governance. Governance refers to the systems by which companies or initiatives are directed and controlled. It's about decision-making. For your accelerator program, having the right governance structure in place is the best way to ensure good stakeholder management and continued support.

In your accelerator program, who makes the decisions? How is decision-making integrated into the larger company's governance structures? Are you reporting to the board of directors? Do you have your own advisory board? Who decides on the companies selected for the program? This is a very important part of stakeholder management. Formal governance structures are a comfortable way for corporate leaders to manage, and it is usually seen as an honor or a professional accolade to be asked to serve on a governance board of some kind. There are several possible governance structures by which to engage stakeholders in your accelerator program.

Board of Directors

Start at the very top. Who does the CEO report to? That's right, the board of directors. Are they aware of your program? Sometimes accelerator leaders report regularly to the company's board of directors, especially if there is an innovation committee on the board. If so, this is an amazing opportunity to get visibility and support at the most senior level. These are usually extremely well-connected and influential people, which gives you an additional level of support and recognition. While it can be a formal and time-consuming process to report regularly to the board, it is generally worth it because it means that the company is serious about innovation and working with startups. If you are not reporting to the official board, it's worth asking your C-level sponsor if this is something of interest to the board and how you should be sharing information with them.

Accelerator Board

You can also create your own board for the accelerator program specifically. This is an effective and efficient way to manage your most senior and important stakeholders. It should be small enough to be manageable, meeting roughly quarterly, though possibly more when the accelerator is in session. As the accelerator manager is essentially the CEO of that program, it should be similar in reporting to the board of directors, though on a smaller scale and less formal. These are the people who accelerator leaders can rely on to help provide insight and make key decisions.

Investment Committee

The selection of startup participants is an essential part of an accelerator. and the investment committee decides on which companies to select for the program. Sometimes accelerator program managers select the companies unilaterally, but this is a wasted opportunity to garner buy-in from stakeholders. It will be much easier to integrate the startups into your company during and after the program if these stakeholders are invested in them from the beginning. A best practice is to include both internal and external stakeholders, including external experts such as VCs, your corporate customers, or startup CEOs operating in the same industry. It should be an honor to serve on the investment committes so also be selective.

Partnership Team

A newer trend is to form a partnership or commercialization team that focuses on enabling partnerships resulting from the accelerator. This is particularly helpful in a partnership accelerator archetype, as the accelerator teams may not be the best resources to navigate the path to partnership. This team should be half biz dev, half special ops – they know how the machine works and can make the pilot, contract, test, or deal happen. While partnership teams are just starting to emerge in the world of corporate accelerators, they are much more common in the world of corporate venture capital. If your CVC team already has a business development function built you can tap into it. But if not, it is worth building to follow through on the momentum you create with the accelerator program.

MAPPING STAKEHOLDERS ON A QUADRANT

Once you know your stakeholders, you need to figure out how to engage them effectively. It is neither possible nor desirable to engage with every stakeholder on every conceivable issue, but you do need a way to monitor and manage this squirrely collection of stakeholders around the company. This can be done by plotting them out on a quadrant where the y-axis is the level of influence, and the x-axis is the level of engagement needed. This will allow you to bucket people together and streamline your communication plans.

The four quadrants are:

1. **Impacted**

    In the top right corner are people with a lot of influence and a high interest in your accelerator. This usually includes the program sponsor and perhaps the innovation leader, and all of your governance committees. These are usually your biggest champions or most effective saboteurs! This will be the quadrant where you will spend the most time, and your communication is likely to be two-way and frequent. These are people who require high engagement and close management.

2. **Informed**

   The top left corner contains people who have a lot of influence but are not interested in spending much time with your program. This is likely your C-level sponsor, board of directors, or BU leaders who are less engaged but important for your success. They have a lot of other stuff on their plate! However, they don't like surprises so communication should be formal, frequent, short, and direct. You need to keep a steady drumbeat of information flowing one way, with occasional (say quarterly?) in-person or virtual check-ins. Build trust and rapport, then when you really need something, like removing a blocker, you can make a clear ask.

3. **Included**

   People in the bottom right work well with a medium level of engagement. These are your mentors, experts, and financial owners who may need high communication on a specific thing (e.g., budget approval), and minimal communication on other things. They can also be difficult blockers if they are antagonists, such as a highly risk-averse lawyer or a BU manager who is needed to work with the startup. They should be communicated to regularly to encourage engagement when needed, such as in an update email or internal newsletter with specific asks and timelines.

4. **Interested**

   This is the easiest category of people, because they are not important for your success and have no impact on decisions. Many times there are people in this category who think they have influence but actually don't. They can be needy and want to be kept in the loop all the time. This may sound harsh, but accelerators are a lot of work and you cannot let these people suck up much time and energy. You can add them to a passive update email that takes zero effort from you. If they persist, make them demonstrate how they can help and possibly convert them into a different category, or politely and respectfully tell them that you have a lot on your plate and aren't able to respond to their requests. Or just ignore them. Whatever you do, do not let them distract you.

STAKEHOLDER QUADRANT

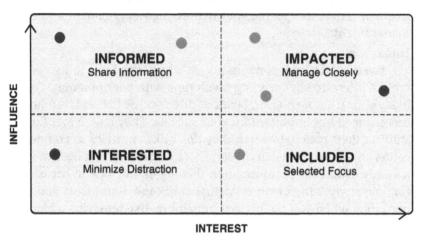

Source: IFI; Nasdaq[3]

HOW TO COMMUNICATE

How do you engage all of these stakeholders along the way? Communication is critical. Much of the long-term success of accelerator programs comes from effective internal communication. Stakeholder engagement is essentially a combination of internal marketing and governance. Deep engagement of your key stakeholders involves more than just a one-off meeting or the occasional update session. It requires an ongoing dialogue and consistent engagement. Whenever possible, it is extremely useful to have a dedicated marketing and communications person on your accelerator team. This person should handle internal marketing and communications as well, not just external marketing. It's even better if you can have different people to focus full time on both of these functions.

You have options – some of this is based on style and preference, but the most important thing is that it's thoughtful and consistent. Use your stakeholder quadrant to create a formal engagement plan.

Communication Type

There are many types of communications that can work here. Different stakeholders have different needs. Some will require mostly one-way communication to keep them informed, but will communicate very little back to you. Others will also communicate a lot to you (e.g., experts who educate you on a particular topic) but may not require regular information in return. Most often engagement requires two-way communication, where there is a constant flow of information between you and your stakeholders. These are typically one-to-one communications like meetings and reporting sessions. You can also have one-to-many communication, where you're pushing the same information out to multiple people at a time, typically in the form of a newsletter, presentation, or event.

What you choose depends on your resources, style, and goals. Here are some options to help develop your plan:

STAKEHOLDER COMMUNICATION OPTIONS

	ONE TO ONE	ONE TO MANY	MANY TO ONE
ONE WAY	• Executive memo customized email for specific people • Budget updates	• Email update • Newsletter • Shared file or folder of "current state" updated regularly and people can check themselves at any time • Board meeting presentation • Summary report or presentation • KPIs or metrics scorecard	• Feedback survey • NPS score request
TWO WAY	• 1:1 meetings to share updates, discuss specific topics, work through challenges	• Event with panels, discussion • Pitch events with feedback	• Post-mortem report to CEO

If you are a practitioner of Agile methodology – which includes scrums, standups, playbacks, and so on – and your organization understands this process, apply it to your communication style.

Cadence and Timing

How often will you communicate? The frequency may be different, depending on the stakeholder or stakeholder group. Make sure it doesn't seem random. A monthly or quarterly update may be appropriate for most. However, when your accelerator is in session, frequency may increase. Consistency is also important, and helps to build credibility and trust. Taking a systematic approach that is grounded in the business strategy and operations increases the likelihood that engagement will earn credibility and respect.

Things should appear to be intentional and collaborative, not transactional. If you're only communicating to people when you need something from them, they will be less likely to help you in the long term. Set ground rules for frequency and meet them – someone expecting a weekly update will not want daily alerts or monthly summaries.

Materiality

All stakeholders don't need all the information. Decide which issues are material to each stakeholder or stakeholder group. In accounting, information is considered material if its omission or misstatement could influence the economic decision of users taken on the basis of financial statements. For the purposes of stakeholder engagement, material information is anything that, if unknown or misunderstood, would prohibit that stakeholder from making sound judgments and taking the appropriate action you need to succeed. Communicate only the critical information, but you can provide more detail and ongoing reference material in an easy to access area such as Dropbox or a shared drive.

Learning

Stakeholder engagement is also extremely useful as a learning and information tool. Ask for feedback: How can you improve? What did they like about the program and what didn't they like? Of course, you don't have to do everything they suggest, but their feedback can be extremely useful in helping you continue to improve the program.

PRINCIPLES FOR STAKEHOLDER ENGAGEMENT

Now that you have identified the stakeholders, and how and when you will be engaging them through your communications strategy, it's important to keep some key communications principles in mind. The goal is to align the stakeholders for success; this means communicating not just the successes but the learnings from things that don't go as well. Some companies in the accelerator cohort – most of them – won't work out, but the learnings from these market tests will make the outcomes of the rest better. An accelerator can help to spread an innovation culture to the broader corporate DNA as one notable benefit, and stakeholder engagement is part of making this happen. Give people the information on successes and failures – and guidance on how to interpret the learnings – through these key stakeholder management best practices.

Build Trust

Trust takes time to build but is critical to your long-term success, especially for innovations such as corporate accelerators that are often a leap of faith for corporations used to more concrete, predictable, and short-term initiatives. To build trust, you must build real relationships with your stakeholders. Start early – relationships take time to build. Trust and mutual respect are established over time. Trust is also much harder to build if stakeholders are only consulted when there is a problem or crisis.

Listen

Ask your stakeholders for their input – often they have a lot of ideas about what you're doing! Sometimes you'll learn something, but even if you don't, just listening to their feedback can build strong relationships and establish trust.

Be Vulnerable

Though this can be difficult in a polished corporate environment, you're in the startup world too! The power of vulnerability allows people to connect with you and know how to help you.

Be Responsive

For your important stakeholders (top right and left quadrant), make sure you respond quickly to any requests. And follow up - don't just leave people without the answers they need. Make sure the accelerator team looks like they're on the ball.

Follow Through

Integrity, or doing what you say you're going to do, is important to any relationship. If you state your goals or claim something will happen, report back. Even if it didn't happen, close the loop. It's better to share this information and learn from it than to ignore it (unfortunately common in the corporate world). Make it clear that stakeholder concerns and interests were heard, considered, and valued. Show that you're someone who follows through on your promises.

Be an Open Book

Try to be up front with your team about your own personal development goals. It may not be relevant to their immediate project, but they need to know that you are a person too. Let them know that you're working toward improving the way you support both them and yourself. The key here is to always lead by example. Want your team to be more open? Start sharing yourself.

Have Patience

As with any long-term relationship, patience is required to weather the bumps in the road. The process can't be rushed. Building consensus and creating an environment of open dialogue can only happen on a foundation of trust, and trust takes time to build and demonstrate. If something is wrong or you don't have the appropriate stakeholder support, *wait*. If you do not have the critical stakeholders on board, while painful, it is better to wait until you do than to launch the program without them. While it can be tempting, especially with an entrepreneurial team, to just launch it and get it out there, it has a much higher chance of failure if not supported properly from the beginning.

Problem-Solve

Accelerators, like startups, never go according to plan. There will be a million unexpected problems that will come up. Share these with your stakeholders – this will give them empathy for the difficult job of running an accelerator. It's like whack-a-mole. Working together on this process makes all stakeholders feel like change agents and increases the chances of buy-in later in the development cycle. Paired with an effective communication plan, showing how you've jumped over every hurdle thrown at you can help to build trust and increase connectivity with your stakeholders.

Fail in Public

It never feels good to fail, but well-managed failures are integral to the process of innovation and learning. During the accelerator program, and your professional life in general, you will need to take risks to succeed. Taking risks means failing every once in a while, maybe failing all the time. How you pick yourself back up, acknowledge it, and learn from the experience makes you stronger and earns the respect and trust of your colleagues. Set the expectations that this will happen and then make it part of the normal process. This helps to normalize it as part of an innovation culture.

Ask for Help

Though it can be tempting to gloss over the details and project that everything is always perfect, everyone knows that this is not the case. If you need help, ask for it. For example, when a stakeholder you need is not engaged in the right way, or is actively blocking you, ask for help from your executive sponsor. That's why he or she is there!

STAKEHOLDER ENGAGEMENT AS CULTURE CHANGE

In the corporate environment, the most dramatic innovation usually comes from the bottom up or outside in. There can be a lot of hubris in big, traditionally successful companies that think innovation can only come from seasoned internal leaders and their teams. They've created successful new products and services before (or maybe their more entrepreneurial predecessors have!), and they can do it again. This pride can be good, as it means the executives truly believe in their company, including the existing products and teams. But it also causes an unfair negative assessment of external technologies.

The longer-term change that you can start to seed and grow is one that embraces external innovation and is proud of it. The opposite cultural disposition of Not Invented Here Syndrome is sometimes called Proudly Found Elsewhere (PFE), which embraces the fact that ideas and innovation outside the company can be more valuable than expertise and ideas from within the company. An accelerator can be this bridge to the world of innovation that slowly lets in a new cultural paradigm.

Managing your stakeholders well can help to create these cracks in the culture with support from an influential and diverse group of people within your company. An accelerator can be a safe sandbox to test new ideas and ways of doing things, which slowly changes the culture to embrace more of the entrepreneurial mindset.

CHAPTER 8

RESOURCES

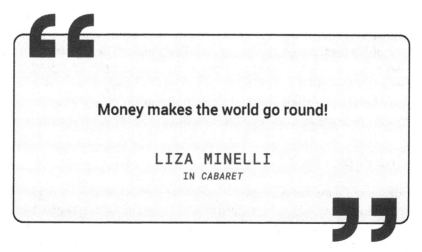

Money makes the world go round!

LIZA MINELLI
IN *CABARET*

Source: John Kander[1]

Creating a strategy is often the easy part, the execution is where most big companies struggle. Achieving the strategic vision for an accelerator is more complicated than it seems at first. It requires gaining deep internal buy-in, long-term commitment to experiment and learn, finding and retaining the right internal talent who understand both your company and the startup world, recruiting top-tier startups that are appropriately aligned with your strategic goals achieving results for both the company and the participating startups – this is an enormous undertaking! It's a lot of work and requires the right financial and talent resources to make it happen. When the time comes to get to work building the corporate accelerator, just like a startup, you need two key resources: people and money.

YOUR ACCELERATOR TEAM

Finding and retaining the right talent for corporate innovation programs is always an issue, and it is even more pronounced with accelerator programs. "My suggestion is really to get buy in around trying a few different things, get the capital to do it, get the resources to do it," says Jenny Fielding, managing director of Techstars–New York City and The Fund. "Then go pick partners who have done it before. Don't just promote someone within who doesn't have an innovation bone in his or her body. Make sure that you get someone from the outside who's built a company. Make sure that you get the right people for the right job." There are several key skills that this person or team should possess.

Startup Experience

The ideal profile for the accelerator leader is an entrepreneurial person who has first-hand knowledge of the startup world, usually having been a founder, a VC, or an accelerator manager themselves. It is extremely important to have the pattern recognition and network necessary to recruit and select the best startups, which is nearly impossible if you have not seen a high volume of startups and have not made investment decisions with limited information. The startup world is an apprenticeship model – you only learn by doing, and there is no substitute for direct experience.

Take it from your authors, who have founded five companies between the two of us, raised millions in venture funding, and have also been on the other side as VCs and accelerator managers. We can tell you with 100% certainty that if you haven't done this yourself, you do not really understand startups. It's a very particular experience. You cannot learn about startups from a book or even just by going to meetups and Demo Days. And for the love of all that is good in the world, please don't equate starting something new within a big company as the same experience – it's not and it minimizes the experience of actual entrepreneurs.

Startup experience is like becoming a surgeon – you can study for it, you can observe others do it, but without practice and actual experience, you should never perform surgery. The accelerator leader must be a licensed startup doctor in order to do their job properly. It will serve you and your accelerator better if the leader, or at least a few of the key stakeholders, have first-hand experience as a founder, VC, or accelerator manager.

Deep Corporate Knowledge and Connections

In addition, the accelerator leader needs to deeply understand your company and how to navigate its complex processes, bring in the right colleagues to participate, and close deals effectively. They should ideally have strong pre-existing relationships with key executives and other stakeholders within the company where they have built trust and respect. This will allow them to ask these stakeholders to take some risks, such as experimenting with a startup partnership or committing to an early pilot of an untested technology. The accelerator leader must have the powers of persuasion and enough career capital to gently nudge people on board with the uncomfortable new terrain of innovation and working with startups.

The person needs to have enough seniority and gravitas to "manage up," with the right credibility to get internal approvals, manage governance of senior executives, get on the radar of the sales team and other internal stakeholders to successfully make "asks" as needed, manage a budget, and lead/manage a team.

If you're thinking that this insider skill set sounds like a contradiction with the external experience required as a founder or investor, you're correct! Someone with years of experience both at your company and in the startup world is nearly impossible to find. Most people who have reached a certain level in their careers have long since decided that they prefer one path or the other.

Project Management Guru

And wait, there's more! This person also needs to be an efficient and effective project manager. After the accelerator is conceived, the execution of the program is extremely administrative. It's event planning, endless communication, juggling multiple resources and stakeholders that may or may not report to them, marketing and branding, and a million more tiny details. It can be a grind.

This type of work generally lends itself to someone with a more junior-level skill set who does not mind rolling up their sleeves and doing the administrative tasks. This is yet another contradiction, this time with the senior-level skill set that is also required.

Collaboration Is Key

Running an accelerator effectively requires a unique background; the best way to do it is to have done it already. Even if you find this magical unicorn with all of the required skills, they might not want to run an accelerator program or be motivated by the compensation you are able to offer.

However, if you can't find this mythical being, don't worry. There is another path: collaboration. If one person doesn't fit the bill, you can pull in people with complementary skill sets to build the accelerator together. Innovation initiatives, especially corporate accelerators, can rarely be built by internal teams only. But they also cannot be entirely delegated to an external consultant. The best-case scenario is to pair an internal aficionado with an experienced entrepreneur from outside the company – a new hire, an entrepreneur in residence, or a third-party consultant – who can work together well, then build a team around them.

Finding the right pairing can be a challenge, but so is building an accelerator in the first place. This is the nature of the game of investing in and partnering with startups, where things are hard and the odds are against you. If finding the right talent (or talent partnership) to lead it scares you, perhaps you're not in a position to launch and sustain an accelerator at all! The right team running the accelerator is a critical success factor – your first innovation challenge is to get it right.

Commercialization Lead

There is an exciting new type of role that is worth considering on an accelerator team: the commercialization lead. With an acknowledgment that corporations must achieve some sort of financial returns – whether from market intelligence, direct sales, or something in between – from accelerator programs, it makes sense to have a dedicated, full-time resource focused on this purpose.

The advocacy of this role comes from Andrew Goldner, co-founder and CEO of GrowthX. GrowthX is a venture capital fund in San Francisco run by operators with extensive go-to-market experience. They have a special Market Acceleration Program (MXP) for their founders focused on go-to-market and finding product-market fit.

"A classic mistake that we see corporations make, which seems like a very logical decision, is to assign top salespeople from inside the company to take new things that result from innovation initiatives to market themselves," says Goldner. "But top salespeople at big companies are used to doing business in a certain way, utilizing the brand halo that's been established over decades and sometimes centuries to sell in the same way that they've always sold with a product that already has a market and a track record," he explains. "They know how to sell a commodity, and they have systems and processes in place to grow incremental revenue, not introduce something that's disruptive and new to a market where learning precedes revenue. And their KPIs are misaligned with the process of taking something disruptive and new to market."

By having a dedicated person on the accelerator team to focus on commercialization, someone who understands how to sell disruptive technologies, there are much stronger commercial results. "We now advocate for corporates to hire a dedicated commercialization lead," said Goldner. "This is what we would refer to in the startup world as the market developer or, what Mark Leslie refers to as the Renaissance Rep." This is an emerging trend that can make all the difference in your strategic results.

SOURCING AND PAYING TALENT

Many companies have now established pipelines for bringing former founders and entrepreneurs into their organization as accelerator leaders, and also to serve as coaches and mentors to startups. While corporate roles do not offer the financial upside of the startup world, it may be easier to recruit from this talent pool than a big company might expect. For many founders, after a long journey building a company, a safe harbor with a dependable paycheck and health insurance is often a very attractive place at some point in their career.

Citibank, for example, has taken to hiring former founders to become entrepreneurs in residence (EIRs) through its structured D10x program. They have built an army of EIRs to provide an outside-in perspective, contributing to the cultivation of new skills and new ways of working that they actively want to instill across Citi.[2] Many entrepreneurs relish these opportunities to put their skills to work on big problems that have corporate resources behind them. Entrepreneurs are motivated by solving big problems, though the compensation should also be fair and have some performance-based incentive.

Also these jobs typically have a lot of flexibility, so an entrepreneur can also work on other projects – investing, advising, serving on boards, or starting their next company – at the same time. Make sure to bake in this flexibility and avoid the typical corporate restrictions on potential conflicts, or it will be harder to recruit the best talent, who generally want to continue with other entrepreneurial projects at the same time.

Compensation can be a bit tricky, as you are benchmarking it not only to corporate roles, but also to the startup and VC world that offers significant upside for financial success. For the key talent of running an internal accelerator, the model of independent accelerators may be worth copying. Though the concept of carried interest (upside on equity returns) is difficult to implement in a corporate setting, some sort of performance-based compensation is critical. For example, Techstars and other accelerator operators provide their teams, in addition to market-based salary and benefits, with a stake in the upside of the cohort of investments through warrant coverage or direct equity participation.

If this is not possible, then bonuses tied to the performance goals of the corporate accelerator – number of pilots or customer partnerships established, for example – can be a great substitute. There is also a concept of phantom carry, which tracks the upside that would have been earned from a particular percentage of carried interest and instead pays out in bonuses that are directly correlated. Regardless, you want to have the team feel and act like owners, as opposed to just employees. This aligns everyone's interests and properly motivates the team to succeed and stay at the company.

FUNDING THE CORPORATE ACCELERATOR OPERATIONS

After you determine the why and map out the accelerator archetype and customizations for the program that you want to build, getting the appropriate budget approved is critical. Many accelerators attempt to achieve big goals with extremely limited resources. In truth, the total amount of budget to be spent on a corporate accelerator program is often nominal for a big company in the grand scheme of things. But there is fear that it might not work, and small budgets are allocated at the beginning to experiment. Like a startup, this can force a team to be creative and scrappy, but can also set it up for failure, especially if it is staffed with people who are used to big budgets and don't know how to be scrappy.

As a critical best practice, it's important to get a multi-year budget approved, as these programs take time to achieve their goals. Ideally this would be for at least five years, which is about how long it will take for a subset of the participating startups to start achieving real success. If this long-term commitment is not agreed on at the outset, there is a major risk of the program being shut down before it can yield any results, in which case it would be better for your brand, your team, and the participating startups to not do it at all. It's simply not possible to deliver on long-term goals with a short-term focus.

There's no one-size-fits-all budget, but generally speaking, the best programs allocate $1–$3 million to execute on and invest in one cohort of 10 companies per year. This is a sliding scale and can increase dramatically with multiple cohorts, larger cohorts, or larger investment or grant checks. While the budget can also be lower, it should be clearly understood what costs are eliminated and why. Too many accelerators are given tiny budgets, such as $250K, and expected to make miracles happen. Expectations must be aligned with budgets.

For many corporations, these numbers may appear daunting at first. But when compared to the broader cost of research, development, and launching new products, the budget is a tiny speck on the corporate P&L. The costs are all relative to results as well, so embedded in any pushback on budget is a fear of not achieving results that will produce a return on the investment. This is a good opportunity to have a conversation on why the person pushing back thinks this might be the case. A cost of even $2 million a year to get under the hood of market trends and emerging potential competitors is surprisingly cost effective when put in that context.

One study from Deloitte noted a general guideline for an accelerator budget: "A rule of thumb for the financial estimation is to set aside 5–10 percent of the money that the organization would like to see a business to create. For example, if the goal is to build a 100-million-euro business, the organization should be looking to set aside 5 million–10 million euros for building and running the accelerator."[3]

Taken in context, accelerators are actually highly efficient ways of identifying new areas for growth. Startups can experiment with new ideas in an extremely low-cost and low-risk way, producing outsized returns for the organizations who invest adequately and have the patience to see them through.

CREATING A BUDGET

When it comes to funding, we've already stressed the importance of planning for the long term – five years is a good target time frame to get an accelerator program firmly established and begin to see some of the participating companies emerge as success stories. In addition, another best practice is to fund the accelerator from the balance sheet, not the P&L; otherwise it will lead to short-term thinking. Finally, although it can be tempting, never charge startups for the program. Your goal here is not to make money from startups, who are broke anyway; it is to prove an innovation model that works.

We will talk about outsourcing budgets in the next chapter, but for an accelerator built in-house, the rough price tag here is somewhere between $1 million and $2 million per year for one cohort. This can change dramatically depending on many decisions you make to structure the program, such as investment amount and the number of startups in each cohort, but should be a good guiding benchmark. It can also change based on the seniority of the team and company band salary guidelines. However, as a rough estimate to understand a possible budget in detail, here's a sample budget:

EXAMPLE CORPORATE ACCELERATOR BUDGET

DESCRIPTION	YEAR-1 COST
Equity Investments or Grants (10 × $50k)	$500,000
Program Director	$175,000
Portfolio Manager	$125,000
Commercialization Lead	$100,000
Associate	$75,000
Community Manager	$60,000
Website	$30,000
Social Media/Marketing	$25,000
Guest Speakers/Outside Mentors	$45,000
Food, Entertainment, Social for Startup Events (excluding Demo Day)	$30,000
Demo Day	$75,000
Purchase of Startup Products	$100,000
Travel	$40,000
Space Build-Out or Rent	$30,000
Equipment	$30,000
Legal (Program Docs and Advice)	$50,000
Marketing Sponsorships	$30,000
Other/Misc	$50,000
	$1,570,000

While of course this can be done on a more limited budget, this sample includes some key people that we don't normally see on corporate accelerator teams but believe should be, such as portfolio manager and commercialization lead. You can start with a scrappier team and build up to this, which will support a smaller budget in year 1, and some of the costs such as building out new co-working space are in year 1 only.

Securing the right talent and financial resources is one of the hardest things to do for an accelerator program. When a company decides to dip their toes into the corporate accelerator water, some may think that the time of a few executives and a few sponsorship dollars is all that it takes. However, launching an accelerator in-house will require a multi-year, multimillion-dollar commitment to do right. Identifying and retaining the right resources makes all the difference between a successful corporate accelerator that lasts for decades and one that fails after two years with no results.

CHAPTER 9

OUTSOURCING AND DELEGATING

The best executive is the one who has sense enough to pick good men [and women] to do what he [or she] wants done, and self-restraint to keep from meddling while they do it.

THEODORE ROOSEVELT
26TH U.S. PRESIDENT

For those of you who are just starting down the path of considering an accelerator as a tool for innovation, we're aware that we probably just freaked you out by showing you all the work you have to do to launch a corporate accelerator. Don't worry – grab a handy paper bag and catch your breath if you're hyperventilating. It's not all or nothing. Fortunately, you have many options. Many corporates start by getting involved in other ways, or they work with partners – experienced accelerator operators – to jump in and get things going when they lack the internal capacity right away.

ACCELERATOR ENGAGEMENT OPTIONS

With a dedicated corporate accelerator program, corporations have two main options: run the program in-house or outsource its administration to a partner such as Techstars, Plug and Play, or 500 Startups. In the partnership model, the partner markets the program (often to a community of start-ups applying to their other accelerators), reviews and selects start-ups for each cohort based on shared criteria, provides mentors, and manages the program. Partners may charge several hundred thousand dollars to several million dollars to set up and operate an accelerator on behalf of a corporate sponsor, and they will typically direct the corporate investment in the start-ups admitted to the accelerator, often participating themselves as well. An analysis by Deloitte shows that half of corporate accelerators launched over the past three years have utilized an outsourced partner.[1]

Perhaps equally important, as an alternative to actively running an accelerator, many companies simply elect to become a sponsor or partner of an existing accelerator. In this model, corporations can lend mentors or other resources to startups and in turn get access to those startups' activity within that program. Unsurprisingly, the company typically has less influence over startup selection and program structure than if it were the sole sponsor.

Sigma Labs, which has corporate sponsors such as EMC and Yahoo, is one example of the sponsor model. This allows an innovation team to get started without a huge budget and full buy-in: they can begin to develop the key skills, understand the operations on a day-to-day level, and begin to see if the benefits are likely to be worth it for their own company to take the plunge. By engaging with a live accelerator, key innovation personnel can see what they are getting into before taking the plunge themselves. They can observe the formal and informal interactions, see the logistics of events and mentors first-hand, and even learn if the startups can be potential partners for further exploration.

After participating in an existing accelerator, innovation executives can then pragmatically assess their own organizations' capacity for success. If they can't muster the resources internally, or simply need time to develop capacity and experience, working with a partner can be an option.

Getting involved can also help the team putting together a proposal for a corporate accelerator really nail down the reason they want to launch one. General responses like "innovation" are not getting to the heart of the problem or understanding if accelerators are part of the solution. Also, it is highly recommended that before launching an accelerator on your own, you actively participate in the market, so you can learn and engage before making the big commitment needed to run your own program. Having a clear set of goals, understanding the expectations and outcomes, and budgeting time, personnel, and financial resources effectively can all be excellent reasons to start with a partner or as a sponsor.

The Three Innings of Innovation

The different stages of engagement and internal readiness are for innovation are summarized nicely by Jenny Fielding, managing director at Techstars–New York City and The Fund, who outlines three different innings of innovation. "If you're in the first inning, which is exploration, working with an external partner is probably not the best idea," she says. "There are so many processes internally that a corporate needs to figure out first, such as really basic stuff like contracting. You can't put a 50-page enterprise-level contract in front of a startup, they're not going to be able to work with that." Fielding advises, "If you're in the exploration stage, you need to look within, get all the right stakeholders, really get your house in order, and try some small experiments. Those can take many different forms, but get your house in order first."

Exploration can be a lengthy, but important, process. "Then when you move into the second inning, you can really start working with external partners," says Fielding. "That doesn't mean you shouldn't be doing your own internal ideation as well, but you can start partnering effectively once you have a sense of what works for you culturally."

Some accelerator programs stay in the second inning if the model continues to work, and for some there's a third inning. "What I've found working with corporates is that after spending a few cycles with them, they can really get up to speed," says Fielding. "After three or four years they might decide to try something internally, which usually looks slightly different than the original programs. For instance, some corporates have transitioned into a later-stage program utilizing some of the format and ideologies from the early-stage accelerator, but apply them to a later stage."

Participate as a Mentor

As a corporate executive tasked with innovation, if you just want to skim the surface to learn without much commitment, you can start by having a few people at your company (including you!) serve as mentors in other accelerator programs. Look for programs that are closely aligned with your business and areas where you can add value to the startups. Then specifically try to generate at least one "win" for your company – can you be a customer of a company you mentor? Can you bring the startup to one of your customers? Can you get senior executive engagement on

this? All of this can help test the waters and generate some early successes to help you make the business case for a substantive investment
by your company.

The benefits of this are that it's extremely easy, usually there is no cost,
and there is a lot of education and learning along the way. The cons are that it
highly depends on the company you get matched with (often not under your
control), it has no real brand impact, and it's harder to generate wins between
your company and the startups. An additional benefit to the participating
executive mentor is the experience itself, as well as being able to observe the
broader program. It's a lightweight way to dip your toe in the accelerator water.

Sponsor Accelerator(s)

Another easy entry point into the accelerator world is to sponsor an existing
program. This can be in the form of cash and/or in-kind products or services.
If your company offers a product that startups can use, and you are thinking
about launching an ecosystem accelerator to increase adoption of that product, then sponsoring a program and giving free or ultra-discounted product
to the participating companies is an excellent starting point. You can see if
there is natural adoption, or if you have to add on additional services or go-
to-market efforts in order for the startups to use your product.

Either way, typically a sponsorship would include benefits like speaking
engagements, hosting events, branding, or whatever else you ask for. Again,
if you have a clear understanding of why you want to do an accelerator
program, this is a good first way to test your assumptions on whether an
accelerator can achieve your objectives.

Invest as an LP in an Accelerator Fund

Another method of investing is by being a limited partner in an accelerator
fund. This is particularly useful if you are planning to invest in the startups but do not have an experienced CVC team at your company or anyone
with direct venture capital experience. You can invest in the fund that the
accelerator then uses to invest in their program's participating startups. If you
tell the accelerator up front that it is intended to be a learning experience, and
request a seat on the investment committee or another useful way to engage
in the process, this can be a great way to up your ability to launch and manage
an investment vehicle of your own eventually. Or it could simply be a learning
experience to understand that this is not something you want to take on, and

you can then decide to either offer an equity-free program or outsource the investment management to a third party.

Corporate Accelerators as a Service (CAaaS)

If you want to run an accelerator program that is customized to the needs of your own company but are not ready to take on the significant commitment of doing it in-house, you can outsource it.

Many of the most prolific accelerators – including Techstars and 500 Startups – have expanded their model to include corporate accelerators as a service (CAaaS) consulting functions. These can be a great way to get started, and the teams there certainly know what they're doing after seeing thousands of companies pass through dozens of programs. They are especially skilled at venture accelerator programs, which is essentially a replication of what they do in their own programs. They tap into the same curriculum, recruitment process, deep networks, and brand to jumpstart the process for their corporate clients.

For most of these programs, there will be an expectation of a seven-figure commitment – often as high as $3 million per year – over multiple years, ranging from about 20% higher to more than double the budget you would need to build a program in-house. However, you are getting experts who have been there, done that, and can easily tap into established networks on your behalf. As seasoned operators, they will expect a multi-year commitment, knowing that success in the accelerator space will take time. The premium price taps into a wealth of operational experience: general managers, networks of mentors, community personnel, support teams, operational and financial documents, preexisting processes for selection, programming, and investment. And of course, they bring a pipeline of startups and a brand name to attract them.

Techstars is the most prolific player in this space, starting with a 2015 partnership with Target to now having launched more than 50 corporate or industry accelerators around the world, ranging from Amazon to Ford.[2] There are also many other excellent options, including 500 Startups, Plug and Play, Highline Beta, Boomtown, Village Capital, and more. Each has a slightly different spin on their offering, but will work with corporates to manage the program and rely on their significant experience to skip some of the novice mistakes.

There are a lot of pros to working with an existing operator – you can launch much faster, tap into their existing networks for mentors and recruiting top startups, and access experienced professionals who have run programs before to maximize your chance of success.

The cons are also obvious – while big companies may be less concerned than financial investors about the shared upside, there is less control of the accelerator, and also less understanding from the outsourced teams of the complexities within your own organization. The operator may be an expert at getting startups into and through an accelerator. However, someone who is mostly experienced working with very early-stage companies may not have the skill set at the next stage when partnership with and integration into your parent company is important. They can also be quite expensive if financial resources are limited. In addition, the outsourced CAaaS providers tend to excel at venture accelerators for early-stage companies. For ecosystem or partnership accelerators for growth-stage companies, they may not be the best fit.

Using an outsourced partner can be a good way to start a corporate accelerator for the first few years, and then we see companies eventually moving this function in-house.

Outsourced Portfolio Management

An emerging trend is for corporate accelerator programs to work with an established third-party fund to manage the investment piece in particular. This allows corporates to focus on building the program and curriculum, which big companies tend to be good at, while partnering with a sophisticated investor and portfolio management expert to handle the piece that is a bit more difficult for big companies.

This usually looks like a limited partner (LP) investment in a VC fund, where the corporate provides the capital and the fund manages it. They deal with the term sheets, manage or at least participate in the investment committee, work with the founders directly and consistently over many years, and write detailed quarterly and annual reports on the portfolio.

Based on our research and experience, this lack of a sophisticated portfolio management component after the program ends is one of the main reasons that corporate accelerators fail to achieve their goals. It can also harm the brand and reputation of the corporation in the startup community. Startups don't stop working after the accelerator program, and if you own equity in these startups, you need to be in it with them until they exit or fail. We will discuss this topic in more detail in Chapter 16.

Outsourcing the post-program portfolio management is a compelling new solution to a problem that has been plaguing corporate accelerators since the beginning.

Launch/Own Your Own Program

If you've already tried the previous options and are ready to have more control and autonomy, then it's time to launch your own program! However, before launching your own program, make sure that you have a clear understanding of your objectives, a dedicated budget, commitment for at least five years, and the right talent who understands both your company and high-growth tech startups based on real-world experience in both (this can be a team of people). This requires support from senior leadership and active engagement by the business unit leaders to be successful.

We recommend launching your own program if you have the internal support and resources available for the obvious benefits: complete control, total autonomy, and the company can receive all of the upside. Most importantly, the experience accrues to the corporate innovation team and the institutional knowledge stays within the company. This direct involvement makes it much more likely that the innovation activity can change the culture and mindset of the parent organization to be more open to innovation in all areas of the business, which is often a key long-term goal.

There are plenty of challenges as well, but the cons represent problems that corporations need to solve anyway if they truly wish to be more innovative. Big companies need to develop long-term commitment to innovation, as well as a pool of talent that understands how to execute effectively. It's also difficult to maintain continuity for the third party when senior sponsors change. Shielding the innovation activities from short-term politics and metrics of success is also difficult.

One major improvement of going it alone more recently is the sheer number of corporate accelerators that have launched and gone before. Sometimes the pioneers, as they say, get the arrows in the back. But the trail has been blazed, and the process and programs are much better understood. It's even possible to hire people who have experience from other accelerators directly with more than a decade of programs already in operation.

FROM OUTSOURCING TO INTERNAL INNOVATION

Building an accelerator in-house can, slowly but surely, help to develop a culture of innovation and train entrepreneurial talent that can be deployed in the rest of the organization. While it might make sense to start by sponsoring or working with an outside team, the ultimate goal should be to bring the skills in-house to have the benefits accumulate in the corporate parent.

The skill sets of fostering innovation and working with startups as partners take time to develop.

The best practice for a corporation truly committed to cultural change, however, is the messy middle of launching the program in-house. Building the accelerator yourself develops the internal talent to manage and integrate innovation that is necessary to create lasting change over the long term. Culture change isn't easy and writing a check can't buy that type of experience. However, this is a massive commitment of time, budget, and team. For many, partnering with an experienced partner is a much more appealing option, especially in the short term.

When to Outsource

So when and why should you bring in a third party? "It comes back to knowledge, network, and expertise," says Vijay Rajendran, head of corporate innovation and partnerships at 500 Startups. "It's knowing the topics that matter to startups and will also be relevant for you, experience in curriculum design and delivery, and the power of activating networks that maybe your corporate doesn't have because of the limits of your presence in the startup ecosystem. Those are three really important things."

If the previous chapters seemed overwhelming, it's probably a good idea to outsource, at least at first. Accelerators are complicated and take a lot of work. They require a rare set of skills and have a high failure rate. Outsourcing to experts who have a strong track record of building successful programs can de-risk the first few cohorts, and corporate leaders can learn along the way.

In addition, when launching or expanding to geographies where you may not have a strong local team who is embedded in the local startup market, it can make a lot of sense to outsource. China, Southeast Asia, and many other developing markets are brutal to companies that are not authentically in the ecosystem. When corporates attempt to launch a one-size-fits-all program in a complex ecosystem without local partners, it is a recipe for disaster. Local partners can collaborate with you to customize your program to the specific place and execute with authenticity in that market.

Another good reason to outsource is when the budgets are there but perhaps the organizational buy-in is not. In these cases, outsourcing an accelerator to an expert might be the quickest way to bring the program to life. Techstars, 500 Startups, Plug and Play, and others can spin up an accelerator program with standard operating practices, a recruitment pipeline, and a pool of operating talent in a relatively short time frame. This can generate quick wins and often allow the initial need of building awareness of innovation to get moving quickly. Also, if it is successful, you can slowly gain organizational buy-in by demonstrating results with an outsourced partner first.

However, according to Fielding at Techstars, you need to have your internal ducks in a row before working with an external partner. "The real point to understand is that you've got to clearly define your metrics," she says. "There's no way to work with an external partner if you're still not sure what you want. The worst partnerships happen where the metrics or the ROI haven't been clearly defined."

Companies short on budget or just getting started should send potential program champions to the field to begin learning and making the business case. Those with resources and senior level buy-in, but more difficult corporate structures resistant to change, can start with an outsourced program. Companies that can muster the human and financial resources and the senior-level commitment to innovation as a long-term cultural shift can roll up their sleeves and get to work on an in-house program.

Translating for Corporates and Startups

Another benefit of working with an external partner or an experienced startup expert is to quickly gain credibility in the startup world by combining your corporate team with seasoned entrepreneurs who can attract top startup talent and work with them effectively throughout the program. This skill set is often lacking in the corporate world and it is very difficult to hire this type of talent. "Often there's a real cultural divide," says Fielding at Techstars. "An organization like Techstars can help be that translation point between the founders who may act and operate in one way, and the corporate partner who is quite different. They can be that bridge." By outsourcing to third parties with experienced entrepreneurs on the team, the combination with your internal skill set can be highly effective.

"We have a great reputation for being founder friendly and really helping founders, which allows us to attract great talent," says Fielding of Techstars. This can be a shortcut for corporates as an authentic brand in the startup world takes a long time to build. "The ability to attract great talent has been developed over time through our brand, through our track record, and through some of the people that we hire. Our DNA is quite different. I'm a three-time tech founder, and all the MDs at Techstars are founders, which is probably why people hire us. We're not McKinsey MBAs who are thinking of this clinically. We are all founders, and ultimately it works because we can speak that language and help translate between the two cultures."

Having people involved with a founder mentality is critical to building a top accelerator program. "Having empathy to understand that founder journey really helps us attract and work with some of the best founders out there," says Fielding. "Just having that experience, having grown companies, having raised capital, having gone through all the trials and tribulations as founders is really what makes Techstars unique as an organization. This is not something that is science, there's a lot of art to really understanding founders, being able to help them, and having them open up and blossom during the program."

Budget for Outsourcing

Outsourcing to a more turnkey provider will also have a clear price tag – a request for proposal (RFP) process can yield the specifics, but planning on $2–3 million annually for one cohort a year, for a minimum of three years, is in the right ballpark. The partners cannot do it alone, and must work hand in hand with your internal team to make sure they are connecting to the strategic opportunities. Therefore, it will also include significant time commitments from multiple people on the corporate team.

Regardless of how you start, the most important thing to do is start. It is especially important to go into it with a learning mindset. No accelerator will be perfect the first time around, so continue to iterate and improve until it is serving your needs. Corporate innovation is hard, messy, and slow. Whether you decide to go it alone or work with a partner, just know that you are leading your company down the rocky but rewarding path of innovation, one cohort at a time.

SECTION IV

BEFORE THE PROGRAM

CHAPTER 10

RECRUITING AND SELECTION

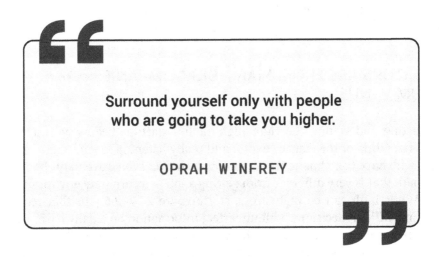

> Surround yourself only with people
> who are going to take you higher.
>
> OPRAH WINFREY

Recruiting and selecting the right startups is another crucial part of accelerator programs. As any venture capitalist will tell you, people are the most important factor in startups. When so many things could go wrong, you're making a bet on the team to work it out and get stronger as they grow.

Like any recruiting process, you'll need to spread the word to where the desired candidates are, explain the value proposition, and make it easy to apply so that you get enough qualified applicants. Selecting among the applicants and filtering down to those who can truly make an impact comes next.

IF YOU BUILD IT, THEY MAY OR MAY NOT COME

The goal of most corporate accelerators is to achieve strategic returns. This starts with attracting the best startups to your program who have the potential to scale quickly and disrupt your industry – the same startups whose goal is likely to replace your company!

Just because you build an accelerator program that works for your own company doesn't mean the right startups will want to join your field of dreams. In order to attract the best companies, you need to have a clear value proposition with compelling reasons for the startup to participate. It has to be worth it for these budding competitors to potentially work with you instead of against you. This is not always so easy, as big companies and startups usually have very different goals and expectations.

STARTUPS ARE FROM MARS, BIG COMPANIES ARE FROM VENUS

Attracting and vetting the right high-quality startups begins with a deep understanding of the startup world, and really listening to your team members who have this experience. Founding a startup is an extremely challenging path that is very different from getting a job in a corporate environment.

While both can be high-stress, startups are 24-7-365 jobs that require making difficult decisions with imperfect information on a daily basis. They require 100% commitment, and there is no such thing as work/life balance. Startups founders will tell you that it can destroy personal relationships with friends and family due to the stress and required commitment, and there is an extremely high rate of divorce among entrepreneurs. This is not just a job for most founders – it's an all-consuming way of life. And the chances of success are extremely low – only about 1 in 10 startups are able to raise VC investment, and only about 1 in 10 of those succeed. And for the ones who do make it, the path to success is messy and chaotic. As Max Ventilla, a Google alumnus who founded an edtech startup, noted, "We're kind of flying the plane while building it."[1]

Corporate leaders come from a different planet. There is a traditional and well-worn path to follow, and those who make it to leadership positions are typically good at following rules, patiently waiting for promotion opportunities, and navigating corporate politics. There is a general level of competency (usually) in the employee base, whereas in the startup world the talent can span the extreme, from world-changing genius to grossly unethical or ineffective buffoon. The mindsets are totally different.

While neither path is better or worse than the other, the challenge for corporate innovation leaders is to understand the startup world well enough to select the best startups for their particular accelerator, aligning with their goals and resources available (their simple innovation machines). And in order to attract the right companies, corporate accelerators need to offer the right incentives for those startups and speak the right language. Building a credible brand in the startup world is important because the startup world is binary – only a very small number survive, and an even smaller subset succeed at a scale that is relevant enough to have a meaningful impact on a large corporation. If your accelerator is not working with the top 1% of startups, it is usually a waste of time.

BAD HABITS ARE HARD TO BREAK

While well intentioned, many big companies have bad habits that are sabotaging your ability to build a strong brand in the startup world. At large, complex organizations with thousands of people, these behaviors are nearly impossible to change, which makes life difficult for the accelerator leader and innovation team.

We've seen this over and over at big companies, and have also witnessed it first-hand at accelerators we've been involved with. At a partnership accelerator set up by a Fortune 500 company, we actively recruited top growth-stage startups from our personal networks only to get an earful about their bad behavior. It was startling at first when in one of the early conversations, a well-known founder who had already raised $30 million in venture capital funding said (paraphrased): "I'm talking to you out of courtesy to [our VC mutual friend], but I would *never* work with [the company] and tell all of my founder friends to avoid [the company] like the plague. I really wanted to work with them a few years ago, but they completely wasted my time in several meetings over many months, then weirdly stopped communicating. Months later, I find out that they tried unsuccessfully to build a competing product based on our discussions. Why would any startup ever even talk to them if that's the behavior that [the company] thinks is okay?"

While this was shocking, what was even more shocking was that this conversation wasn't unusual and happened several more times in the span of a few weeks. Obviously, it was a systemic problem, and there were surely dozens, if not hundreds, of other companies out there who had similar experiences that just didn't get a chance to say so. However, this is difficult to avoid, especially at companies with technical and product development talent in-house. The best outcome is that the accelerator, CVC, or other innovation team, who should understand both the startup world and their own company, are the gateway for all interactions and act as relationship managers between the startup ecosystem and the overall company.

This is hard to do if you don't have a software tool managing interactions, or at a minimum a shared database to track startups that anyone at your company engages with. It is highly recommended to use a sophisticated CRM system such as Salesforce, or some of the custom tools used in the CVC world such as Affinity and Proseeder. This is a good start, but only works if the accelerator team doesn't feel like a middleman – they need to be providing value by helping executives who are out in the market interacting with startups. One best practice, however, is having a single source of truth for the many contacts a startup may have with your big company.

EVALUATING STARTUPS IS A LEARNED SKILL

Big companies are usually not equipped to distinguish between a high-potential startup and one that is missing some of the critical pieces of the puzzle to succeed. It's not because the corporate doesn't have smart people, it's that distinguishing between a top startup and one that will likely fail is a skill that is developed over time. In fact, distinguishing between a good startup and a bad startup is the entire business of venture capitalists, and most of them still aren't consistently good at it! Though the ones who are have reaped the financial benefits in a massive way.

It takes years, if not decades, to fine-tune fine tune the skill of distinguishing good startups, and is nearly impossible to know for sure until the startups succeed and achieve that exit event, which means tracking your initial judgments over 10-plus years. This requires seeing a high volume of startups and placing bets, then seeing them through over several years. Bets mean an investment or selection into an accelerator program – beware the service provider who thinks they know startups because they've sold to them, which is a very different experience that doesn't require the same judgement call. Most VCs say you need to actually invest in 30 or more deals to develop your gut instinct about startups. This means, based on an average VC fund pipeline, evaluating 1,500-plus startups and actually placing bets on them where you have skin in the game. This is not something typical corporate executives have the time or capacity to do, and it's also not the best use of their time.

Selecting startups is a talent that takes a long time to perfect, so make sure you have people involved in the program who have already developed this skill. It's worth nothing that it is much, much easier for corporate executives to assess later-stage companies, which have more data – revenue, metrics, financials – that can be compared across companies. This is another appealing benefit of a partnership accelerator focused on growth-stage companies.

HOT OR NOT: SHORTCUTS TO IDENTIFY TOP STARTUPS

Startups are a special type of business that can move mountains, change industries, and create enormous wealth at lightning speed. The entrepreneurs can learn more in a couple of years running a startup than in a couple of decades working at a bigger company. To start one, you have to be overly optimistic, unequivocally driven, and a little bit crazy. And as accelerator leaders, you're looking for entrepreneurs who choose this mad path, understand what it means, and are able to execute under the insane conditions.

It is extremely hard to tell at first who is good and who is not – it takes one to know one! Unlike a public company where you have plenty of available information to assess a company, including audited financials and 10K reports, the startup world is opaque, and they do not have to share critical data with you. Often founders will optimistically embellish performance, and too often just flat-out lie. The most promising founders aren't necessarily those who present well; that's just one skill set. Execution is the key – getting things done, consistently, with slim resources. While there are still institutional biases, especially around gender, race, and ethnicity, if a startup has been able to raise VC funding, especially from top-tier investors, it's an indication that they are one of the best and most promising startups out there.

Very few people on the planet have the skill to vet startups effectively, and it's safe to say that it's rare to find corporate employees, who have been working at big companies for most if not all of their careers, with this skill. So, how do you identify the best startups for a corporate accelerator? Looking at VC funding is the easiest proxy. Let the people whose job it is to vet startups do it for you! When top-tier VCs invest in a startup, it reduces the risk for you because you are relying on their years of experience and pattern recognition, and you also know the company has money in the bank. Differentiating between good startups and not-so-good startups is the job of VCs, as they have refined the skill by investing in less than 5% of the several hundred startups they look at per year.

Another way to do this is to build an investment committee for your accelerator that includes seasoned VCs. You can also hire talent from the startup and VC world on your accelerator and innovation teams. However, be aware that the best people can make significantly more money at VC funds or accelerators where they get carried interest (i.e., a piece of the action!) on their investment successes, so it is extremely difficult to hire and retain people who are good at recruiting and selecting the best startups.

Finally, evaluating and selecting startups is the entire purpose of an investment committee (IC). By bringing in experienced investors and founders alongside your internal stakeholders, you can all learn from each other and rely on your collective skills to select the best startups for your accelerator.

WHAT IS YOUR VALUE PROPOSITION?

In order to attract top startups, there must be an authentic and attractive value proposition. If not, the best companies have options and will choose to participate in other accelerators with a better track record and brand, or even not participate in an accelerator at all. "I think what happens with corporate accelerators today is that they get tier 3 deal flow. They get the companies that don't get into the tier 1 or even tier 2 accelerators . . . that's not what you want," explains Anand Sanwal, founder and CEO of startup research firm CB Insights. "You want the best entrepreneurs and the best ideas."[2]

Corporate accelerators must make the case to those tier 1 companies that their accelerator is going to add value and improve the startup's chance of success in a way that is significantly better than an independent accelerator or none at all. "Corporations must think about the unique things that they might offer," says Vijay Rajendran, head of corporate innovation and partnerships at 500 Startups. "That usually comes down to just a few things, if you think about what startups want. We've published our *Unlocking Corporate Venture Capital* report, and at the top of the list of startup priorities is, not surprisingly, sales and distribution support. After that, there are other things that have to do with scaling people or scaling into new markets or knowledge sharing and R&D support. Many corporates think that startups just want to have a corporate logo to show next to them, but brand recognition and reputation was halfway down the list. It was not even among the top five things that founders said they wanted."

Corporates need to actually line up a strong value proposition that startups want. So the accelerator leader's job is to assemble and articulate a unique value proposition to the startups. This is not an easy task.

Competing against established independent accelerators, corporates have a few strengths. A Deloitte report[3] found there were four main reasons startups were attracted to corporate accelerators over other options – and these are some of the best ways to attract top startups to your program.

1. **Equity-free funding** – While it is still common for corporations to acquire equity from startups they bring into their accelerators, Deloitte's analysis found that Samsung, Microsoft, Google, and many others have adopted equity-free funding. This is compelling for startups that are hesitant to part ways with their equity, especially on an unproven program with a potential competitor.

2. **Industry-focused mentors** – Startup founders often cite mentors as the single most important element of an accelerator program. When corporations focus their accelerators on their own industry, entrepreneurs can tap into your verified experts in the field, from executives and business unit leaders to product managers and technical experts.

3. **Corporate resources** – Access to proprietary resources can be a critical differentiator for an accelerator program. For example, Qualcomm, Samsung, and Barclays all provide startups with data, internal tools, and intellectual property. These ready-to-use established resources are not available elsewhere and are integral to rapid startup development.

4. **Customers** – The corporate host and its customer base are obvious early customers for a startup. A clear path to customer relationships is usually the most compelling incentive, as brand-name customers bring credibility and revenue quickly to a newly formed startup. This is usually your most persuasive value proposition, but corporates have to actually follow through on this promise.

Each of these four benefits is extremely compelling for startups, and can be unique to your particular company, therefore making the case for top founders to participate in your accelerator program. Independent venture accelerators can have a tough time competing if these are executed well – meaning not just saying they're a benefit but actually delivering on the value consistently. This is particularly true for customer relationships.

DEFINE YOUR CRITERIA

Before doing any outreach to startups, it is important to define your criteria. This should include industry, company maturity, customer profile, and many more details. You should also brainstorm about what type of results you and your team would be thrilled to see at the end, and whether this vision aligns with the startup profile you expect.

Note that the industry of the startup doesn't necessarily have to be directly aligned with the big company's main business. We have built energy industry accelerators for financial firms trading commodities, for example, seeking innovators for information on the market's direction. Sometimes a particular technology, such as blockchain or AI, is interesting strategically and applications can be translated from adjacent industries. Generally, though, the corporate accelerator will be defined by a specific area or theme that your corporation seeks to develop for strategic reasons.

Source: JLabs[4]

Consider JLabs; Johnson and Johnson's (J&J) network of accelerators provides a global footprint to work with innovators across the wide range of businesses they are in. Their goal is "empowering innovators across a broad healthcare spectrum including pharmaceutical, medical device, consumer, and health tech sectors to create and accelerate the delivery of life-saving, life-enhancing health and wellness solutions to patients around the world."[5] This broad approach is a series of venture accelerators and co-working incubation spaces designed to cast a wide net across many of the company's interests to generate market intelligence.

Source: Verizon[6]

Verizon approaches things slightly differently, with targeted labs focused on specific technologies and verticals. For example, they have a big bet on 5G technologies, and focus their programs on innovators building things that will take advantage of this investment. An ecosystem accelerator at its essence, this allows Verizon to attract startups that will invent use cases to fill the networks' capacity. The Los Angeles lab focuses on gaming and entertainment, whereas the DC lab focuses more on smart cities technologies.[7] These are diverse applications that align with wider innovation trends targeting startups that have the potential to use Verizon's technology.

Class Size

You will also need to make a decision on class size. The standard accelerator program has about 10 startups per cohort, but this varies greatly. Y Combinator boats over 200 startups in each cohort, while The Cage has only two.

The Cage is a 12-week program from The Lane Crawford Joyce Group, one of the biggest luxury fashion and retail brand managers and distributors, headquartered in Hong Kong with 1,500 brands across 50 cities throughout Asia. The Cage was created to support early-stage technology startups that enhance the customer experience in the fashion and lifestyle retail industry, offering a $50,000 grant with the goal of securing a commercial contract by the end.

"Our main goal is just to take two to three startups maximum every year. We are very, very selective," says Cristina Ventura, chief catalyst officer and head of The Cage. "It's not only about the more the better, it's about quality and having a 100% success rate. We really want to be close to them, to make sure that we are part of the journey and that we together create this ecosystem. And that, of course, they get a commercial agreement and/or partnership with us, which is our main goal."

There is no one-size-fits-all cohort number, but the decision should be made intentionally based on your goals and stakeholder expectations.

DESIGNING YOUR APPLICATION PROCESS

Once you know what you're looking for and what you will be offering in return, it's time to create an application process and timeline. Creating a formal application is the first step, because you need a standardized application to compare startups fairly against each other. This reduces bias, and by tracking over several cohorts you can learn from past decisions to continually improve the process.

Open Application or Nomination

Most accelerators use an open application process, meaning there is a public website and application that is available to anyone who wants to apply. This can be useful, especially for venture accelerators or ecosystem accelerators where you want a broad swath of candidates and they may be very early-stage companies with limited connections to your corporate network.

However, we are also a big fan of using a nomination process, especially for later-stage programs, and have used this effectively in partnership accelerators in particular. For later-stage companies, they should have enough contacts to have a nominator that is connected to your company in some way, and it also means that the companies who apply are generally higher quality and vetted in some way by the person who nominates them. We always allow for self-nomination as well, but find that the strongest nominations come from people inside the company or in the ecosystem who already know the type of startups that would be great partners for the big company. This also reduces the number of applications, which alleviates some of the burden on an accelerator team to review sometimes thousands of applications within a short period of time.

Application Questions

The key for applications is that less is more. Startups usually apply to multiple accelerators and are also fundraising, so if the application is too complex it will create friction and prevent good companies from spending time to complete it. Stick with the standard questions asked by all accelerators that align with information they already have for fundraising. Adding one or two key filtering questions around unique elements of your program is fine. The balance must be between information needed for a decision versus additional complexity that deters participation due to its time-consuming nature. Information that a startup has handy, like founder backgrounds, is fair game and needed; detailed financials, future projections, or essay questions might be less useful. Startups may also be hesitant to share sensitive financial or customer information with big companies in an application.

One interesting example from the independent accelerator world is Antler, which selects cohorts of individual founders using a data-driven process before they officially found their company, helping them go from "zero to seed." Antler was created in 2017 in Singapore, and now operates in Amsterdam, London, Nairobi, Oslo, Stockholm, Sydney, and New York City. Unlike most accelerator programs that have set recruiting requirements for the company and co-founders, Antler selects its cohort based on the individual founder, using LinkedIn profiles, personality tests, video interviews, and problem-solving puzzles. The criteria they articulate as important for applicants are inner drive, spike (which they define as the ability to "stand out from the crowd" with deep expertise in a specific area), and grit.

The unique Antler application process starts with the candidates simply sharing their LinkedIn profile. If the Antler team finds it compelling, they will send an online assessment for the candidate to complete, and if they pass that threshold they'll be asked in for an interview. According to Ryan Sommerville, director of growth and portfolio for Antler in the United States, "In some of our locations we use personality tests as part of the selection process, but in the US, we do a behavioral interview-style selection process."

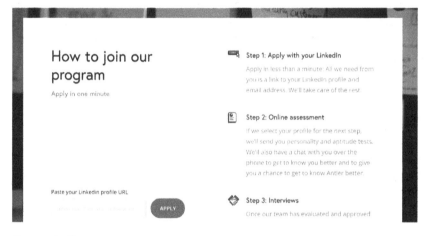

Source: Antler

Antler then builds out a dashboard for each participant based on a lengthy questionnaire that includes a personality test as well as background information that includes things like what each person has built in the past, what startups they've worked at, and how much money they've raised. Everyone within the cohort has visibility to the other members and how they answer the questionnaire. This data-driven approach to recruiting is an interesting trend that we expect to continue.

Application Tool

The next step is deciding how to collect the information. Many corporates want to build and host their own application. Although this can be done by a moderately capable tech team, it adds very little value and is not recommended. The best practice is to use a simple technology tool – a microsite or survey software – that can be assembled quickly by the accelerator team. There are many existing commercial solutions out there, some of which are used by multiple accelerator programs and have ready-to-go templates to make the process extremely easy. Our recommendation is to go with one of the existing community solutions, which not only has the process down pat, but it has customizable templates and other ways to shortcut the process and save your team valuable time and resources.

We have steered many accelerators to one of the popular providers in the space, F6S, which is a startup accelerator directory and community. The application tool is free, with only a modest fee for additional administrative and analytic capabilities. Best of all, they have existing templates for Y Combinator and Techstars, which you can simply adopt or customize. This allows companies that have already thought of applying or submitting another application to simply copy that work over. Think of it as essentially a common application for colleges, but for accelerators.

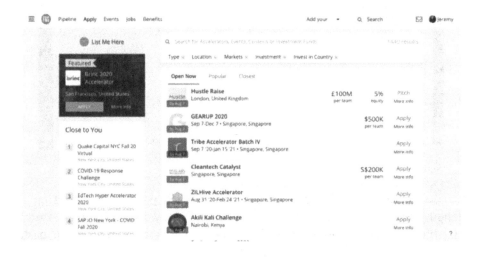

Source: F6S[8]

All of the application software programs will include the application, pipeline tracking, and an evaluation tool to distribute to and collect feedback from multiple reviewers. As your program grows, there's even a capability to compare cohorts and analyze changes. Finally, when leveraging an existing application platform and community, you provide convenience to startups already on the platform. We strongly suggest using one of these tools and resisting the inclination to build something in-house.

RECRUITMENT: GENERATING INTEREST

You've defined your accelerator archetype, the profile of companies to recruit, and the value proposition. You've built out your application process and have a plan to review and select the companies that apply. Now you need to get the word out. This will require a combination of communications channels, from organic and existing networks to straight-up ads and sponsorships.

As a corporate innovator, the things you do are newsworthy in the industry. It's no surprise that one of the first things corporate accelerators do is announce their program launch with some splashy marketing. Discussing the vision, the types of innovators you're looking for, and the value add you'll provide are all great elements in an initial press release. This can also be the kickoff of your recruiting, and best practices here are to align with an event – an open house at the accelerator space, a panel discussion with hot industry startups, or just a local meetup.

Each accelerator has its own process. Village Capital, an impact-focused independent venture accelerator, describes their process as follows: "For each accelerator program we launch, we intentionally develop a specific problem statement – a clear, robust definition of the issue areas we want to focus on in terms of stage, sector and region. This is defined by a program-specific advisory board, which is typically a group of 20 or so sector experts, including investors, successful entrepreneurs, community leaders, and representatives from our funding partners," explains Dustin Shay, senior director of partnerships at Village Capital. "That problem statement is then used as a recruitment guideline for the program. We use those guidelines to identify and directly reach out to entrepreneurs within our network that are a good fit. We then solicit our networks of many earlier stage investors and accelerators across the U.S. This is essential. We work with a wide range of partners that are very focused on different affinity groups or demographic groups. We also release a public call that is put out on social media." There is no right way to recruit, as long as it attracts top startups in your target area.

Leverage Corporate Strengths, Be Aware of Weaknesses

Key elements here are to leverage corporate communications' ability to get traditional and digital press mentions – key blogs and industry news channels – but also to capture as many emails and social media referrals as possible. All should reference a simple URL to apply and not go through a series of complicated instructions from your corporate homepage – use an easy-to-remember address or link shortener and make it easy to find on the company homepage.

One common blind spot for corporate communications is that they will focus on the usual suspects for big companies, but aren't always connected in the channels that are popular with startups. Getting mentions in the regular industry press is great. However, make a special effort to find out what the innovators read in terms of media. Be an authentic part of the startup communication channels. Blogs, podcasts, social media – there's an ecosystem of startup and entrepreneur media that you'll need to tap into to get the best applicants.

You can also focus on local events that entrepreneurs in your industry target might attend. There's almost always some local meetups or panel series where you can find the aspiring, early-stage founders. Sponsorship dollars judiciously applied can cut through the clutter and get the message noticed.

Advertising in general doesn't work well, but the exception to this rule is the startup communities themselves. Targeted sponsorship in the email newsletters and front pages of the application-based communities can yield quick and effective results. Expect to spend a few thousand dollars at most and focus on the key month before your deadline to spread the word.

Finally, ask for referrals from your employees, customers, and wider ecosystems. They know your company well. However, be aware that they might not be experts in the startup world, so make sure to vet the candidates with experienced investors and founders.

Quality Over Quantity

Remember that it's not important to get a high volume of applicants – it's more important to get the right kind of applicants. An accelerator we worked with had fewer than 30 applicants for a half dozen spots and found a great class. Others have thousands of applicants but struggle to fill 10 seats with the quality of startups they seek, and also spend many, many hours wading through the applications. Spread the word, but don't sweat the numbers.

Referrals, of course, are the best source of high-quality applicants. Tap into your industry networks and company personnel to make suggestions first. Encouraging recommendations from employees can help you get access to thir own networks and can also benefit the nominator – they can get a friend or colleague noticed.

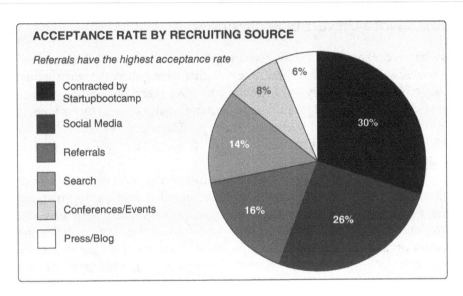

ACCEPTANCE RATE BY RECRUITING SOURCE

Referrals have the highest acceptance rate

- Contracted by Startupbootcamp
- Social Media
- Referrals
- Search
- Conferences/Events
- Press/Blog

30%
26%
16%
14%
8%
6%

Source: Startupbootcamp[9]

Startupbootcamp, a popular accelerator program for early-stage founders, confirmed that referrals also have the highest level of acceptance rates of all recruiting sources. Overall, the most common sources accelerators cite for recruiting top startups are:[10]

1. Referrals from entrepreneurs affiliated with the accelerator
2. Investors
3. Entrepreneurial associations
4. Universities
5. Sector-specific industry associations
6. Sector-specific conferences
7. Entrepreneurship conferences
8. Inbound requests from program marketing efforts and social media
9. Outbound direct, "cold-call" recruitment (e.g., finding and contacting entrepreneurs directly with no reference, via their website, or through LinkedIn)

However, not all sources are equally helpful, and a corporation should decide where its outreach efforts will get the most bang for the buck in terms of attracting quality applicants, not quantity.

Tapping into University Ecosystems

Another excellent resource for recruiting is universities and their alumni networks. Many college and graduate students have gotten the startup bug, in large part because they have friends who have taken the plunge or have heard stories of the novel products and extreme wealth created by their peers who started or worked at successful startups. Educators have followed suit with many opportunities to take ideas and develop them with the goal of building a startup.

Many universities have entrepreneurship centers (Jeremy ran one at Columbia University!) and most now have included lean startup-inspired classes in their curriculum. There are also active alumni networks and entrepreneurship clubs. These provide good opportunities to publicize the accelerator program and tap into a pipeline of talent. As an added bonus, the pipeline is not only repeatable cohort after cohort, year after year, but can also yield interns and early employees for the companies emerging from the accelerator. Student clubs and organizations can also be very powerful tools for spreading the word and attracting founders.

The most difficult to reach but potentially game-changing source of innovation are the departments and research centers pursuing new ideas. They have incredible intellectual property and often formal programs to encourage entrepreneurs to commercialize it. Programs like I-Corps train academics and researchers to use the lean startup methods of customer discovery to build prototypes and consider launching companies themselves, and tech transfer offices look for entrepreneurs to use university-created IP. While many academics are right where they want to be – producing research in their labs and offices – some are being enticed to take the plunge into entrepreneurship. These front-line researchers can be the source of defensible and game-changing innovations.

The Entrepreneurs Are Coming from Inside the House

While some corporates have separate venture studio programs for internal innovation, we're seeing more and more programs incorporate "intrapreneurs" along side the external entrepreneurs in the same accelerator program.

"With our Launch program for idea-stage entrepreneurs, we encourage our own employees to apply as well, facilitating intrapreneurship that can lead to cultural change," says Dan Sinclair, head of MDR LAB at London-based law firm Mischon de Reya. "We've previously had two people who launched businesses from within the Mishcon umbrella, so now it feels like we're in a stage and a maturity where we should formalize that so people don't have to leave the firm entirely." This is a great way to engage internal stakeholders and budding entrepreneurs within your company.

Diversity

No matter your method of recruitment, it's important to be extremely conscious of the diversity of your pipeline. This is a hot topic in the wider startup and VC world and it reflects badly on accelerators that do not include diverse founders. This relates both to the accelerator team and within the cohort itself, in terms of gender, race, geography, and background. Research conclusively shows that within a startup team, diversity can help improve performance and decision-making. Even just explicitly saying "we encourage diverse founders to apply" helps, and having diverse leaders on the accelerator team makes it clear that diverse founders are welcome.

Unfortunately, the vast majority of founders who seek out accelerators tend to be white, male, and young. Especially for partnership and ecosystem accelerator programs, which may be recruiting companies who don't typically seek out accelerator programs, it can take some additional outbound recruiting efforts to achieve a diverse cohort. Based on our interviews and personal experience working with multiple accelerator programs, it takes about five times more effort for each successfully recruited female founder than it does for the male founders. It is important to make this effort as a commitment to diversity, and both your program and the founders will benefit immensely.

Village Capital is particularly focused on this area, boasting an incredibly diverse portfolio, with more than 45% women-led companies and more than 30% Black and Latinx entrepreneurs. "Diversity is the strength of our programs," said Shay. "We seek to build a better, more equitable system that doesn't overlook the vast majority of people who are starting a business." They have an intentional selection and recruitment process that purposefully levels the playing field for founders with nontraditional backgrounds.

Diversity can also have a positive impact on performance. The Village Capital portfolio "is not only more inclusive, but we've also seen that our partner fund is on track to outperform venture capital funds of its vintage year," says Shay. "It currently has an 88% survival rate, and has had 16 early and profitable exits to date." This is way above market for accelerator and VC portfolio survival rates, which are about 30%, demonstrating that equitable representation can be a major advantage.

EVALUATION AND SELECTION

Once the applications start coming in, you'll need a process for winnowing them down to a short list of candidates and for ultimately making your selection. You can begin the review process right away, but keep the notification process separate and wait until the end. Just ensure that when an application comes in, you communicate that it's been received and your best sense of the timeline for decisions. This should be as quick as possible – hot startups will be considering other accelerators and will need to make a decision rapidly once they have one offer. A standard guideline is about a month between when applications close and the class is confirmed, which usually includes several stages of the application process such as phone screenings and in person interviews. It's a whirlwind!

When applications close, a good first pass by the accelerator manager or associate can screen out those who simply don't meet the criteria – wrong industry, wrong stage, or clearly a bad fit for some obvious reason. This can cut the pipeline in half or more. Then, a review of each company by two to three people – some from your company and some experienced outsiders – that includes a numerical scoring function for different categories can quickly provide a simple ranking based on key factors. Usually it's pretty easy to bubble up the top tier of candidates. Next, a phone or video call screening can be done to meet the founders and ask deeper questions about fit and direction. Final candidates – all of whom would be possible fits – should ideally do a final round and "sell day" in person, to see the space, meet the team, and ideally pitch the senior decision makers and/or investment committee to get buy-in.

SELECTION FRAMEWORK

There is a mix of art and science to selecting startups for an accelerator program. Startups, by their very nature, are works in progress. They won't be perfect, and in fact most of the startups will have major red flags compared to more mature businesses. This is fantastic, because it further confirms the benefit of your accelerator program, where participants can continuously improve and work through some of these areas as they grow. This can make the selection process challenging, but also further aligns potential partnerships between startups and corporates, where they can solve each other's problems. Be clear about what things are deal breakers and what things are acceptable.

A good framework for selection comes from OrangeFab, the accelerator connected to the French telecom company Orange. "We have a framework called the three N's: The Now, The New, and The Next," says Guillaume Payan, VP of startup outreach and head of OrangeFab at Orange Silicon Valley. "When we meet startups, we try to classify them into different categories."

- **The Now** – Startups that provide the service that we already provide, but in an innovative way (it's better, cheaper, more efficient, or faster).
- **The New** – Startups that provide an additional service to what we already offer, and that Orange would like to offer to its customers, such as additional features on a product.
- **The Next** – Companies that are leapfrogging business models and technologies, coming sometimes out of nowhere, and, in some cases, competing with or trying to replace Orange.

This is a great example of a strategic framework customized to Orange that categorizes the startup applicants. What works for your company? When managing a variety of stakeholders, a clear selection framework is extremely helpful.

Interview Process

After filtering down the applications to a short list of companies that meet the criteria, typically there is a multi-stage interview process. This can be in person, virtual, or some combination of both. It also takes many forms. According to a Deloitte report, "the selection procedure can be rigorous with multiple interactions such as interviews, pitch events, and Q&A sessions, or it can be a simpler two-step pitch and choose model. It can be focused around specific verticals or it can be open to any topic, allowing admittance startups in batches or on a continuous basis."[11] There are many ways to do this, and consistency is the key.

A typical process may look something like this:

- Review all applications with a peer review process or working with a CVC team.
- Select top 20 to 30 companies for a cohort of 10, or two to three times the total number you anticipate accepting.
- Decline all others – it is important to communicate to the ones who do not make it and possibly keep them in your ecosystem or encourage them to apply to the next cohort.

- Engage investment committee (IC) to review short listed applications.
- Invite remaining companies to a phone screening.
- Cut the list down by 25–50% and invite them to in-person interviews, including all co-founders.
- Hold investment committee meeting and review all interviewed companies in detail; select final cohort.
- Make offer to selected companies, but do not decline companies until all slots are filled with a signed acceptance letter or term sheet (sometimes startups decline to participate).
- Announce the program participants after onboarding them with any paperwork or investment involved.

The more people from your parent company you can engage in the process, the better. Make sure everyone understands the process and memorialize the discussions in writing or recorded audio so you can look back on it afterward, when the selected or passed-on companies either succeed or fail, which will help you to learn and continuously improve.

BU Sponsorship

Some corporate accelerators require business unit (BU) sponsorship, or at least signoff, on the companies where that BU would be required to work with them in a partnership. Many accelerators avoid doing this at first because it is extremely cumbersome and slows the selection process. However, if the time is taken to do this properly, the chances of a successful partnership increase exponentially after the program. The BU feels engaged with the company from the outset, since they were involved in the selection process, and then is set up to work with them throughout the program. It is well worth the time and effort up front to do this, especially for partnership accelerators.

Investment Committee

Once a very short list of companies is whittled down to no more than three times the total number of slots for your cohort, the investment committee usually makes the final decision. In some instances, the accelerator manager makes the decisions alone, which is tempting because it simplifies the process enormously. However, especially for partnership-focused accelerators, investment committees are the best practice because they are all about generating buy-in from your stakeholders. You want the extended team of senior executives to feel responsible for the companies selected and be engaged in the process.

In addition, it's a very good learning experience and an opportunity for relationship development with key external stakeholders. It is a great practice to include experienced founders, VCs, or customers in the process, especially if they will be critical to the success of the participating startups and the resulting partnerships. SAP.io Foundry, for example, notably involves its customers on the investment committee.

Village Capital brings in external experts from a variety of corporations to their selection committee. "I think the best advice is to be as inclusive as possible," says Shay. "Take our Finance Forward committee, which is about 30 people. It ranges from representatives of our funding partners – MetLife Foundation, PayPal, Moody's, and major financial institutions like JPMorgan Chase – to leaders of community groups or affinity groups like Native Women Lead. They're very geographically diverse, from all across the US. The main KPI for our programs is impact on specific populations, and these advisory boards allow us to get a very good understanding of what the major issues are that the target population is facing. It allows us to create a much better overall program."

The investment committee is an excellent way to engage key stakeholders to get them excited about the participating startups even before the program starts, and a way to learn what is important to their businesses, which will help you to recruit even more aligned companies in the future.

Selection Criteria

Before going into an investment committee meeting, it is the job of the accelerator team to be extremely clear about the selection criteria.

One template suggested by a Deloitte report, "Design Principles for Building a Successful Corporate Accelerator,"[12] lists key questions to discuss with the investment committee that mirror closely how VCs select their companies. It differentiates between questions focused on financial return or strategic return:

Questions for financial returns:

1. Will the startup integrate or exit within the next five to seven years?
2. Does it have the potential to return 10 times the funds invested?
3. Does the team have a prototype and traction in the market?
4. Is the founding team visionary, ambitious, and able to scale this business?

5. Is the founding team receptive to criticism and ready to pivot from the original idea if the market demands it?

6. Do we have a network of experts that can help this startup in its specific vertical?

Questions for strategic returns:

1. Is this a venture representing the edge of our business?

2. Is the marketing moving in such a way that this innovation could become the core of our business?

3. Do we have the specific resources the startup needs to develop the technology?

4. Do we have a network of experts in this vertical?

5. Is the founding team visionary, ambitious, and able to scale this business beyond borders?

6. Is the founding team receptive to criticism and ready to pivot from the original idea if the market demands it?

For all startups, the founding team is a critical component. Many corporate teams fall in love with the idea, but don't properly assess the founding team, as this is less critical in a corporate environment. But in the startup world, the founding team is everything. The startups are not yet fully-fledged businesses, so you are really betting on the teams' ability to execute on their vision. The earlier the stage of the startup, the more critical the team is in the decision.

The former president of Y Combinator, Sam Altman, lists specific characteristics that he looks for when selecting startups: clarity of vision, clarity of explanation, determination, passion, and evidence that applicants have done something great in the past. They particularly emphasize determination, which is an absolutely critical trait for startup founders creating something from nothing and facing many challenges along the way. According to his colleague founder Paul Graham, "That's the myth in the Valley . . . as long as you're over a certain threshold of intelligence, what matters most is determination."[13]

Selection Fatigue

If any one person has more than about 10 companies to review, be aware that they will likely get selection fatigue. You'll have more mental energy and may be more likely to spend time on the startups you first look at than the ones at the end of the process.

Expect the first 25% to attract way too much scrutiny and debate, and the last 25% to get way too little. That's not fair to either of those groups of applicants. Remind yourself to reserve your mental energy, and be strict about time limits on review and discussion of each applicant.

There are ways to deal with this, including:

1. Require nominations to reduce the overall applicants and increase quality.
2. Have someone (e.g., intern or associate) do first screening to filter out any companies who obviously do not meet the baseline criteria.
3. Vote on yes/no with investment committee for first round instead of discussing at length.
4. Don't discuss (or limit the discussion) of the ones you agree on, either yeses or nos, and only discuss the companies where there is dissent.

The Cohort Is a Reflection of You

For accelerator programs overall, the programming itself matters less than the companies participating. The companies you select tell the world how you are approaching innovation. Recruitment of startups is a new skill for most corporate executives, as the criteria for success are very different than in hiring a corporate employee or partnering with a more mature company. However, it can be an amazing opportunity to learn, form stronger relationships with internal and external stakeholders, and learn market trends by engaging a wider audience than just the accelerator team in the selection process. Your goal is to find what works best for your company, and pick startups that are a good fit for your goals.

CHAPTER

INVESTMENT

**Never go into venture capital if
you want a peaceful life.**

GEORGES DORIOT

FOUNDER, AMERICAN RESEARCH AND DEVELOPMENT
CORPORATION (THE FIRST VC FIRM, FOUNDED IN 1946)

A corporate accelerator is a program for high growth startups, and these companies all need one thing to achieve that growth: money. This can come as revenue (sales) or investment (equity), but it is absolutely necessary to facilitate this high growth. Capital and customers are two of the main reasons that startups join accelerator programs. Investment is a keystone feature of accelerator programs, and one that corporates must be thoughtful about to ensure that their spending aligns with strategic goals.

There are multiple ways to invest in startups through an accelerator program and simply copying the investment model of independent venture accelerators is often a simplistic and ineffective way to invest for large corporations. Competing on the amount of investment dollars is also less likely to be successful than focusing on resources where corporates can provide unique advantages to startups. In fact, there are many more options on the table for corporate accelerators that can be compelling to top-tier startups and can give corporate accelerator programs a true competitive advantage over independent accelerators.

STRATEGIC INVESTMENT

The accelerator model grew out of the venture capital model, so most independent accelerators invest in a similar way to venture capital funds. However, this is aligned with being a financial investor versus a strategic investor. This model only works with a large portfolio and a long-term commitment; combined with a bit of luck a handful of the portfolio companies become massive successes and achieve lucrative exits.

Independent venture accelerators can be successful through a high volume of bets in very early-stage companies, as they can attract the best companies and wait for 5–10 years until they mature or fail, expecting a 60–90% failure rate. Most corporates do not have this same risk appetite, nor do they want the same volume of portfolio companies that independent accelerators need for this model to work on financial returns alone. For a corporate accelerator, a partnership with a company that enhances revenue, increases operational efficiency, or simply makes the company more able to defend against the competition can be a valuable strategic outcome.

Investing in participating startups for equity is only one way of doing things. It may be one part of a larger benefits package to the participating startups, or it may not be needed at all. In addition, the investment can come in the form of standard equity at a predetermined valuation, in-kind products and services with an attributed value, performance-based vesting, or a non-dilutive grant. There are also many ways to invest without equity involved at all that can achieve your strategic objectives better than cash.

Alignment with Innovation Goals

It should go without saying, but any investment should align with your why and your goals for the program. Are you looking for a financial return from the investment? Are you structurally equipped to understand, manage, and support the investments? Is partnership the most important thing? Does that partnership need development or dedicated people that are not already in the corporate budget?

Often corporate accelerators copy the investment strategy of independent accelerators to take a flat equity percentage because they believe they have to follow that blueprint to be competitive, but this is not the case. In fact, blindly following this model can (1) harm the corporate parent and the startup if the investment is not managed well, and (2) miss out on even better opportunities to invest in different ways that are more aligned with achieving corporate strategic objectives. Be intentional about why and how you invest.

When to Invest

There are multiple options on when to invest, and it can be a good idea to split up the investments to align with different inflection points.

Investment before the program begins is typical of a venture accelerator and is a key benefit to participation. This usually comes in the form of a flat investment for all participating companies – it's often too complex to customize unless you have a very small class size and are able to do full-blown investment due diligence on each company.

While some programs try to avoid investing at all, the reason for investing before a program begins is to incentivize startups to participate. There is usually a cost for the startup to participate, such as flights and accommodation for the city in which the program is held, or at minimum an opportunity cost on the founders' time, which is their most precious resource. You also want the startups to have enough resources to focus on your program and be able to follow through on the opportunities that arise during the program, and not be distracted by the need to fundraise (at least for a short period of time).

Investment during the program can also frequently come in the form of in-kind products and services, such as cloud credits, expert consultants who would otherwise have been out of budget for a startup, or amenities during participation such as office space. This is also part of the benefit of participating in the program and demonstrating the value of access to things that can help the startups grow faster than they could on their own. This should still be paired with a cash investment of some kind and is not sufficient alone.

Finally, many accelerators invest heavily in a subset of the participating companies after the program ends. This is most commonly in the form of a traditional CVC investment for equity, which can either be managed by the accelerator team or, even better, by an affiliated CVC arm who knows what they're doing. This can also be outsourced. Alternately, an additional grant or prize for the top companies can be awarded for their performance at demo day, which is also an incentive to complete the program and perform well in a splashy public event that reflects on your company.

Finally, a corporate can invest resources to cultivate a partnership that was developed during the accelerator, such as a joint research and development agreement, a product POC, or a go-to-market partnership that requires internal and/or external resources. Moving to phase 2 with a smaller portion of the companies is a goal of many corporate accelerators, and this is when the strategic benefits start to generate results. This can take a cash or internal budget allocation to enable.

The best corporate accelerator programs have some combination of investment in multiple categories along the way.

It's Okay Not to Take Equity

While nearly all independent venture accelerators take equity for participation in their programs, this is due to their business model requiring a financial return from the equity. Corporate accelerators, on the other hand, do not need to do this. In fact, it can often be counterproductive and cause more of a headache than a value.

First and foremost, any return on equity investment from an early-stage program will take several years to achieve, so it is unlikely to be useful in justifying the program in the short term. It's also common that the corporate goals are around additional revenue or increased efficiency, so equity does nothing to achieve this.

Big companies also commonly overlook the practical aspects of managing and administering a portfolio of illiquid private company stock, which can take years to mature, exit, or shut down. A shareholder has administrative and management responsibilities that accelerator teams are not usually set up to handle. Someone has to look after the investment for years, if not decades, after the accelerator ends. Usually this is a CVC team or corporate development resource, but if they are not involved in the program at the outset, they may be reluctant to give the right amount of attention to the accelerator portfolio and this can sour relationships.

Finally, the time frame of successful investment is long enough and risky enough that the net present value and eventual liquidity of a private portfolio may be simply too small to justify all the accompanying long-term management challenges and costs.

Based on our research and personal experiences in this space, we strongly recommend only taking equity in a company if there are dedicated and experienced resources who can manage the portfolio over the long term, usually 5–10 years or longer. This can be a sophisticated CVC arm at your company that has agreed to own and manage the portfolio after the program, or even an outsourced third party specifically hired for this purpose. If neither of these resources is available, it may be best to avoid taking equity in the participating startups at all.

HOW TO INVEST WITHOUT EQUITY

This doesn't mean that there is no way to invest in and benefit from the startups participating in your corporate accelerator. There are plenty of ways to make an investment in the startups without taking equity.

Office Space

Many accelerator programs offer a dedicated place for startups to work during the accelerator program. This can be beneficial to the startups, who otherwise would have to use their limited resources to pay for space. It can also give them easier access to corporate executives, as well as the other participating startups, both of whom they can learn from and collaborate with during the program. While the space itself is not necessarily a differentiator against independent accelerators, access to the parent company's space is – especially if it includes access to specialized spaces like labs, warehouses, or executive offices.

The benefits to the corporate of offering this space is to keep an eye on the startups, to get to know them better, and to build community and culture for the cohort that supports the success of the program. It also makes it easier for your corporate colleagues to engage with the startups, as simply walking down a floor in their office is much easier than driving across town for a meeting. There is usually an exciting buzz about startup workspaces that is a positive thing for overall corporate culture.

In-Kind Products and Services

Every corporate accelerator program should offer things that highlight their unique assets. It is important to get creative and play to your strengths. What can you offer the participating startups that no other company can? This can be a compelling reason for a startup to join your program. This falls into two categories: in-kind investments offered by your company that are unique to you, and third-party in-kind investments that you negotiate in advance of the program, usually with companies who you already do business with.

As an example of a product that is unique to the company, you may have access to data sets that can help a company develop their product faster or better. Another example is companies such as Google, Microsoft, Amazon, and IBM, which all have cloud services in their core product suite, and as part of their accelerator program they offer free cloud credits to use those cloud services. This is extremely strategic, because if the startup becomes massively successful they will be built on their company's products, spending more as they scale. For ecosystem accelerators, it is access to the technology that is the basis of that ecosystem and specialists that work at your company who have agreed to dedicate a certain number of hours above and beyond that of a mentor.

Alternately, you can negotiate unique benefits from third parties, such as services from experts including public relations, marketing, or pitch preparation. For example, the Mars Accelerator funds best-in-class service providers (marketing, branding) that the startups would otherwise not be able to afford. If you're not Google, Amazon, Microsoft, or IBM, all of those companies also offer their cloud credits to other accelerator programs for the same reason.

These in-kind products and services should be translated into a dollar amount as part of the value offered as a package to participate in the accelerator program. For any services offered by your company or third parties, this should be more hands-on than mentorships with actionable deliverables, as they would with "real" clients. Many accelerators put a tangible value on this package of in-kind products and services.

People

Some accelerators have dedicated people resources on the accelerator team to work with the startups on a particular topic as an extension of their team. This can be a floating pool of software developers to support speedy product development during the program, a PR or marketing person to help with the company press releases or blogs, or someone dedicated to helping with pitch preparation and fundraising. This is highly valuable to the startups, otherwise they would have to hire people for those roles. Often accelerators can build a team of entrepreneurs in residence (EIRs) who enjoy working with startups and are either compensated for their time or driven to do it as a path to being hired by one of the startups full time after the program.

Become a (Paid) User of the Startup

One of the easiest ways to invest in the participating startups, and one that they are always thrilled about, is to simply be a customer of their product. The best accelerator programs have a line item in their budget to purchase the startup products, if they are able to be users, and have a dedicated resource to use, test, and provide feedback on the product. This helps the startup by showing revenue, along with an early customer (you!) who can be referenced to give them credibility with other potential customers.

This can also give the corporate an advantage by being an early adopter of innovative technologies, which will improve your detailed knowledge of the new trends and offer your customers early access to an emerging technology. It is extremely important to pay for the products and not demand them for free, and to be prepared to give feedback to the startup team so they can improve the product. This is a good way to keep an eye on the company without getting too entangled. Then, if or when it makes sense, you can cultivate a deeper partnership.

Although the amounts transacted may seem negligible to a corporate budget, the simple fact of becoming a paid client can be a game-changer for the startup; the revenue generated can meaningfully extend the life and enhance the value of a small company. Likewise, live customer feedback can improve the product for the rest of the market in ways that a free trial simply can't and won't.

Invest in a Partnership

For corporate accelerator programs that have the main strategic objective of partnerships, one of the best ways to invest is to allocate capital to enable the development and roll out of a pilot project or go-to-market partnership.

Much of this may be internal budgets not cash on hand to pay third parties. But any substantive partnership will likely require resources from the corporate team that need to be incentivized with the right internal budgeting to dedicate their time. This can also be adding external resources, such as developers, to a team that supports product development or integration. If you need colleagues to commit time to make the partnership work, someone has to pay them! At some companies there is an internal proxy currency that is exchanged between P&L holders, allowing people to commit their time to a particular internal project. If the work is volunteer based, there will be less commitment and more likelihood of failure when the person's "day job" gets in the way as a priority – this is what they are paid to do, after all! This is an excellent use of capital and often where corporate accelerators get stuck, so allocating investment capital for this in advance of the program sets management expectations and clears the path for a smooth partnership.

In addition, if you are engaging in a pilot with the startup that will require significant time on their end for development or other work, it is a best practice to pay them for the pilot. Although it does not have to be market rates, it is important to pay the startup for the work they do, as your company would expect to get paid by your partners and customers. Again, the power and financial dynamic is in favor of the bigger company, and it goes a long way to develop a good relationship with the startup, and builds a stellar reputation in the market, if you pay for the pilot.

For any partnerships that will be revenue generating, such as go-to-market efforts that push the startups product through your corporate sales or distribution channels, the parent company should invest or co-invest in getting the partnership up and running; then the reward (revenue) can be shared.

Offer a Grant

Many corporate accelerators offer non-dilutive grants to participate in their program. This avoids the need to deal with small amounts of equity in early stage companies, and still makes it competitive for the startups who expect some capital infusion from an accelerator. You want the founders to be focused on participating in the program and not distracted by fundraising to survive. Grant programs, with their non-dilutive nature, can be an advantage when competing against the independent venture accelerators. Startups like to keep their equity.

For resource-strapped startups, there can be significant cost to participate in your accelerator program. This includes physical relocation of the founders and team members, product development in alignment with your program (e.g., integrating with your company's products or developing a POC), and doing any activities required by the program (e.g., customer discovery). Though these activities may be beneficial, they are doing them on your time and in your way.

For early stage entrepreneurs, there may be a real cost to leaving their job and launching a startup that a grant can lessen. Dan Sinclair, head of MDR LAB at London-based law firm Mishcon de Reya says, "For our Launch program for idea-stage entrepreneurs, we pay a stipend for individuals that join for the first two months so that they've got a bit more comfort to take the plunge."

Grants are usually relatively small, ranging from $5,000–25,000, and tend to be more common in accelerator programs that focus on early-stage startups who are operating on shoestring budgets and have not raised significant venture capital to date. However, it's also worth noting that because many startups participate in more than one accelerator, non-equity grants can capture the attention of those who have already achieved some market success.

Help with Fundraising

Even if you don't offer funding directly, startups are always looking for it. Accelerators can help to route startups to appropriate sources of capital, including angel investors, venture capital firms, or even debt financing providers who do things like inventory financing. This can even be directing companies to funding sources within your own company who are not affiliated with the accelerator. According to Guillaume Payan at OrangeFab, "We do have several investment vehicles with Orange, so what we do is systematically connect the startups in the program with different entities to see if there is an investment opportunity."

HOW TO INVEST WITH EQUITY

While equity participation for independent accelerators is the main way they generate a return, a corporate accelerator is not in the investment business. It is there to support the objectives of the parent company, such as market intelligence, new product development, invigorating sales channels, or similar strategic objectives. Investing for the financial return from equity ownership is rarely a main goal for corporate accelerators.

While it is not always necessary to invest in return for equity, many corporate accelerator programs do so because it allows the corporation to participate in the upside of companies who succeed in part because of the knowledge and/or partnerships resulting from the accelerator program. While some invest for purely financial gain, most are simply strategic, with an investment demonstrating faith in the startup and solidifying a strong relationship with aligned incentives.

Some companies invest as a way to generate an ecosystem and support the scale or network effects of their business. This is the case, for example, when companies support distributors, aftermarket tools or add-ons, or other third parties that support the business. It also helps to capture the upside that the corporate partner helped to create – startups can often experience a step change in valuation from partnering with an incumbent or large customer, validating their business model, even if it is not yet experiencing perfect product market fit.

The main scenario where this is advisable is during or after the accelerator program if there is a resulting partnership between the startup and the corporation, in which case the motivations are aligned and the corporation is also able to capture the upside of value it helps to create in the startup. If there is no partnership or ongoing relationship, it is not advisable to take equity.

Upfront Investment in the Full Cohort

An independent venture accelerator typically invests $50,000–150,000 for 5–7% equity in all of the participating startup in exchange for the benefits of their network, programming, and investor introductions. Most of these programs focus on preparing a company for VC investment, and this is the intended business model of the accelerator programs. The mature ones have set up funds that operate very much like a VC fund, with some even raising larger opportunity funds to double down on their winners by investing in later rounds of the best performing companies. Most independent accelerators follow this model of investing in the entire cohort at the same terms, which many corporate accelerators have adopted. Although this is not the only model available for equity, it is a model that startups are comfortable with.

As an alternative to the flat percentage for all companies – because they may have different funding levels, valuations, and performance before they enter the program – you can invest a flat amount at different valuations. This is slightly better, because it shows an appreciation for the traction and previous funding. The best way to do this is to offer the same dollar amount (or it will cause problems with the other startups) at their prior valuation or convertible note/SAFE terms if they have raised a round in the previous six months. If they have not raised money or it has been more than six months, then you can set up a simple convertible note or SAFE with a standard discount of 20–30% on the valuation of the next priced round with no cap. We would advise against setting valuations or caps yourself. Either way, you should be working with your CVC arm (and their lawyers) to draft the term sheets and set the terms.

Please note that for any investment in return for equity, you must use an experienced venture attorney at a credible outside law firm to do the transaction. Many times corporations try to use in-house attorneys who do not have this experience or panel firm members without a strong venture practice, and this can lead to real issues with the terms (we have seen the wreckage from this first hand). It will also damage your reputation with the VC community and potentially prevent the startups from receiving follow-on capital when VCs do diligence in the future and see the legal documents of the company and previous round terms that are off market.

Equity for In-Kind Services

Sometimes, in addition to a cash investment for equity, accelerators bundle together the value of the in-kind services with the cash investment to take equity of the total all-in value. For example, they may make a $100,000 cash investment, paired with $400,000 worth of in-kind services, and call it a $500,000 investment on the cap table of a startup. The aforementioned valuation rules would apply here as well.

Although this is possible, we advise asking for equity only in return for the value of the cash unless there are some incredible in-kind benefits that are so out of the ordinary (and expensive to the corporate parent to procure) that they would warrant this arrangement. Otherwise it's simply part of the benefit of joining your accelerator program to incentivize the best companies to join.

Investment in a Subset of the Cohort

As long as expectations are managed properly, you can also only invest in a subset of the companies involved in each cohort. Based on our research and experience, this is the best way to achieve upside from equity ownership in a startup that has participated in your accelerator program. Typically this would include a small upfront grant or stipend to all companies who participate in the program, with the expectation that only a few will receive funding at the end of the program based on their performance and whether a partnership results. These selective investments after the program has ended are a sort of phase 2 of the program, and you can share in the upside achieved from the value created by the partnership. It is also a positive signal to the market that you believe in the company enough to "put your money where your mouth is" and can help them gain momentum for a fundraising round. This decision is usually at the discretion of the accelerator team or investment committee, though you should be clear about criteria so the startups are not disappointed if they do not receive investment.

Another interesting model was created by Village Capital, which has "democratized entrepreneurship" by teaching its accelerator cohort to evaluate their peers' investment readiness. Village Capital's partner fund provides the capital, distributing investment capital according to the peer evaluations of the participating entrepreneurs themselves. Village Capital has facilitated more than 100 of these peer-selected investments, creating a portfolio that is both more inclusive (46% women-led, more than 30% led by Black and Latinx founders in the United States, and more than 88% outside of the major venture hubs of Boston, New York, and San Francisco) and that is financially outperforming funds of it's vintage year (86% survival rate, 16 early and profitable exits). This process, in addition to resulting in a more inclusive and high-performing portfolio, has been shown through an academic study[1] to mitigate bias in the investment process.

Be careful on valuations – these should only be done by people with years of experience investing in and valuing startups – and always use an experienced outside law firm with a strong venture practice. Also, if you do not have an experienced CVC team who can manage the portfolio afterwards, you will have to build up that internal capability or hire a third party to manage this. If internal, it requires getting headcount approved for 5–10 years after each investment, which is the life cycle of that equity ownership. Try to avoid passing it off to corporate development or others who have investment experience but are not venture capital or startup experts!

If you know that this is your strategy and you want to achieve the upside of investing at the valuation of the company *before* they go through the accelerator program and you created value for them, this is also possible. This would be in the form of an option to invest the intended amount at the valuation of the company prior to entering the program.

MDR LAB in London uses options successfully for this purpose. The option should expire in a reasonable time frame after the program ends (3–12 months). That way, if a partnership results, you can make the investment immediately and see the upside, especially if they are able to raise capital at a higher valuation immediately after the program ends. Then, if no partnership results, the options expire when you do not invest, and it does not cause any negative signaling to future investors. There are also programs that include pro rata rights, meaning they have the right to invest in future rounds at their discretion.

Performance-Based Vesting and Buyback Clauses

A newer option that we're starting to see more frequently, and one that we think works well with the corporate-startup dynamics, is investment that vests based on performance or has the ability to be repurchased. The investment should only occur if the corporate and startup continue their relationship in some way after the accelerator program, but there is often a risk of a partnership falling apart or the corporate becoming a direct competitor down the road. It can be extremely bad for the startup to have the corporate on the cap table in either case and can harm them in future fundraising. This fear can prevent top tier startups from participating in your program.

Therefore, performance-based vesting includes funding where vesting is based on the performance of the partnership. Usually startups are eager to partner, so this depends on the corporate partner's performance and can be based on sales milestones or activities such as meetings with X number of potential customers, and should be expected over the course of one to five years.

A buyback clause can be included so that if the corporate becomes a direct competitor, the startup can repurchase the shares at a particular multiple or at the most recent valuation if VC funding rounds have occurred, or even at the original purchase price if one or both of the partners is dissatisfied. For example, Techstars offers an Equity Back Guarantee if any participating company is dissatisfied with their experience in the Techstars program.[2] This permits companies to repurchase some or all of the equity purchased by Techstars at the same price per share paid by Techstars, and can be exercised within a few days after the Demo Day. Indie.vc, a nontraditional venture fund (where Jules is a scout) also offers a redemption clause where entrepreneurs can buy back up to 90% of their equity at a 3x multiple. They open sourced their legal documents on github as a reference point for others who want to replicate this model.[3]

A buyback can benefit the startup because it gives the startup the contractual ability to get a dangerous competitor off their cap table and to get out of any information rights or other problematic clauses if the relationship turns sour. It can be good for the corporate parent because it saves the time and hassle of managing an adversarial investment, and it gives liquidity to claim a return on the investment. This can go back into the operating capital of the accelerator, to the BU that sponsored the deal, or to whoever put up the budget in the first place for the investment.

Although this is not an ideal situation, it is a way to prevent things from going very wrong and alleviates the concerns of startups who are unsure about getting into bed with a huge company when they are at an early stage of their growth and unsure of the future plans. Although an adversarial investment is not a good outcome, from our experience it does happen in large corporations and no one enjoys it. Having an out is a better outcome overall for both parties and alleviates concerns for startups.

Partner with Third-Party Funds

If you do not want to or do not have the capacity to manage equity investments at your company, you can outsource this to a fund who will manage investments for you. This can be their money or yours (ideally a combination of both to align incentives), but the third-party fund should be a sophisticated investor who is committed to managing the portfolio in the long term as a traditional VC investor would. This model is starting to become more popular and is a benefit of most CAaaS programs, who manage both the investment and the program management. It can also be done exclusively as a fund, not including the accelerator piece, to focus on the post-program portfolio management. (More on this in Chapters 9 and 16.)

INVESTMENT DO'S AND DON'TS

When thinking about your investment strategy, keep in mind that they are many ways things can go wrong. While some decisions seem reasonable at first glance, and may even make sense in other parts of your business, the world of startup investments is tricky. Many well-intentioned corporate accelerators have bungled things badly with amateur mistakes that seem logical, but do not work in the startup world. After studying dozens of accelerators, running them ourselves, and participating as founders, here's the hard-earned best practices we have learned around investment.

Manage Expectations

One of the biggest mistakes we've seen corporate accelerators do is promise the world to startups. Especially for programs just starting out and building a brand, accelerator managers need to recruit the best startups that fit their criteria, so they pitch them hard on the benefits of participation.

Startups come in expecting to have partnership, investment, and/or massive success after the program. Often this is not the case, nor is it the intention or desired outcome from the corporate side. Accelerators are a filtering mechanism to get to know a startup and maybe invest small amounts before diving into a larger partnership or investment. So be clear that it is intended to filter, and this can even stoke the fires of competition in startup founders who tend to be highly competitive by nature.

In particular, if you do not invest capital in all companies, be very clear about the criteria for investment during or after the program. We've seen this lead to upset founders on too many occasions to count. In general, do not over-promise results. Everyone will appreciate the program more and leave with a positive experience if expectations are managed properly. Your reputation, and ability to recruit in the future, is at stake.

Do Not Charge

Some giant, multibillion-dollar corporations have thought that it was a good idea to charge tiny, cash-strapped startups a fee to participate in their accelerator program. This is a terrible idea, and even suggesting this means that the company does not understand the startup world.

The vast majority of corporate accelerator programs are focused on strategic returns, so charging a few hundred or a few thousand dollars to startups means that the strategic incentives are not aligned properly. If accelerators work well, the strategic objectives should exponentially outweigh the potential benefits of charging for a program. Program fees make corporates essentially a consulting firm and event organizer for startups, which is a bad business and not one that most corporates should be in, especially if it's not their core business.

Some argue the rationale that they need to cover costs of the program, but this is where strategic goals come in. At a large corporate you have scale, and a few thousand dollars means nothing to your firm's bottom line. Meanwhile, cash is a scarce resource for startups. The strategic benefits of the accelerator to your organization should *far* outweigh the costs of the program. If not, you're not doing it right.

Another excuse for charging is that the corporates want a filtering mechanism to ensure the startup is serious so that they know they can pay the corporate for the products and services they plan to hawk during the program. If your strategic goal for the program is to sell things to startups, then do not run an accelerator program. If you absolutely must, at least be transparent that this is your goal so that the participating startups know it from the outset and provide resources for free at first to incentivize this usage, such as in an ecosystem accelerator.

Charging startups is a quick way to kill your brand, because entrepreneurs are not shy about sharing their opinions publicly or privately. For example, a major global professional services firm (that is not known for being entrepreneurial) launched an accelerator with a $7,500 entry fee, and top entrepreneurs called this bad behavior out in public via LinkedIn and in private to investors and other founder, ensuring a negative stigma that will be hard to shake for this corporate. As startup founders often adapt the Madeleine Albright quote, "There is a special place in hell for big companies that think they can make money from selling things to startups." We repeat: *do not charge startups* for accelerator programs.

Use the Product (if You Can)

Startups take a major risk joining a corporate accelerator program – namely, that the competitors of that corporate will not partner with them or buy their product. They are choosing to be aligned with your company and brand, and there is a responsibility on the side of the corporate to not screw them over as a result.

If you could use the startup's product as a customer and do not, it is an extremely negative signal to the rest of the market. Other potential customers and investors wonder why the corporate, who liked the company enough to put them in an accelerator program, is not a customer. The same goes for potential investors. They wonder, "Do they know something we don't?" or "Does the startup's product not work as well as they are claiming?" Don't put your startups in this bad situation.

The accelerator team and the parent company must understand this weighty responsibility and not unintentionally harm the startups. This is compounded if you are a shareholder on the cap table, and overall it is a very bad, company-killing situation for founders. Use the product if you can.

Only Invest as Professional Investors

While it can be tempting to take equity as a corporate innovation team, it requires a deep understanding of VC investment and the implications and responsibilities of that equity ownership over the duration of its life, which can last more than a decade. **This should not be taken lightly.** Unless there is a sophisticated CVC program at the corporation that has experience, talent, and commitment to manage the company's portfolio longer term, the equity from an accelerator program can be orphaned or mismanaged, which can have meaningful consequences for the startup and damage your reputation.

For example, if startups need their shareholders to vote on a particular resolution and require a certain percent of the share class to approve a resolution, and the corporate is not actively managing the investment and does not participate in the voting, it can prevent the startup from getting approval for decisions it needs to make for the company.

Alternately, if inexperienced corporate executives are participating in the governance and they do not realize the implications of their decisions, as is often the case if well-intentioned people do not have experience with the nuances of venture capital and startups, it can create a bad relationship at best or drive the company to failure at worst. This is all counterproductive to the goal of an accelerator and investment program, which requires the best startups in the world to want to work with you.

An accelerator program should only make equity investments if there is a sophisticated, professional, experienced CVC arm or third-party fund partner managing those investments.

INVESTMENT BEST PRACTICES

Based on our research and expertise with multiple accelerators, we recommend the following rough guidelines based on the type of program you operate and your objectives.

For a venture accelerator that is focused on marketing or market intelligence, consider:

- Non-dilutive grant for participation ($5,000–25,000); flat investment of $50,000–150,000 in exchange for 5–7% equity
- Package of in-kind services that focus on marketing and PR
- Ad hoc equity investment after the program if partnership or other longer-term relationship results, usually through CVC arm

For the ecosystem accelerator, consider:

- Non-dilutive grant for participation ($5,000–$25,000)
- Offer dedicated development resources

- Generous credits to use your software/hardware/etc. needed to develop in the ecosystem (enough for 12–24 months of usage)
- Access to users who can test the product and be early adopters
- Investment for equity at market valuations if a POC results

For partnership-focused programs, consider:

- Non-dilutive grant for participation ($5,000–$25,000) or refund of expenses; investment of $1 million or more at market valuation
- Include funding to support product integration or preparing for go-to-market together
- Invest directly at market valuation after the program if a partnership results, with performance-based vesting and buyback rights, usually through the CVC arm

Overall, an accelerator is an investment in long-term relationships with startups and a filtering mechanism for corporates to find alignment with innovators. Although the mechanics can be altered, the personal relationships will last. The startup world is based on relationships, so at minimum go into any investment with the idea that this could be a multi-year, if not multi-decade, relationship and do what feels fair for both parties.

CHAPTER 12

METRICS AND KPIS

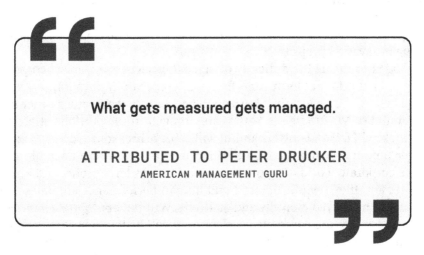

What gets measured gets managed.

ATTRIBUTED TO PETER DRUCKER
AMERICAN MANAGEMENT GURU

Source: Peter Drucker in The Practice of Management, 1954.

Anyone who has worked for a large corporation can tell you that what gets measured is what gets managed. When it comes down to it, whatever gets tracked and mapped to personal and business performance will get the attention. Individuals want career progress through promotions, as well as good reviews and the raises that come with them. Business unit leaders want to increase their responsibility and budgets. All of this depends not just on what leadership says is important, but what metrics they track and monitor to determine success.

Peter Drucker's quote is notable for a few other reasons. First of all, he never actually said it, according to the Drucker Institute.[1] Notwithstanding, this is actually a closely held belief in management. Things that get measured get managed. In fact, that is sometimes the problem. Things that get measured do get managed – even if they are useless or actually detrimental to the company and its goals.

For your corporate accelerator to set itself up for success, it's important to set goals first – the " why" of the accelerator – then translate them into quantitative measurements that showcase the positive impact of these goals on the wider corporation. Select the wrong measures, and it will be easy to dismiss and shut down the program at the slightest change of fortune. A change of leadership or economic downturn can easily be used to justify killing innovation projects.

Added to this is the difficulty of achieving success by typical corporate metrics in the longer-term time frame of corporate innovation. As we've noted before, the typical time horizon for startups to yield returns after their first round of VC funding is 5–10 years. Implicit in the portfolio strategy is that most will fail and only a handful will achieve breakout success. Both the longer time frame and the high attrition over time are very uncomfortable in the corporate world. Corporations measure quarterly profits and annual growth, and they review financial and human performance annually. Sales targets are measured monthly and quarterly. Without appropriate metrics to track success for the corporate accelerator, it will be tough to show progress and maintain senior-level commitment over time, and the inevitable early failures that are part of the path to the successes.

What's needed, then, is not just a clear why with goals and a vision that senior management can buy into. We also need metrics that can be used as a proxy to meet our long-term goals. These metrics need to be both short term and longer term. It may take 10 years to see an IPO for a portfolio company that makes a big financial return for the program, but you can show progress along the way toward goals that support the vision but can be tracked in shorter periods.

You need good metrics for several reasons: to support and track progress toward your goals, to provide measures that can confirm and continue the support provided by senior management, and to track the operational success of the accelerator to know you're doing a good job of running it. Choosing the right metrics to measure the performance of the accelerator is critical to effective management within the context of the wider corporation.

QUANTIFY YOUR WHY

As we reviewed earlier, accelerator leaders must first start with the overarching question: Why are you launching an accelerator for the corporation in the first place? This will be the north star that guides you in setting your goals and then turning those goals into metrics that track success. You can then filter these through the time horizon to arrive at a set of metrics that are both trackable to your goals and actionable for improvement. The benefits from an accelerator can be both financial and strategic. Since corporate accelerators are so often modeled on their independent counterparts, it's easy to adopt financial metrics like return on investment (ROI) as a judgment of their success. This then forces a comparison to other investment-driven accelerators – where the corporate accelerator is likely to compare poorly. Return on investment is most meaningful, after all, if you are an investor and need to return funds to limited partners.

When examining the why, a separate category of metrics emerges. Driven by the more strategic goals and operational impacts of the corporate accelerator, they allow a different set of tracking measures to evaluate success. For example, impact on revenues, costs, or efficiency through successful partnerships can have an impact not only on profitability but on long-term survival for companies in traditional industries disrupted by change and innovation. Revisiting the why and quantifying the desired outcomes will provide you with guidelines for the right metrics of success.

A newer concept is that of return on innovation. "Based on our observation, there are a few things that reflect a concept of return on innovation," says Vijay Rajendran, head of corporate innovation and partnership at 500 Startups. "Those fall into broadly three buckets: exploration and learning, commercial gains, and operational savings." This anchors returns in both strategic and financial metrics, and aligns with our simple innovation machines.

Reputation and Brand

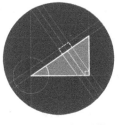

INCLINED PLANE

Reputational impact can be a key reason – if only one of many – that companies launch accelerators. Key stakeholder groups take notice when a corporation begins to embrace innovation, and an accelerator provides a newsworthy platform with a variety of opportunities to showcase the process. This impact should be measured, then, in a few areas. Press and communications metrics should show an increase in earned media as well as more associations of the brand with innovation and its relevant topics. Customer, vendor, and partner attitudes about innovation and their willingness to engage on forward-looking projects can improve. Human resources may notice an increase in interest from younger candidates who are more mission-driven in their careers, as well as improvements in recruiting candidates from key disruptors or competitors in the industry – employees want to work for a future-minded company. And ideally, investors will take note and begin rewarding the company with a multiple reflecting a commitment to innovative and long-term growth.

Culture and Talent

WEDGE

Changing the culture of a company is a common goal, but it is often challenging or downright impossible to measure. A more innovative culture can show up in many ways – more ideas but also more failures as new things are tested and cast aside. Human resources, however, often track metrics that have a direct impact in the battle for human capital. Employee satisfaction at work can often improve just by being associated with innovation, much as corporate social efforts can improve employee morale. Innovative employees feel more at home at your company and stick around to contribute rather than jumping to a startup or faster-moving competitor. New recruits choose the company and bring fresh energy, because of the work challenges, not just the paychecks.

Revenue

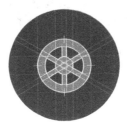

WHEEL & AXLE

Strategic partnerships that yield revenue are the most common why for corporate accelerators, based on our research and experience. This benefit can be directly measured in the short term, though it's important to keep a long-term time horizon. How many new products or services come from partnerships with accelerator participants or the insights they provide? How does this track over multiple years?

Less obvious but equally important are operating impacts. Better, faster, and cheaper ways of delivering the same products are all trackable through dollars-and-cents measures of improved performance against the company's baseline. Less obvious, but also impactful, are sales won due to the perception of innovation and the implied future-proofing of commitments to a company's platform, as well as partners choosing to work with your corporation due to the innovative ethos.

Sometimes innovation is a category on RFPs, and this should be tracked as well. A best practice is to create a templated response about the accelerator and startup partnerships for sales teams responding to these RFPs to use easily. The halo of innovation from the accelerator can indirectly bring broader opportunities to be a market leader as companies translate the accelerator mindset into a willingness to try new things.

Market Intelligence

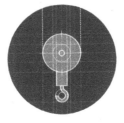

PULLEY

The knowledge gained from working with startups forces a reckoning for the corporation of the direction in which the industry is going. This is a motivating factor for information-driven accelerator goals. However, it is the ongoing deal flow and interaction with alumni that can provide the early data and new approaches that allow the company to incorporate new thinking and be prepared for disruptive waves – because they can see them coming from farther away.

Equity Returns

Of course, if the accelerator is taking an equity position and participating in the startup's upside in any way, there are clear metrics for financial success. These investment driven metrics don't just validate the choices of the accelerator in the public markets, but can provide financial returns and benefits even when the startups in the accelerator don't end up being successful partners for the parent company. An alumni startup may find success outside the parent's sphere despite the hope and promise initially, and the financial returns of that success through equity upside can reward the risks taken.

It's also worth noting that this same goal of financial success can be supportive of your CVC and M&A teams as well. They get early access and data on the most promising candidates downstream from where they usually pay attention. This success should be credited back to the source accelerator wherever possible as an indicator of success.

SAMPLE METRICS BY WHY

GOAL (YOUR WHY)	SHORT	MEDIUM	LONG
Reputation and brand	Media mentions	Inbound innovation	Investor sentiment/ stock multiple
Culture and talent	Job applications Retention	Employee surveys Tenure	Innovations from internal sources
Market intelligence	Insights and data Research partnerships	Innovation area Cultural adoption	Trends over time Informational advantage
Revenue	RFP requests with innovation mentioned Operational efficiencies	# of pilots # of partnerships	New products launched Revenue from accelerator company partnerships
Equity Returns	$ raised by cohort	NPV of portfolio Markups	Return on investment via exit (IPO/M&A)

KEY PERFORMANCE INDICATORS TO MEASURE SUCCESS

In most corporate innovation teams, especially related to equity-based investments in startups through a corporate venture capital (CVC) or corporate accelerator program, there is always a discussion of whether the team is looking to achieve strategic or financial returns as a metric of success. The truth is that you have to do both, which makes the job much more complex and difficult than traditional (non-corporate) venture capital funds or accelerators.

Added to this difficulty is the longer time frame required to invest in startups. Both the investment dollars and the partnership process often require years to pay off. It's challenging to track private companies' value before an exit provides a verified success. It's even harder to track the potential value of partnerships, and standard corporate operational metrics usually don't apply. However, we can lean on metrics from the VC world, and there is also an opportunity to develop new mechanisms to track innovation success.

Financial Metrics

Financial returns are relatively easy to track. Calculating a return on investment (ROI) is basic math for business students; similarly determining an internal rate of return (IRR) can also be easy. Calculating multiples of investment cost (MOIC), distribution to paid-in (DPI), or total value over paid-in (TVPI) are common measures of performance in venture capital and private equity. This can show the success of an investment based on the dollars returned. But with startups, it's not that simple. Since an actual outcome can take many years, measuring performance in the earlier years will take some work.[2]

There are multiple ways to value a venture capital portfolio, which is absolutely what you have if you are making equity investments into the startups participating in the accelerator. With the private markets you can't get an up-to-the moment enterprise value, so instead you must rely on markups (most common) and 409a valuations (less common). A new round of funding, for example, provides a market-driven data point. But what is the right way to value a private portfolio?

There is very little agreement, but VC firms, like corporations, are usually required under Generally Accepted Accounting Principles (GAAP) in the United States or the International Financial Reporting Standard (IFRS) everywhere else to "mark to market" the value of their underlying company holdings on a quarterly basis. According to Scott Kupor[3] at Andreessen Horowitz (A16Z), one of the most revered VC firms in Silicon Valley, there are three main "mark" valuation methods used by venture firms:

1. **Last round valuation/waterfall** – uses the company valuation at the last round of financing.

2. **Comparable company analysis** – for companies that have substantive revenue and/or profits, VC firms sometimes use a public-company comparables analysis to reflect how the broader public market values this set of companies; that metric is then assigned to the portfolio's company's financials.

3. **Option pricing model (OPM)** – the newest and most complicated method, and the one that A16Z prefers, uses the Black-Scholes model to value a portfolio company as a set of call options whose strike prices are the different valuation points at which employee options and preferred shares all convert into common stock.

Sometimes these methods are also combined and weighted, adding to the complexity. Regardless of your preferred method of valuing your portfolio, make sure it is consistent and reported quarterly to your management team.

Strategic Metrics

Strategic metrics are even more difficult to track than financial metrics. There is no commonly used set of metrics here, and even if you create key performance indicators (KPIs) that make sense for your business, clear attribution and accurate data collection is nearly impossible. For example, if sales revenue from startup partnerships is one of your metrics, how do you confirm the attribution of each sales dollar that comes as a result of the partnership? Sometimes it is clear; often it is not. And there are secondary and tertiary revenue streams that come as a result of the partnership but not directly. How do you measure this consistently? For reputational impact and cultural change, it's an even greater challenge – how do you quantify a company culture becoming more innovative?

For most executives setting up a corporate accelerator, the biggest challenge is identifying metrics that are short-term enough to be indicators of success in what is by nature a long-term initiative. Even companies emerging from the corporate acceleration program with clear areas of impact on the parent may take years to have an impact big enough to matter to the bigger corporation. There is no easy answer to this.

For startups, these metrics can be tracked only over the long term. The challenge is to create a spectrum of metrics that span the short-, medium-, and long-term time horizons to provide initial indications of success; further measures of ongoing progress, and ultimately the financial return measures as they impact the bottom line. Sometimes proxy metrics are the closest we can get to the metrics we want. In the short term, it may simply be counting the number of promising pilots, or how many convert to successful partnerships.

Measuring strategic returns is difficult for every company, but it is not meant to cause despair, it just means there is work to do. "For a corporate to work with startups there are always potential challenges and opportunities to learn from," says Cristina Ventura, chief catalyst officer, who runs The Cage accelerator in Hong Kong for The Lane Crawford Joyce Group. "But if everybody works with the same purpose, which for us is to enhance the customer experience and get a commercial agreement to benefit the customer experience, then we can work together toward the same goal. It's important to have a common understanding from the very beginning with very clear KPIs of what we intend to achieve and what they want to achieve at a personal and professional level."

Nielsen for Innovation Is MIA

As a benchmark, in the marketing and advertising space we've seen a similar transformation. In the *Mad Men* era, marketing and advertising gurus sold a concept to big companies, which paid high prices for their campaigns. Sometimes they worked, sometimes they didn't. They used focus groups to gauge some insight, but real user metrics were extremely difficult to get.

It took Nielsen to establish baseline metrics and analytics for television, which had actual figures for "eyeballs" watching each program and ad, clear numbers (ratings), structure, and analytics. It may seem basic now in the time of programmatic advertising and sophisticated analytics, but at the time it was revolutionary to get any data on advertising results, and to understand the reasons for success or failure. Billions of dollars in advertising spend now depend on metrics like these for determining decisions and payments. Marketing became a much more data-driven science, and now there are sophisticated models to figure out where to put money in those campaigns. Now no one argues today that they need to do targeted marketing and have a data-driven marketing strategy.

In corporate innovation, strategic metrics are still living in a pre-Nielsen world. It's still the Wild West in the sense that corporations are often spending millions of dollars on programs that they aren't sure are working. There is tremendous opportunity for those who want to put structure and analytics behind this in the same way marketing has developed. Until a Nielsen for corporate innovation is created, we will do the best we can and continuously improve as we go.

INTEGRATING WITH THE CORPORATE MISSION

Corporate accelerators are different from independent accelerators in many aspects, and one of the clearest areas of this divergence is consideration for the metrics that matter to the larger parent company. Independent accelerators do not have to deal with this extra layer of expectation. There is almost a gut-level understanding that strategic results are an important element of corporate innovation success, not just financial, but how does a company track these aspects? Avoiding innovation theater demands defining areas of impact and metrics that can be tracked against them.

Know Your Own Metrics and Goals

Before developing metrics for your accelerator or wider innovation initiatives, it's important to make sure you know your overall company metrics. As you would instruct the startups participating in your accelerator program, you need to do user research and know your customer. Once you know who your internal stakeholders are, talk to them! Ask them what they want out of a startup partnership and how this relates to the overall company goals. Ask them to talk about their biggest pain points. Ask them what technology gets them excited that your company doesn't do well but wants to. Ask them what it takes for them to meet their annual bonus. Find out what success looks like for the stakeholders, and make sure your metrics align with the impact they need.

You can and should do this type of heavy one-on-one engagement with any key stakeholders and develop KPIs together. Ideally you will get an understanding of the overall company and individual business unit's goals and metrics, with greater attention paid to any BU that is likely to be engaged in the accelerator program. As an added bonus, these will be the exact people you'll need to get buy-in from to support your startups, and this process is closely aligned with stakeholder engagement (Chapter 7). By framing the requests in terms and metrics that meet their day-to-day operational goals, you're far more likely to get what you need.

You will be best served as an innovation program if you can align with the overall corporate goals. In particular, growth in revenue and/or reduction in costs over the long term, so pay careful attention to your revenue and growth metrics.

Once the innovation goals are aligned with the overall company goals, they must be quantified and turned into trackable metrics. By aligning the goals for a corporate accelerator's success with the greater goals of the parent company and its business units, accelerator executives essentially translate the innovation laboratory into the language of the boardroom. There are a few key categories of information that are commonly tracked and used as KPIs.

Client Acquisition

Look at the new customers your company brings on board on a monthly and annual basis. Where are they coming from? How are you marketing to potential clients (digital marketing, conferences, sponsorships, direct sales, etc.)? Is it working? From where are you getting sales leads (clients, personal relationships, etc.)? Why are they sending you these leads and are you compensating them for it? On average, how much does it cost to close a new client (CAC – customer acquisition cost)? How long does it take between the time you first meet a potential prospect to the time they start spending money? Who on your team is involved? How long does it take to close a deal once it's qualified? What is the velocity? Are there any target clients that you have not been able to make progress in? This information should be easily available in your customer relationship management (CRM) system (e.g., Salesforce) or sales ops team.

Look for areas of opportunity for the accelerator to drive meaningful impact in any of these areas, and always be thinking about how a startup might be able to help improve these numbers. This is the easiest way to get internal support for your initiative.

Account Management

Once a client is on board, try to understand their behavior as a client. How much are existing clients spending? Does this vary by business unit, account manager, or geography? Are there any noticeable trends? How much does client spend increase or decrease each year? What touch points do you have with your clients when not on a specific deal? Is your sales team transactional (e.g., only engages when they need to sell something) or relationship driven? What feedback are you getting on the product or service? Have you been able to upsell successfully? What is your churn? How long do clients remain with you on average? What is the total expected lifetime revenue of each client (lifetime value [LTV])? If you can increase the revenue from and strengthen the relationship with existing clients by dropping a startup product into your suite of offerings, everybody wins.

Competition

It is important to benchmark yourself against your competition and keep tabs on what they are doing in the realm of innovation and startup partnerships. Who do you compete with? What is their revenue and expenses? What technology are they using? Why do you win business? Why do you lose business? How do people view your brand versus your competition's brand? What is the client profile of your firm versus your peers? What is your net promoter score? Do a SWOT analysis, identifying your firm's strengths, weaknesses, opportunities, and threats. Understand what the startups' other options are.

Ratios

Once you have these numbers, compare them to each other in meaningful ways. For example, in the startup and venture capital worlds, there are critical metrics that executives and investors regularly track to measure ROI and peer comparisons. One widely used ratio for software as a service (SaaS) companies is lifetime value (LTV) to customer acquisition cost (CAC). This starts with the LTV of a customer, which is the average revenue a single customer is predicted to generate over the lifetime of their client relationship with you. The exercise of calculating these types of ratios gives you a better understanding of your business and where you have inefficiencies. The goal is to pull as much baseline data as possible to understand where you stand so that you can identify opportunities to partner with startups that have a direct positive impact on something that matters to your top-line or bottom-line revenue. If you don't have this type of baseline of information, it's impossible to assess whether investments in new technology actually produce a return on your investment.

The point of all these exercises is to zone in on the key areas that matter to the business units and senior management that are key to the support of the corporate accelerator. The preceding suggestions are not a checklist but a starting point for discussion to zero-in on what's important. Fear not – most innovators are facing the same challenges, trying to design impactful metrics around often difficult-to-measure long-term goals. One McKinsey study found that the average number of KPIs tracked for innovation is eight. Not all meet the high standards we have discussed; many are easy-to-track vanity metrics.

While 71% of executives claim to be satisfied with the innovation metrics they are using, they don't seem to be able to use the metrics for anything. When asked if the innovation metrics have enabled them to use data for actionable purposes, such as for improving overall innovation performance or assessing their progress against goals, the majority said no. Less than a third (32%) reported the ability to use any single one of their metrics to influence action, let alone all of them.

Best practices require that innovation metrics track the goals of the accelerator alongside those of the parent company so that the accelerator can easily show success and impact against the things that matter for the larger corporation. Providing these numbers directly or through proxy metrics is a way to bridge the gap between the long time frame of startup success and the inevitable need to show success and progress before then.

CUSTOMIZING YOUR CORPORATE ACCELERATOR METRICS

Ava Lopez spent a lot of time understanding her stakeholders and the overall goals of FabCo with a blitz of one-on-one meetings, and it became clear that the most important goal for the company is growth. When she pressed her executive team on the timeline, it was "medium term," which they defined as two to three years. She knows that she wants to launch a partnership accelerator first, then maybe after a cycle or two launch an ecosystem accelerator, so these should give her the best chance of success in terms of revenue during that timeframe to FabCo.

She decided that her strategic metrics should be as follows:

- **Short term** – media mentions, amount of VC dollars raised by the participating startups, RFP responses that mention the accelerator or the resulting partnerships
- **Medium term** – number of pilots, number of partnerships, responses to a new question about innovation that she added to the annual company-wide survey

- **Long term** – revenue from startup partnerships (though she wasn't quite sure how she was going to track it yet), operational savings from using the startups products, innovation scorecard results from the Investor Relations team (she offered to help them develop this)

In addition, FabCo does not have an established CVC arm. They've made a couple of random investments here and there when executives got excited about a market trend, but then moved on to the next shiny object shortly after the investment. Most of these investments were abandoned and were being looked after by a junior finance professional in the corporate development team. Coming from the VC world herself, Ava wanted to start the slow process of educating her team about venture capital and startups.

As an experienced investor, she decided that she'd make investments in any company that participated in the accelerator program that led to a meaningful partnership. She got approval from her boss, CEO Jordan Burns, to invest off the balance sheet up to $1 million per company and hire an experienced associate from the VC world to focus on portfolio management once she had made five investments. Ava also decided to include some clear financial metrics around equity returns, including NPV of the portfolio using the most recent company valuation to keep it simple, as well as IRR and DPI.

Ava knew that tracking these metrics would not be easy, especially as they related to sales, but she was optimistic that it was the right set of KPIs for her program. She put together a "board pack" in PowerPoint with charts and graphs of all of these metrics, and set up quarterly meetings with her advisory board and investment committee to review them regularly. Metrics, managed!

DURING THE PROGRAM

CHAPTER 13

PROGRAMMING

I believe you have to be willing to be
misunderstood if you're going to innovate.

JEFF BEZOS
FOUNDER OF AMAZON

Source: Apr 28, 2018, Jeff Bezos interview with Axel Springer CEO Mathias Döpfner. Retrieved from: https://www.cnbc.com/2018/05/17/jeff-bezos-on-what-it-takes-to-be-innovative.html.

One of the advantages of a cohort-based accelerator is the ability to leverage resources and experiences across multiple companies at once. The learning experiences and training aspects of an accelerator are a key benefit for founders, especially with the earlier-stage startups or if there is a very particular industry vertical or technology tool that is the focus of the program. From formal instruction in lean startup methodologies, practical clinics on new technologies, and office hours with experts and professionals, accelerators can leverage the time and expertise of the teachers across an entire cohort of founders at once.

Building a curriculum and related programming is fortunately not complex, though it does take a lot of work to coordinate. Thanks to the lean startup movement and the many years of accelerators operating in the real world, we have an established body of materials to draw upon.

These fall into four main areas:

1. Basic entrepreneurship and lean startup methods
2. Expert-level best practices around startup topics such as recruiting, product development, and fundraising
3. Industry- and domain-level expertise, such as on an industry vertical or new technology
4. Hands-on technical or design workshops

It's in these last two areas that corporate accelerators can really differentiate themselves. If the accelerator theme is in an area where your company has particular expertise, this provides unique access to practitioners and insights that other accelerators can't provide. Executing on this requires getting people from within your company engaged in the curriculum. A corporate accelerator needs to plan the timing and location of the program to enable this engagement by others in the company.

PROGRAM LENGTH AND TIMING

When designing an accelerator, one of the defining elements is a set time. There's a duration for the program and a milestone that moves the fledgling companies out of the nest and into the real world. But what's the right amount of time?

While accelerators can be as short as a couple of weeks and as long as a year, most of the industry has settled around a standard duration of three months. Paul Graham, founder of Y Combinator, said "We discovered [the three-month program length] by accident. When we first started YC, we began with a summer program. We were trying to learn how to be investors, so we invited college students to come into Cambridge and start startups instead of getting summer jobs."[1]

The three-month "summer school" program may have been discovered accidentally, but it helped create a new dimension of startup support that leverages the time constraint and creates urgency. One benefit is that it allows for a two-cohort-a-year program schedule, including time for preparation, recruiting, post-program activities and a short break between cohorts. But while the exact timing can still be finessed, the key factor is the constraint of a limited duration itself. All good things must come to an end.

The goal for accelerators is to have enough time for participating startups to hit a noteworthy milestone – but only just.

Three months creates enough time to build something that can impress potential partners and investors, keeps costs constrained, and provides a convenient two-cohort rhythm for accelerators each year. The relatively short time frame allows for achieving goals but simultaneously excuses shortcomings and gaps in development. For example, early-stage companies can be expected to ship a minimum viable product (MVP) in three months, but a longer time frame would raise expectations for the product significantly.

LOCATION AND STRUCTURE

Where an accelerator happens can set the tone of the program. Consulting firm BCG found that, from a broader innovation perspective, there is also some correlation between the type of innovation vehicle and its location.[2] Innovation vehicles that focus on transforming the core business, such as venture studios and partnership units, are usually geographically close to corporate headquarters because they require easy access to corporate assets and business units, whereas accelerators and CVC arms are mostly held – about 75% of the time – in the cities that have strong startup ecosystems. They may have some decentralization if they require access to facilities or assets, such as in the pharma industry. For most companies, the corporate accelerator location involves trade-offs and benefits that need to be discussed.

AN INNOVATION VEHICLE'S PURPOSE DICTATES ITS LOCATION
Key findings about each innovation vehicle

INNOVATION LAB OR DIGITAL LAB	• Close proximity to HQ to more easily impact the core business • 25% of digital labs centralized in major cities, with the rest decentralized in smaller cities
ACCELERATOR	• Concentrated in startup hubs to access ecosystem • 74% of accelerators in major cities
CORPORATE VENTURE CAPITAL UNIT	• Centralized in startup hubs to access ecosystem, but decentralized if access to facilities or assets is required (as in pharma) • 53% of CVC units centralized in major cities, with the rest decentralized
PARTNERSHIP UNIT	• Close proximity to HQ to impact the core business more easily • Decentralized
INCUBATOR	• Centralized in startup hubs to access ecosystem • Major cities hold 48% of incubators

Source: BCG[3]

Corporate Office versus Co-working Space

One of the benefits of the accelerator being housed in the corporate office is the cultural transfer of the startup mindset to the more traditional corporate workforce. Employees, whether they are involved in the accelerator or not, can be inspired by the perpetual energy and creativity that happens when several entrepreneurial startups are working in the same space side by side. This influences the corporate culture, slowly but surely.

Company spaces also have the benefit of proximity and often are cost-free from the company perspective – sunk costs on a lease or owned outright. Proximity can provide access to experts and even lunchroom conversation, but this needs to be facilitated and actively encouraged by the accelerator team. Also, most large corporations have multiple offices around the country or the world; proximity for some is still distant for others. Finally, many corporate offices are in locations that are off the beaten path for startups and their founders. Many startups are located in the classic industry centers of innovation, Silicon Valley, or major metro centers to meet and have access to employees, financing, and industry contacts. Locating them next to a rural factory may not be appealing.

If companies decide to use existing space, the best practice is to invest in sprucing up the space – ensuring not only basic amenities but ones that you might find at a top startup office or a co-working space. Easy access to good lighting, fast internet, conference rooms, and stocked kitchens are a must. Usually retrofitting it to look a little cooler is also advised – something similar to a WeWork space is a minimum threshold.

It also goes in reverse. If a startup is participating in your accelerator, they probably have an interest in partnering with your company. Being in your office allows them to understand your culture and get into the corporate mind hive, which can be extremely valuable. It also gives them access to people within the company who they may need to work with in the future, and makes it easier to grab a coffee or lunch to meet with the folks who otherwise wouldn't venture offsite to a co-working space. Yet finding space in key company sites can be difficult or impossible – and they may not be located where the innovation centers are. Corporate accelerators are often either dropped into leftover space wherever it may be – often neglected floors or buildings – or the company finds a new space to set up operations.

Many companies choose to go where the startups are, however, because they both need space and want access to the ecosystem. These spaces are modeled after the co-working trends pioneered by WeWork and others, with open desk plans, communal spaces, and perks like coffee and activities to appeal to founders. This can limit the interaction with corporate employees, as many won't make the effort to venture to the co-working space. However, the ones who do can really benefit by seeing startups on their home turf. Often, the company will simply take over a floor or area of a prominent co-working space – solving the problem with the benefits of a shorter-term lease commitment and someone else to manage the physical space. This method is usually the best of both worlds – it allows the manager of the corporate accelerator to focus on the programming and not stocking the kitchen.

The decision to operate an accelerator at your office or at a co-working space depends on your goals for the company. Our general advice is that if you have an office in a major startup ecosystem, it's best to have it there to benefit from the interaction with a wider swath of the company. Make sure to redesign it a bit, though. If you do not have offices in major startup hubs, then go with a co-working space in one of these ecosystems.

Module-Based Approach

One option that is becoming more popular is a module-based approach, versus a full program in one location. This makes it easier for entrepreneurs who are not local and do not want to move or disconnect from their entire teams and families to the location of the accelerator.

This approach includes a series of modules, usually once per month during the course of the program, consisting of an intense three to five days on-site. The entrepreneurs go home afterward and may have some virtual programming in between. This tends to lend itself better to later-startups and partnership-based accelerator programs, and also gives you flexibility to hold different modules in different locations.

The IBM Blockchain Accelerator-Network program, which Jules launched in 2018 with the first cohort starting in January 2019, is a partnership accelerator for growth-stage startups participating from around the globe. It holds three in-person modules of three intensive days each, with an additional two days of optional on-site work space and operational support for meetings with mentors, potential customers, or otherwise if the entrepreneurs wanted to make the most of it and stay for the full week. It was designed to host two of the modules in New York City, where the majority of the IBM Blockchain team is located, then one of the modules in San Francisco around IBM's annual THINK conference, where the companies have a speaking slot and can also tap into both the attending IBM customer and the Silicon Valley investor ecosystem. This would not have been possible if all programming was held in New York only. This allows for greater flexibility and diversity of networks, which can be a huge benefit for the participating startups.

Virtual Programming

What about virtual programming? After all, with the rise of remote work, is a physical space even needed? This question has come up more and more during the COVID-19 crisis as the world has been forced to work remotely. Accelerator programs have adapted by going remote as well. These work to a degree, but the in-person networking and impromptu meetings are often the most valuable part of accelerator programs. The best practice continues to be building an in-person program. Alternately, there is a way to host the majority of the program virtually, with some opportunities to meet in person (at least in a post-COVID world).

The serendipity of interactions, the camaraderie of the community and shared experience, and even the visibility of the site visit to the cool startup lab, help build the culture of innovation for accelerators. While virtual can increase access to startups around the world and does happen, the benefit of bringing everyone to one place is undeniable.

DESIGNING THE SPACE: THE COOL FACTOR AND CO-WORKING

It's important to note that innovation culture has its own signifiers and language. Open spaces, non-traditional hours, communal areas with social aspects (like the proverbial foosball table), and other social outlets are all statements that break free of corporate culture. Although some of this may seem childish and feel like a simple design choice, the space communicates the culture. Snacks in the kitchen speak to late nights and staying in the office; communal areas allow for informal creative meetings.

Equally important are the facilities needed for getting work done and collaborating. An ample number of conference rooms, from small ad hoc meeting rooms with whiteboards for creative brainstorming, to more formal classroom and teleconferencing facilities, is critical support for programming. Ample offices are needed for mentor meetings, venture capital drop-ins, and interviewing of new recruits. Newer functionality like phone booths for sales calls are also key components, especially in open-plan office environments. And don't overlook support staff who provide basic reception and office management support but also can ensure that happy hours and team lunches happen smoothly as well – the informal transfer of culture and ideas.

CURRICULUM

The curriculum is a key element of the program. For most accelerators, this comes down to a few key areas of focus for the content.

First, for early-stage companies the basics of business and entrepreneurship in general can be extremely valuable. For many entrepreneurs, particularly those just out of school or with a more technical background, the skill sets they have around developing a technology, programming an application, or engineering a technology are essential to developing the innovation. However, they may lack the skill set to commercialize – to turn an innovation into a product that customers want, then that product into a company that can deliver it. Even for those with a more business background, the unique aspects of startups are often alien to those who come from traditional corporate environments.

Finally, there are many best practices, from vendor selection to building a sales team, that require experts who have done it before. An accelerator can provide all of this training, but needs to balance the beneficial in-class learning with the downside of too much time spent sitting in a classroom and not building the company. Startups win through execution, not reflection. This means the programming should focus on the practical, not the theoretical.

Venture accelerators for early-stage startups generally rely on content from the lean startup method, with exercises around going into the market immediately to gather user data and perform customer development, along with iterative and agile MVP launches. Although many founders have proactively read the popular *The Lean Startup* by Eric Reis and related texts – the holy grail of the lean startup movement – accelerators often offer a curriculum that allows the founding team to use their company as a living laboratory to bring these principles to life. The later the stage of the participating startups, the less important this type of curriculum becomes.

Another important part of the curriculum at all stages is developing, perfecting, and practicing the pitch. Startups should present their pitch deck so many times during the program at events, demo days, and curated meetings that they can recite it by heart. And along the way, they should be getting feedback from their mentors and anyone who hears it to continuously improve. At least weekly sessions help practice and hone the message and identify weak spots. When Jeremy participated in the ERA Accelerator, all of the companies had to pitch before they could attend happy hour! This was very motivating. Practical progress in the business and the pitch, which explains the business, are parallel. The best programs spend less time on general business skills and more time on developing deep expertise, honing specific technical skills, networking, and presenting.[4]

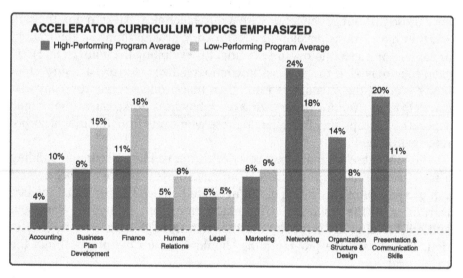

Source: Based on Village Capital, GALI.

One of the important benefits of accelerators is that many high potential entrepreneurs simply don't have access to the right networks, whereas they can learn double-entry bookkeeping in any online course or university. These networks are often what makes the difference between a successful startup and an unsuccessful one. In fact, research has shown that most of the benefit from accelerators comes from indirect learning, so entrepreneurs build a set of skills, awareness, and connections to be able to address future known and unknown issues as they build their businesses.[5]

If you are at a large, highly complex organization, it's highly recommended that you include some type of training on your company and how it works. Startups may not fully appreciate all of the various businesses you're in or how the internal processes work. In some of the accelerators we've worked with, these are the highest-rated sessions and give the startups a better understanding of how to do business with you, leading to a higher success rate for partnerships.

Finally, deep dives into best practices and more complex issues in all of these areas can be important. Startup-specific workshops on hiring and recruiting – with attention to equity incentives for new hires, legal structures, and requirements to plan for growth – and even vendor selection and contracting, can be critical in saving time and money for the new companies. Recent alumni of the program or local startup icons who have achieved success in these areas often participate in these practical sessions. Their real-world stories and expertise are invaluable.

IMPLEMENTING THE CURRICULUM

After designing the curriculum, you need to put it in practice for an audience of ambitious, easily distracted entrepreneurs. Sitting in a classroom all day is not the best use of time. Accelerators are not intended to be a replacement for education, though there is a component of learning. Rather, they should enable entrepreneurs to *do* in a safe and structured environment. Startup success is not about ideas and knowledge; it's about execution. Improving the founders' ability to execute better and faster is a main goal of any accelerator.

Here is a sample curriculum inspired by The Founder Institute as an initial source of inspiration when putting together your programming.

ACCELERATOR CURRICULUM TOPICS EMPHASIZED

	POST PROGRAMS									
14. SHOWCASE / INAUGURATIONS										
13. EQUITY & FUNDING										
12. GROWTH										
11. HIRING & ONBOARDING										
10. PROGRESS REVIEW										
9. PRODUCT DEVELOPMENT										
8. GO-TO-MARKET										
7. LEGAL & IP										
6. IDEA REVIEW										
5. BRANDING & DESIGN										
4. REVENUE										
3. CUSTOMER DEVELOPMENT										
2. VISION & VALIDATION										
1. ORIENTATION	PITCHING	CUSTOMER DEVELOPMENT	LEADERSHIP & FOUNDER WELLNESS	SALES & CUSTOMER ACQUISITION	PRODUCT DEVELOPMENT	REVENUE MODELING	LEGAL & IP	BRANDING & DESIGN	FINANCIAL PLANNING	TEAM & ADVISOR	FUNDRAISING	POST-PROGRAM ONBOARDING
WEEKLY FEEDBACK SESSIONS	BUSINESS SPRINTS									

Source: Curriculum Table, Founder Institute. © 2020, Founder Institute, Inc.

Lean On the Lean Startup

There are many principles and practices for doing, and the most common for accelerators targeting early-stage startups is by following the principles of the lean startup methodology for the programming. One of the main principles stems from the book by one of the original fathers of the movement, *Four Steps to the Epiphany* by Steve Blank. In it, he espouses the doctrine of customer development as a way to learn what customers want from a product as early as possible, before investing in expensive development and launching a product.

Blank's methodology of four steps was designed to find product/market fit – building a product that the customers in the target market wanted. First, through *customer discovery*, literally "getting out of the building" to speak with real potential customers. This is followed by *customer validation*, which shows that customers are willing to pay for the initial product, then *customer creation* to create a scalable sales and marketing process. Finally, *company building* is the process of scaling and standardizing the company for efficiency in its operations.

Workshops and Studios

The later the stage of companies, the more they will want practical, hands-on sessions. These can be technical workshops, design thinking workshops, studio time where the startups can work with their mentors or other experts, or a variety of other options. The most important thing is that they are not sitting in a classroom all day listening; they are doing.

Path to Partnership

One of the compelling benefits of a corporate accelerator is a path to partnership in some way, and this is a main reason that startups participate. Corporates have the potential to be the customers of the companies in the accelerator, and their employees and decision makers are precisely the people who need to be spoken to in the customer development process. A significant advantage of joining a corporate accelerator is that, with the proper access, this portion of the process can be expedited.

The corporate accelerator curriculum can provide access to a roster of key personnel from the parent for the various startups to speak to and/or engage in one-on-one meetings with. The BU sponsor or mentors should have ample time built into the program to focus on scoping out a partnership, working with the startup teams, and actually getting the partnership set up during the accelerator. Make sure to build in time for this, either in a structured or unstructured way, and it will lead to better results after the program ends.

It's Personal

For executives in big corporations, innovation is usually just a part of their job. For startups, it's their entire life. They live and breathe the companies that they create, and often the lines are blurred between personal and professional. It's important for accelerator leaders to keep this in mind, and the best programs incorporate a human touch with networking events and personal development opportunities.

"This might be unusual, but the personal component is something that we added after a few cohorts because the startups wanted it," says Cristina Ventura, chief catalyst officer and head of The Cage accelerator for The Lane Crawford Joyce Group in Asia. "For example, we have a yoga studio in our building, so we offered a yoga session or meditation every morning. Our startups said please do this with every cohort because it has been one of the best parts of the program. We put a bit more holistic and personal growth experience into the program so it wasn't only about professional growth, including a volunteer trip to SiliconBali.io."

We know that the combination of business and technology is important for innovation, but the humanity or personal side is equally crucial for the long-term success of the humans running the business. Startups can have a great business model with excellent technology and make it work for a certain amount of time, but for the long run they need personal strength, resilience and alignment on values and purpose. After all, startups are all about the people running them.

Standardized versus Customized

As a general rule, the earlier the stage of the participating company in an accelerator program, the more standardized curriculum should be implemented. The later the stage of the participating startups, the more customization and one-on-one engagement should occur. Growth-stage startups need more practical, situation-driven advice and executive coaching rather than the basics.

Vertically focused programs around a particular technology or use case may also provide education on that particular area. Many founding teams are experienced enough to start a business in the space, but almost all can benefit from a broad education in the specific history and technology, its structure, its major players, and important milestones across the industry. A blockchain accelerator, for example, can provide a baseline of the technology and its possible use cases to ensure that all members of the cohort have a foundational understanding and common language. According to academic research, "a major benefit of focusing on teams in one sector is that the ventures benefit from sharing expertise because they are working on related problems or technologies. Similar teams in one cohort also facilitate collaborating with investors and partners who are active in the particular sector."[6]

Corporate accelerators, then, can add additional value by tapping into their industry expertise. Not only can they educate newcomers to an industry with fundamentals and key information, but they can also provide aspiring disruptors the language and background to succeed in getting pilots and customers. Corporate partners provide value as incumbents by helping to educate the startups enough to translate their innovations into a format that industry customers can compare, evaluate, and purchase.

Kill It or Be Killed

It's important to make sure the companies are progressing rapidly during the program. Expected performance metrics should be identified at the beginning of the program, with weekly updates on how things are going. And if for some reason things aren't going well – the company just isn't working, the corporate can't figure out how to add value, or the founders are checked out – then it may not be worth anyone's time for them to continue to the end of the program.

"We are really laser focused on objectives coming in weekly to make sure the startups get the most out of the program," says Dan Sinclair, head of MDR LAB at London-based law firm Mischon de Reya. "Something which might be perceived as controversial, which was inspired by some of the Nordic programs we've seen, is a kill point in the middle of the program. Midway through we do a review to say: are you getting enough from this? If you're not getting the most of it, or we don't feel like we were going to be value added for you, then let's shake hands and find out ways to support you, but you don't need to be with us for the next six weeks."

This may seem harsh, but the most valuable resource for the startup founders is their time. "Introducing this kill switch with a positive angle means that we're really forcing progress," says Sinclair. "It means that we're not wasting anyone's time."

Create, Then Iterate

Ava Lopez is excited to put together a curriculum for the FabCo accelerator, but there's almost too much content to include. She lists all of the possible topics and speakers that she wants to include, and it could be enough for five accelerators! Especially since she's launching a partnership accelerator for growth-stage startups, she doesn't want to overwhelm the founders or keep them from building their businesses. So she streamlines her original classroom-intensive program to be a series of four two-day modules. Each has a theme, and she plans to host them in four different FabCo offices around the world (of course, covering the cost of the founders' travel with a stipend). In each module, day one is in the classroom and day two is in the field, getting hands-on experience at FabCo's manufacturing plants and customer sites. She thinks this will work great! But just in case, she plans to get feedback after every module and continuously tweak the agenda for each cohort until it's perfect.

DEMO DAY AND A PROGRAM'S END

> "Now this is not the end.
> It is not even the beginning of the end.
> But it is, perhaps,
> the end of the beginning."[7]

Winston Churchill delivered these famous words in a 1942 speech at London's Mansion House, just after the British routed Rommel's forces at Alamein, driving German troops out of Egypt. The battle marked a turning point in the war, leading Churchill to write in his memoirs, "Before Alamein we never had a victory. After Alamein we never had a defeat."

One of the signature features of any accelerator is that it is on a schedule. There is a recruitment and marketing process, a kickoff and beginning, an intense program with a curriculum and mentorship, and then the program ends. The ultimate culmination of most accelerator programs is a demo day, when the participating companies pitch the businesses or announcements that they've been hard at work on during the program. This usually takes place in a splashy big event with lots of fanfare.

Demo Day Goals

The goals may vary for different types of accelerators: venture accelerators may seek to fill out investment rounds, ecosystem accelerators may showcase the products, and partnership accelerators may seek to drum up new customers or partnerships. However, all accelerators encourage the companies presenting to show confidence and clarity in their mission, and concrete milestones of progress.

Demo days are essentially a public graduation ceremony. They are an opportunity for everyone involved to demonstrate the progress made during the program. For companies, it's where they can demonstrate that they've achieved their goals: initial investment, key partners, product launch, first customers, or other exciting news to generate interest from investors and customers. Perhaps most importantly, demo day, much like the set term of an accelerator itself, provides a "forcing function" to make sure everyone is aligned on hitting their goals by the end of the program. It creates a sense of urgency to achieve some sort of exciting milestone that founders can announce on stage.

It's especially important to know your why, specifically for demo days. Otherwise they can be a lot of work and expense for little payoff.

The Death of Demo Days?

When there were only a handful of accelerators and the concept of the demo day was still fresh and new, they were often invitation-only events, coveted by investors seeking to get in early to the best companies that had been groomed for success. For top accelerators, there is still a sense of missing out if one does not get invited to the final event.

However, recently demo days have been losing their luster. Compared to early days when people used to hang on every company presenting at Y Combinator and it was covered extensively in TechCrunch and other tech publications, there is less enthusiasm these days, perhaps simply because of the sheer number of accelerators and demo days now. When a relatively small number of companies graduated from a relatively small group of accelerators, the highly screened and trained companies were perceived as the best of the best; now, with Y Combinator classes having hundreds of companies in each cohort, and hundreds of accelerators graduating even more companies, the process has become less exciting with more variability on quality.

"The original intent of Demo Days was to help companies raise capital," says Ryan Sommerville, US program director at independent venture accelerator Antler. "But in the U.S., because it's a sophisticated ecosystem, the Demo Day is more about marketing and PR for the companies with the intention of announcing them to the world and helping the teams get as much traction as possible."

Fundraising is still a priority in the United States, but as Sommerville states, "We help with fundraising on a more one-on-one level with making introductions, bringing in angels, bringing in VCs for more closed door meetings as opposed to a Demo Day where everyone's in the audience." He explains why this is important: "In the U.S., the more established VCs want to see the deals early because it is a competitive advantage for them. By the time it gets to Demo Day and everyone has exposure, then they don't have an advantage. So it's too late for some of the reputable VCs that our founders really want to have on their cap table."

Guillaume Payan at OrangeFab agrees entirely. "I think Demo Days are over. I wouldn't do a Demo Day – it makes no sense to me. Demo Days nowadays are either too short or too long. Now we customize meetings for our partners; when they come to San Francisco we review all the startups and select them ahead of time." These curated one-on-one meetings with potential investors, customers, and partners are almost always way more effective than demo days.

There may be a paradigm shift in the United States away from using demo days for fundraising, and a realization that they are more for purely marketing purposes after the deals have been done in advance. However, in other parts of the world where there are fewer accelerators, the original purpose still stands. This is not to say they are a bad idea, even in the United States. Generating marketing buzz, especially with potential customers and others inside the big company, is extremely valuable. Just make sure to understand the purpose and plan accordingly.

IT DOESN'T END AT DEMO DAY

Although most people think the accelerator is just a three-month (or however long) program that starts and ends in that period, this is not true. It is simply a means to an end.

A startup's purpose isn't to get into a good accelerator, it's to build and scale an industry-changing business. They join a corporate accelerator likely because they want to partner with that particular company. The corporate doesn't just want to run a program, they want to build and scale innovation projects and create partnerships to earn revenue in the short and long term.

The corporate accelerator is just a filtering mechanism to see if there's a good fit for a longer-term relationship between the corporate and the startup. This is when the real work begins.

CHAPTER 14

MENTORS

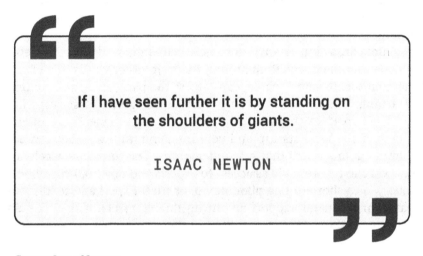

> If I have seen further it is by standing on the shoulders of giants.
>
> ISAAC NEWTON

Source: Isaac Newton

It's often said that the entrepreneurial journey of a founder is a lonely one. In fact, investors often dislike solo founders and instead look for teams where the cofounders not only complement each other's skills professionally, but also support each other emotionally through the challenging ups and downs of every startup's roller coaster journey.

It should come as no surprise that one of the main benefits of an accelerator is the community and camaraderie a founding team can get through participation. Mentors can share their expertise, peers can share their support, and alumni can share their experiences. This provides an incredible network of resources and skills for founders to draw upon both during an accelerator program and long afterwards. While mentors can't replace a co-founder, they are important thought partners for founders.

Many accelerator programs rely heavily on mentors, and many founders say that mentors are the best part of accelerator programs. However, getting the mentor piece right is often the trickiest part of running an accelerator. It's harder to control and reliant on individual personalities and vague expectations. Some teams could love their mentors and receive company-changing advice, and some teams could clash with their mentors or worse, have the mentors not show up at all. The experience is often inconsistent, even among teams within the same cohort. When it works, it really works. But when it doesn't, it can cause a lot of stress and reflect poorly on your accelerator's brand.

Mentors are so important that some accelerators start with the mentors, then construct the curriculum around them. In other words, the expertise of the mentors, to some degree, can inform the pace, style, and content of the learning. The shared experience of the peer group of startups in the cohort itself creates a common bond, but it is access to mentors – often key members of the local startup and venture communities – that can create the shortcuts to success that a founder needs. For corporate accelerators, this access can be as simple as access to experts and potential customers for discovery, or a shortcut to a pilot, demo, or trial. Expert advice, discounts, empathy, and general support are all invaluable assets of the accelerator mentor community.

THE MENTOR'S ROLE IN ACCELERATION

Mentors are often one of the main benefits touted by accelerators. No matter what the focus of a particular program, one of the advantages is the access to other professionals in the startup ecosystem and within your corporation. Those who have built a company before, whether they have achieved success or failure, are invaluable guides through the uncharted wilderness of building a new venture. For internal mentors coming from inside the company, their expertise and help navigating a partnership can make all the difference in a startup's trajectory.

Having the wrong mentor, the misguided mentor, or the inexperienced mentor can often be worse than having no mentor at all. Scott Howard, former founding director of the Chobani Accelerator and former head of acceleration at Mars, could not emphasize the importance of good mentors enough. "Whether your accelerator is dealing with early stage startups working towards their first minimum viable product or startups that have already raised some funding, it is crucial to incorporate mentorship into the program in some capacity," said Howard. "Mentorship has consistently proven to be one of the most valuable assets gained from these programs; it is often the ad hoc relationships that are born from these constant founder-mentor interactions that lead to meaningful development and involvement."

Mentorship is a time commitment for both parties, so the value has to be clear for both the startups and the mentors. The most committed mentors spend many hours working with startups during the accelerator session. Active mentors also commit, at least implicitly, to "take the call" (or email or text) and meet with or speak with the accelerator participants when they need it.

TYPES OF MENTORS

There are many different types of mentors that can be helpful to a startup during their time in an accelerator. Sometimes they work closely throughout the duration of the program or sometimes they have a one-off conversation on a particular topic, which can be equally as helpful. Accelerator leaders should make sure to have a diverse set of mentors with key skill sets that are aligned with the stage and theme of the startups participating in your program.

Experienced Entrepreneurs

The broadest iteration of the mentor network often includes big-name entrepreneurs who have achieved some success. They have been there, done that, and come out on the other side. These are some of the most useful mentors for startups, especially if the mentors are only a few steps ahead of them and the lessons are still fresh. The most dedicated entrepreneur mentors are not necessarily the biggest names, but the ones looking to give back before starting their next company, or are even still active founders at a later stage than the participating startups, who drive the best energy into the program.

Investors

Startups are always looking for capital, and it benefits them to have investors in the mentor pool to be part of their network and help them in fundraising. An accelerator class generally has a free pass to contact the venture capitalists on the roster of mentors, even if it is not a mentor specifically assigned to their company. It's a two-way street because those investors are participating precisely to create the deal flow they need for their own business and to keep an eye on market trends.

Corporate Executives

A corporate accelerator is unique in that it can tap into a vast pool of employees who have varied skill sets. Technical experts, sales experts, and legal or procurement practitioners are all useful, especially if the focus is on how to effectively work within your company or its specific ecosystem. This is also highly beneficial and enjoyable for the employees, as working with startups for a couple of hours a week can be a fun and inspiring addition to their day job.

We find that an open call for volunteers is useful, as unexpected people pop out of the woodwork to share their time in fantastic ways you couldn't have planned. It's also important to proactively reach out to key people within the organization who are relevant for the participating companies and could lead to partnership with them directly. Mentorship is a low-stakes way to start developing a relationship that could eventually turn into a commercial agreement.

Corporate mentors can also be tricky, as most corporate executives have not been startup founders. They do not know how to build or scale entrepreneurial ventures and any advice to this topic may be misguided, if not well intentioned. This is often where problems arise in accelerators, so whoever manages the mentor network should be sure to focus the mentorship of this particular category on their area of expertise and avoid topics where they have no direct experience.

Specialist Mentors

There are a wide variety of technical and business skills that can be useful to the participating startups where people are deep experts. Specialist mentors are also notable for their commitment of time – they love talking about their area of expertise, especially to people who are innovating in their space. In these cases, they often lead specialty sessions and hands-on advisory with startups in the accelerator class that need their particular advice. For example, a sales expert who built the sales team and process at another successful growth company may be called in to explain the process – and work one-on-one with founders in the same space or with the same needs.

One good example of highly engaged specialist mentors is the expert in residence (EIR) program at BMW MINI's URBAN-X accelerator. The EIRs are full stack product development resources, industry experts from the fields of software development, manufacturing, UX, communication, and industrial design. Their focus is to rapidly prototype and test ideas for new solutions de-risking the path to market for startups in URBAN-X.

"When a company joins the program, they go through an assessment with our experts in residents, then they map out a scope of work and a plan to deliver on it over the five month program," says Miriam Roure, program director and principal at URBAN-X. "The EIRs are highlighted by the founders as one of the most valuable parts of the program. Most founders, even if they know about the experts in residence program before they join, they don't realize that they're going to get hands-on work from them. It's very common to get strategy advice from a mentor, but it is very different to get a new interface or a new dashboard design."

The EIRs are also very helpful to the accelerator team because they provide useful feedback from working directly with the founders. "We have meetings where all the experts in residence present their work to the partners and we rely on them to also tell us what it's like to work with members of the team," says Roure. "They are able to raise flags and highlight blind spots that the investment partners might not be able to get to by just talking to the CEO, because they're working with the company directly on their product. The EIRs are very integral to our team."

Vendors

Vendors and professional services firms often provide a range of support to the community around the accelerator. Experienced startup lawyers and accountants often blur the line of vendor support with their expert advice and even training sessions, and more typical vendors of a startup community might be cloud computing providers, human resources, and accounting software, or other services needed by new companies.

However, there should be a no selling policy so startups don't feel assaulted by a sales pitch from their mentor and put in an awkward position.

Attitude is everything here, and the best vendors build up a reservoir of goodwill as trusted advisors to the fledgling companies in the portfolio. Later in the company's life when faced with bigger challenges, they will have the resources and need to properly engage as customers.

Peers

For participants in an accelerator program, it's not just the experts and mentors that provide the support needed, it's often the very peer companies in the cohort or outside of it that provide the most value. Other founders at the same stage are usually not viewed as competitors, but as fellow travelers. It's not uncommon for founders to recommend a peer for potential investment, for example. It's also the more human aspects of late nights, partner, and spousal relationships, and the ups and downs of business where peer support can be so critical. It's worthwhile to recruit some mentors from the startup community who are peers or only one or two steps ahead of the participating companies.

Alumni

For those considering launching an accelerator, one of the assets that builds community most effectively is the alumni network of the program itself. Those who pass through the program, share the experience, and graduate to grow their startup are the backbone of support that newer entrants can turn to for help. It's no coincidence that the older and more established accelerators have the broadest and deepest networks of support here. Y Combinator startups can often find their first customers among program alumni eager to provide them a shot in an effort to pay back the support they received themselves.

Alumni are first and foremost founders who have gone through the same experience as the current crop of the accelerator. They are also a great source of immediate feedback on what works and what doesn't to the accelerator management team. As founders, they provide the participating startups with recent and raw experiences in dealing with challenges others simply won't understand; co-founder troubles, disgruntled employees, client challenges, and the like are all shared and hashed out by peers who have been there before. For many accelerators, alumni are also a human capital resource; when their talent in an area becomes apparent, it may be recycled into a new startup looking to fill a skills gap.

Lead Mentors

Lead mentors are the main mentors assigned or matched to a single company in a cohort. They are the mentors intended to spend time with the companies for a few hours a week during the program, and usually have specific experience that matches the needs of the startup. Lead mentors coach and assist the startup from kickoff to demo day, sometimes even introducing them on stage. Lead mentors rarely number more than one or two per participant, and are often very invested – sometimes literally as angel investors – with the companies they assist.

Selecting and matching the appropriate mentors is nearly as important as selecting the best startups for your cohorts. Recruiting mentors may seem like a gargantuan chore at first, and it is definitely time consuming, but don't look to cut corners here. Fast-growing startups with top talent often choose the programs in which they feel they have a chance at connecting with and getting advice from the best and most successful in their industry. In this way, the mentor roster for your corporate accelerator can act as a beacon to the startup community about the potential quality of the experience.

Mentors also market the program for you, even if it's simply listing themselves as a mentor for your program on LinkedIn, and can also help with recruitment of future cohorts. Having a few big names associated with your mentor community is tantamount to having a diversity of mentors in your program, and both increase the credibility of your program overall.

MENTOR RECRUITMENT

There are few concepts to consider when bringing mentors into an accelerator:

Vet for Real-World Experience

From a high level, it is important to thoroughly vet these mentors before onboarding them to the program. After all, the initial cohort's relationships with these mentors will influence spell the success of your accelerator program going forward both in the advice they are able to share with the founders and in the word-of-mouth marketing that the initial cohort will bring back to the startup community. The last thing you need is a disgruntled startup graduating and talking smack about the mentorship component of your new program, whether it be the quality, quantity, breadth, or depth.

An important tip is to value tangible venture experience such as being the founder of a tech startup, successfully exiting a company, or working as a mentor in previous accelerators over solely academic or aspirational credentials. Founders come to your program to speak to someone they can not only learn from, but also relate to on a personal level. These mentors will be guiding founders coming from a variety of backgrounds at a variety of stages in their personal and professional development. It is crucial that they can learn from an experienced mentor who is drawing advice from a place of experience rather than an armchair.

Avoid those looking for a resume credential or who see this as business development. Dig into potential mentors' experience a little deeper – many people in the startup ecosystem make it seem like they have more startup experience than they actually do. If they don't have the tangible experience we indicated earlier, they may be one of the insidious lampreys of the startup world – the *wantrapreneur*. These posers have never started their own venture and will often try and spin a consulting experience, supporting work on a new product launch, or otherwise into the battle scars of a true entrepreneur. Avoid these people, as they tend to give bad advice and are difficult to manage as they overestimate their own abilities.

Equally dangerous are the lead generators – those service providers who profess their extensive startup experience that they want to share with the group. Vet the topics and experience carefully before accepting as they are looking for clients. Also make it very clear that this is a pitch-free environment for vendors. They can share their expertise, but if they are pushing a hard sell to the founders they will be kicked out of the program and not invited back.

Aim for Diversity of Thought

Another thing we would like to caution against is the shortcut of populating the mentorship roster with mostly colleagues from your big company. If this is your first time running an accelerator it can be easy, and seem logical, to pull mentors from within the corporation. We cannot emphasize enough the negative signaling that a roster chock-full of internally sourced mentors emits.

This is not to say that the advice and knowledge housed within the corporation is not valuable; rather, it is more a testament to the fact that talented founders with rapidly growing startups are wary of advice distilled through a corporate filter. It is extremely important when developing every aspect of the corporate accelerator – not just the mentorship roster – that you establish a culture unique from the corporate body. It is also a missed opportunity to have the mentors from your company interact with a wider part of the startup ecosystem, as many of the mentors meet each other at the various accelerator events and learn from each other as well. We recommend that a bare minimum of 60% of your mentors originate from the startup or venture community external to your corporation.

In fact, some corporate accelerators don't pull from their own ranks for any mentors at all. Guillaume Payan at OrangeFab says, "One of the things that we did in San Francisco was refuse to have any mentors from Orange. We have great people in-house who have been amazing mentors, but you don't want to fall into the trap of having people that were never entrepreneurs but are giving advice to startups based on experience that they never had."

Accelerator leaders should look at the mentor program as an opportunity to broaden the field of influence and diversity for both your startups and your corporate colleagues. "A corporate accelerator should therefore look around its wider network to find people it is comfortable involving in its accelerator program as mentors, but who are from different networks to its own company," says Tobias Stone, PhD in applied social network theory and innovation strategy from The University of Huddersfield. "This may be its lawyers, clients, partner companies, and the wider social networks of its employees. This will create the diversity that will make the accelerator relevant and useful to the startups, and will ensure that the value – the non-redundancy – decays more slowly, so the program remains interesting."[1]

The importance of this non-redundancy in the advice given to founders is key in crafting a program that has the ability to accelerate a wide variety of ventures. Stone goes on further to describe how this inclusion of many external mentors actually manifests itself in other benefits to the corporation through developing more social capital for the program, and its parent company, across the wider ecosystem.

Communicate Expectations Clearly Beforehand

Especially when talented mentors are onboarded to the roster who may not have had experience mentoring, it is extremely important to be up front and transparent with them about baseline responsibilities, expectations, best practices, and even value adds to their own careers. Not formalizing these aspects of the professional and social contract in writing can sometimes lead to mentors who detract more from the program than they add. Creating and communicating these guidelines, which will depend on the specific goals and structure of the accelerator, is a simple task whose benefits can far out-weigh the one-time effort of creating them.

Some important points to include in these expectations are any minimum responsibilities, including but certainly not limited to holding office hours at certain intervals, planning and running a certain number of sessions based on their experience, or expectations surrounding willing-ness to utilize personal networks to make introductions for the startups. Less time consuming for mentors may be formal office hours, sched-uled in-person or virtually, "ask-me-anything" (AMA) rap sessions to share experiences and advice, or informal coaching at pitch practices or other sessions.

After you find high-quality mentors, communicate with them reg-ularly as you would any stakeholder. They share in the successes and failures as they associate their personal efforts with your brand. As the accelerator grows cohort after cohort, the network can speak for itself, and mentors will understand this value add and seek out entry into the strong accelerator network.

KPIs for Mentors

For mentors within your own company, it's helpful if they have some account-ability. Most of the time this is a volunteer experience, but if you can tie the mentorship responsibility into their overall performance reviews, it makes it a more serious and committed audience.

"Our C-level team and people in different teams around the company – such as tech, digital, or legal – are part of our mentors," says Cris-tina Ventura, chief catalyst officer at The Lane Crawford Joyce Group. She launched and ran The Cage, their accelerator for technology companies in the fashion and lifestyle retail industry. "The mentors are measured by how much they are supporting the startups and also must dedicate a specific time to the startup. This is part of their annual performance assessment, even for the most senior executives. We had the chief strategy officer as a mentor, the director of digital transformation and innovation, and others. It's an honor to be part of The Cage and they absolutely love the experience, integrating business, tech, and humanity."

Payment for Mentors

There is always a touchy issue of mentor compensation. Mentors are usually experienced people whose time is very valuable, and they may want to be compensated for spending time with the startups. Typically we don't see accelerators, corporate or otherwise, paying all the mentors involved in the program. This is absolutely true for any mentors coming from your big company, unless it is part of their job description, in which case it will be paid in salary, not your accelerator budget. Most mentors only commit a handful of hours, and they benefit from being connected to the network in some way.

Set expectations and outline the requirements of mentors, such as estimated hours and things they need to participate in as part of being in the program. This should be a reasonable time commitment, usually no more than a couple of hours a week. Many mentors go above and beyond this and sometimes try to ask for equity or cash compensation from their mentee. This puts the startups in an awkward position, especially if they feel like they are already paying for the program with an equity contribution, and it also reflects poorly on your program management.

We advise telling mentors that they will not be compensated for their participation as a mentor during the program, but that they are free to negotiate with the startups directly after the program ends if they both agree to continue the relationship. It helps to give the startups a benchmark of mentor compensation as well so they don't give away too much – generally we recommend 0.10%–1.0% equity that vests over two years, depending on the stage of the company and the value added by the mentor. Overall, it's a great outcome if mentors join as a formal advisor, mentor, or board member to startups after the program. It means you made a very successful match!

There is one exception to this, which is lead mentors or people who will be spending a significant amount of time with the startups – more than an hour or two a week – and have proven themselves to be very effective mentors. For this extra-heavy time commitment, some may receive a consulting payment from the accelerator, not from the startups directly. For example, 500 Startups has an uncompensated mentor program for a broad pool of mentors, then selects a subset to function as entrepreneurs in residence (EIRs) to work in a more hands-on way with participating companies. They compensate these mentors for up to a certain number of hours per week at an hourly rate. (Disclosure: Jules serves as an EIR here.)

BMW's URBAN-X program also compensates their EIRs, who are usually experienced designers, developers, and engineers doing hands-on work with deliverables for the participating startups. "We have one EIR who is a full time BMW employee, and he's the design director for URBAN-X. The rest are part-time experts that we pay as contractors," says Miriam Roure, program director and principal at URBAN-X. "They're compensated on an hourly basis, which is pre-agreed, so it's very stable work for them. We do two programs per year that are about five months each, and for the month and a half in between programs the EIRs also work directly with BMW and URBAN-X, for example on our brand. They're very much like part of the team, and many of them stay with us for years." This level of consistency and quality from stable, highly engaged mentors works extremely well. "Everyone thinks of the program as a great resource," says Roure. "When the founders evaluate the program, the EIRs are always something that they love."

There are also some creative ways that accelerators are compensating mentors. For example, the Founders Institute rewards mentors who make a significant contribution with participation in a pool of warrants from the startups, giving them a small stake in the value they are helping to create.

For the best mentors, it's not about making money, as they could almost certainly make much more for the same amount of time elsewhere. It's about respecting their time and keeping them actively engaged in the program. A little payment can go a long way with the most valuable mentors, but is absolutely not needed for all mentors participating in the program.

MENTOR PAIRINGS

Once a roster of mentors is confirmed and they all understand their expected contributions, now comes the important task of ensuring that the mentor-founder pairings are optimal and lead to the best outcomes for both parties. There are a series of documented strategies that work well, but ultimately it is highly specific to your program. Which strategy to use depends on the startups in your accelerator at the time and the particular skill sets of the mentors involved at the time. We will review a few tried-and-true methodologies.

Hands-Off Matchmaking

One methodology calls for an organic process whereby mentors and founders match themselves. This follows the logic that the ability for a startup to optimize its benefit from a mentor cannot be forced. In other words, a natural relationship must be developed so that the mentor and the founder are able to establish a rapport both on a professional and social level. Accelerators must build the network and put them in front of the startups, but matching can be made from informal networking events or simply sharing a list of potential mentors for the startups to select. This way, the bonds do not confine themselves to the accelerator, but rather persist into the outside world where the startups can parlay these connections for future partnerships, customer/vendor relationships, and potential future funding rounds and/or connecting to VCs for these future-funding rounds. A study from the World Bank[2] found that this was a highly effective way to match mentors, and it also has the added benefit of being less work for the accelerator team.

Assigned Mentors

An approach used by many accelerators with deeper pools of mentor talent is to assign a lead mentor based on a mutually needed skill set. For example, Jeremy is a digital marketing professor and former founder/CEO of a digital marketing company, so he is often matched with companies that have gaps in this expertise and need go-to-market and growth hacking advice. Other mentors might excel at building sales teams, fundraising, or other functions critical to that startup's success.

Alternately, some accelerators create a pool of experienced mentors and then assign them somewhat randomly to the teams. In this case, the role is more often one of coach and confidante. A hybrid of this, where a meet-and-greet is followed by mentors and founders creating short lists of companies and mentors they prefer, is another common method.

Matching Mentors Based on the Story Arc

One compelling approach is from Scott Howard, former founding director of the Chobani Accelerator and former head of acceleration at Mars, who is now on the founding team at Share Ventures, an independent venture studio. He blueprinted each startup's journey through the accelerator programs he has run in a "story arc" structure. This means having different mentors at different stages of the accelerator program.

The beginning of the arc consists of open discussion and workshopping of ambitions, goals, and whys. Much like when a corporate accelerator is created, a startup, too, must identify its whys, set clear goals, and broadly understand how to scale. To this end, mentors who you have identified as being experienced in goal setting, high-level strategic planning, and unstructured, early-stage coaching will serve best here.

As the program progresses and the startups begin to connect with each other and formulate more concrete plans and goals, the learning (and thus the mentors involved) will begin to transform. This is when the mentor interaction starts to change from high-level goal setting to more detailed and operational advice. The remainder of the accelerator's story arc can manifest itself in these types of relationships. According to Howard, these types of bespoke pairings are the ones that make a material difference in the trajectory of the startup's development.

For example, in the case of the Chobani Accelerator, the curriculum would pivot toward specific issues such as geographical expansion, specific product launches, and personalized time horizons. Naturally, it made sense to connect the founders to veterans of cross-regional sales to discuss geographical considerations when selling new goods, or SVPs of product to discuss how to launch new products, or ex-CEO/COOs to discuss how to navigate when and how to scale the company into new products and markets.

At Mars, Howard and his team had the founders do pre-work to establish their biggest short- and medium-term needs. In addition to group panels, they set up a series of one-on-one lightweight interactions and deep dives between founders and mentors. Deep dives were constructed to be purposefully targeting known needs. Lightweight interactions were meant to investigate unknown needs and opportunities. It was then up to the founders to capitalize on those mentors' expertise by continuing ongoing involvement proactively.

The most important lesson, which was core to how Howard designed accelerator programs and specifically parts of the mentorship curriculum, is that time is often the most valuable asset for both the startups and the mentors. No founder wants to be stuck in a seminar on a topic or meeting with a mentor that won't benefit them when they feel like they could be investing their efforts elsewhere. And the mentors are usually senior executives in high demand, and they could be doing many other things with their time. It only works if it's a fit: the mentor has relevant expertise and the startup wants and appreciates this expertise.

While trickier to manage, this ethos can be applied to the mentorship program to foster a turntable of mentors forming ad hoc relationships, then encouraging offline dialogues and longer-term connections if and when it suits both parties.

GO FORTH AND MENTOR

Mentor programs are an integral part of most accelerator programs, and for some they are its core value. We highly recommend that accelerator leaders and key stakeholders participate as mentors in other accelerator programs beyond your own to see how they do things, get inspired, further build your network, and bring those best practices back into your own program. Most successful founders, and most successful people, attribute part of their success to great mentors. If your accelerator can build a mentorship program that works, it will be a major asset to you and create connections for the companies that can help them achieve success in their companies and in life.

CHAPTER 15

MAKING PARTNERSHIPS WORK

> Alone we can do so little.
> Together we can do so much.
>
> HELEN KELLER

Source: Helen Keller

After a fantastic accelerator program where everything was done just right, your corporation decides to partner with one of the start-ups, and you're off to the races! Your innovation goals are hit, and everything is easy from here on out. Well, not quite.

In theory, partnerships between big companies and startups should be a win-win. Corporates can partner with startups to tap into their energy and creativity, experience different methods of working, and learn from their

241

use of new business models and technologies. In return, startups can tap into corporate partners' market knowledge, reputation, customer base and industry expertise. Corporations have the resources, brand, and customers that startups yearn for, whereas startups have agility and innovative mindset that corporations value.

The potential is certainly there, but it's harder than it seems to get these partnerships right. Instead of tapping into each other's strengths, a poorly planned partnership can exacerbate each partner's weaknesses. Startups get bogged down in internal processes of a larger partner; corporations have unrealistic expectations or do not give the partnership a chance to demonstrate its value over a reasonable time frame. Although the depths are not always apparent at first, there are many dangerous asymmetries in culture, processes, and desired outcomes that can cause landmines all along the way to prevent successful partnerships. It's critical to understand these structural challenges in order to give these partnerships the greatest chance for success.

ARE STARTUP-CORPORATE PARTNERSHIPS WORKING?

While partnerships between the big companies running these types of programs and the startups participating in them is not the only goal, it is a directionally correct indicator of success. According to CB Insights, accelerators result in partnerships only 1% of the time. Compare this to CVC investments, which are still low but 10x better with partnerships resulting 10% of the time.[1] This low success rate leads many corporations to quietly shut down these programs before they have time to spread their wings.

CB Insights data also shows that 60% of corporate accelerators shut down within two years, and one-third of new CVCs stop investing after five years. This can often align with changes in management, as corporate leaders tend to change jobs after less than three years and innovation programs struggle to survive the transition. This is unfortunate, as it typically takes at least five years to realize even early returns on innovation programs.

A recent World Economic Forum paper[2] articulates that collaboration between technology start-ups and large corporations can benefit both sides, but there are also significant risks and challenges.

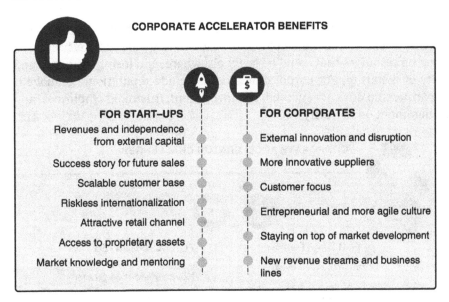

Source: Collaboration between Start-ups and Corporates A Practical Guide for Mutual Understanding, January 2018. © 2018, World Economic Forum.

For startups, the benefits include revenue, referenceable customers, sales channels, access to corporate assets for an "unfair" advantage, market knowledge, and mentoring. For corporations, it's external innovation, additional value to customers, market intelligence, and new revenue streams.

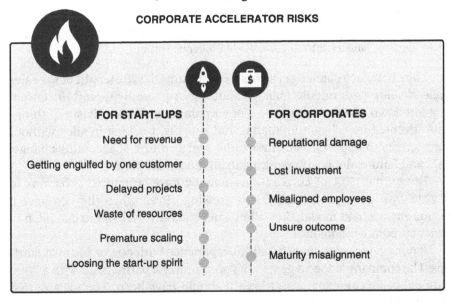

Source: Collaboration between Start-ups and Corporates A Practical Guide for Mutual Understanding, January 2018. © 2018, World Economic Forum.

The risks for the startup include need for revenue in the short term, concentration of the customer base, slow-moving and bureaucratic processes, typing up resources that could be spent elsewhere, and losing the speed and agility of a startup. For corporations, risks include reputational damage if the partnership does not succeed, lost investment, frustrated employees, and misalignment on maturity.

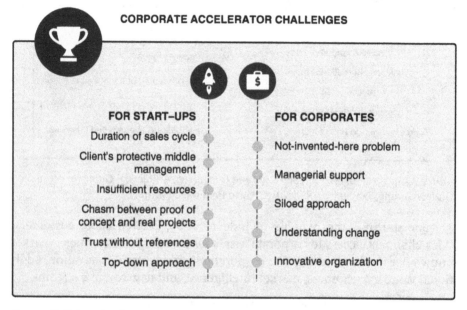

CORPORATE ACCELERATOR CHALLENGES

FOR START–UPS
- Duration of sales cycle
- Client's protective middle management
- Insufficient resources
- Chasm between proof of concept and real projects
- Trust without references
- Top-down approach

FOR CORPORATES
- Not-invented-here problem
- Managerial support
- Siloed approach
- Understanding change
- Innovative organization

Source: Collaboration between Start-ups and Corporates A Practical Guide for Mutual Understanding, January 2018. © 2018, World Economic Forum.

They both face challenges as well. For startups, it's the length of the sales cycle, dealing with middle management, limited resources, and the corporate top-down management style. For corporations, it's skepticism of things "not invented here," gaining managerial support, working in silos without connectivity to important business units, and a culture of accepting change, risk, and failure along with working in an innovative way.

Fewer than 50% of corporations actually have structured programs to engage with startups, though this is growing.[3] Even when they do have a formal engagement model, they often don't execute it well or are beholden to wider corporate roadblocks.

Jeremy had a particularly painful experience with one of his own startups. The company signed a game-changing strategic partnership with a large national cable company . . . at least it should have been. The plan started strong, with six planned city rollouts designed to learn the market for a national launch. Unfortunately, in the middle of launch planning, the big company received an acquisition offer. Everything froze. Calls stopped being answered and returned. Planning halted as corporate execs feared making choices, not knowing where the company would be in a few months. When the deal fell through, planning ramped back up. Delays built up in the rollout due to the company's annual (yes, annual) cycle for testing new ideas, which pushed everything back an entire year. But everything slowly and painfully got back on track. Then . . . another competitor made an acquisition offer. The ice age descended again. Everything froze. Jobs and roles of the contacts changed. And after three years of paying monthly contract minimums with no rollout or benefit, the lawyers and accountants struck back and cancelled the contract. A termination fee became the consolation prize. The merger deal would ultimately go through – but the startup no longer had the contract or the contacts to make a new one.

Jules also has deep battle scars from being on the big company side. For example, she teed up perfectly curated partnerships with four of 10 accelerator participants in one cohort, and they all fell apart one by one in extremely painful and unnecessary ways (which, unfortunately, she cannot disclose). In fact, this is a main reason why she left the corporate accelerator world – the satisfaction of the job is not the whirlwind of programming and recruiting, it's seeing the real business results of all that hard work. In fact, she was so frustrated that the startup partnership process at the big corporation was broken, she refused to run another cohort until she was able to fix the path to partnership. It was a partnership accelerator for growth-stage companies, after all! After nine months of putting the accelerator on ice and working on this with a larger team within the company focused on improving startup partnerships, it was clear that they were nowhere near a place that might work, so she left to join a VC fund. The unfulfilled promise still haunts her.

Unfortunately these stories are all too common. In a report by global consulting group BCG entitled "After the Honeymoon Ends: Making Corporate-Startup Relationships Work," they confirm that corporate-startup partnership intentions often start out strong, but this doesn't last long. There is a "heady honeymoon period during which both sides enjoy some early successes. Over time, however, frustration can set in as one or both partners wake up to the reality that they are not achieving all of their hopes and expectations."[4] According to their research, which focused on the European market but is consistent with our experience and research globally, 45% of corporations and 55% of startups are "very dissatisfied" or "somewhat dissatisfied" with their partnerships. Only 8% of corporations and 13% of startups rated themselves as "very satisfied."

Academic researchers from the IESE Business School in Spain reached the same conclusion from interviewing chief innovation officers, who confirmed that about three-quarters of their own corporate innovation initiatives failed to deliver the desired results.[5]

This means that somewhere between 75% and 92% of partnerships either don't work or are mediocre for at least one of the partners. While we expect some degree of failure in innovation programs due to their high-risk nature, a single-digit-percentage success rate is certainly not good by anyone's standards. Based on our research and experience, a desired outcome should be a success rate of somewhere between 30% and 60%. If it's higher, you're probably not taking enough risks. We are very far from a place where corporate-startup partnerships are working.

What Went Wrong?

According to the BCG study, there is some difference of opinion between corporations and startups on why things are not working, but there are some clear trends as well. The three main factors where both parties agree that things go wrong are (1) difficult and time-consuming corporate decision-making, (2) mismatched or nontransparent expectations, and (3) an inability or unwillingness to move at the same speed.[6]

Where they differ is also interesting; startups are more likely to blame corporate culture, and corporations point at startups' lack of appreciation for or ability to navigate governance.

WHY STARTUP—CORPORATE PARTNERSHIPS FAIL

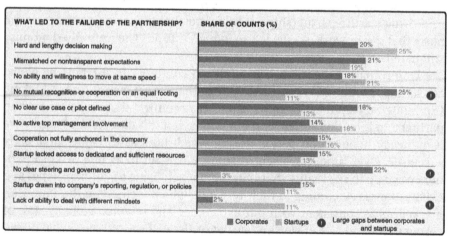

Source: Michael Brigl, After the Honeymoon Ends: Making Corporate-Startup Relationships Work Retrieved, 13 June 2019. © Boston Consulting Group.

FROM FACE TIME TO INTERFACE

After working together directly for a three-month program, both the startups and the corporates get used to a high-touch model from the accelerator. After the program ends, there can be a "what now?" moment and often the partnerships struggle to transition from this high face time model to something that gets attention from anyone on the team after the program is completed.

As you transition to the next phase, where the accelerated startups have completed the program and a subset of the companies is moving to a partnership of some sort, it is critical for corporations to enable a clear engagement model between the startups and the wider corporate team outside of the innovation or accelerator team. Who is the point person on the innovation team? Their job is to simply identify the right person and unblock any blockers that come up (e.g., when the right person doesn't respond to an email for three weeks, they change jobs, or something gets stuck in a complex procurement process). We will discuss post-program portfolio management in the next chapter.

Shameen Prashantham, professor of international business and strategy at China Europe International Business School (CEIBS) researches what he calls "dancing with gorillas" – partnering between large corporations and startups. Leveraging computing nomenclature for a shared boundary between system components, he calls this creating an "interface" between the startup and corporate.

According to Prashantham, "creating an effective interface gives startups a first port of call that overcomes the difficulty of establishing a connection in the first place and increases the odds of meaningful relationships ensuing by giving both parties a shared understanding of the nature of collaboration that might be feasible. Executing an effective startup partner interface calls for genuine and thoughtful effort – not mere lip service – from corporations."[7]

In order to do this effectively, corporations need to help startups bridge the boundaries between both internal and external stakeholders. The bigger the company, the more difficult this is to do, especially with stakeholders who were not involved in the accelerator in some way. He states, "a corporation's partner interface . . . is only as good as its ability to connect high-quality external startups with relevant internal line managers. Once an interface is created, the team running that unit must be skilled at building bridges with entrepreneurs, whose decision-making styles and strategic orientations may differ considerably from those of managers in large corporations. They must also be able to connect startups with their *own* corporation's business unit leaders who have the ability to realize the prospect of collaborating with startups, yet may view this as a distraction."[8]

For any partnership that focuses on go-to-market in some way, either directly through a sales channel or collaborating on a product integration that will be put in front of customers, the interface should also be clear between the startups and the external stakeholders. Startups must connect directly with these folks to get valuable user feedback and iterate on the product or other offering, and to "land and expand" these customers. However, the rules of engagement should also be clear. Many times, we've seen corporate account managers get upset when the startups are introduced to major customers, then start cutting the corporation out of the conversation and working with them directly. Most of this is not malicious; it is because the startups move fast and the corporate middleman was either blocking them in some way or moving too slowly. Corporations need to manage expectations here clearly, and also do their best to add value and move quickly, rather than get in the way of progress on an external partnership.

As with any product or program, this interface should be consistently evaluated and adjusted to make it work in a way that achieves your goals or creates new goals. Ongoing tweaking can continuously improve the interface with individual startups, but also for an ongoing model that supports multiple startup partnerships. As with anything, practice makes perfect! As Prashantham puts it, "corporations are increasingly battling for the hearts and minds of the best startup partners – and building an effective interface is vital to a winning strategy."[9]

TYPES OF PARTNERSHIPS

There are many types of partnerships that can result from the accelerator:

Pilot Project

A pilot project is a test run. It's a small project with specific goals to demonstrate the value of the partnership, with the intention of moving beyond the pilot to a more substantive partnership if everything works well. Pilot projects should take no longer than three months and have clear deliverables or KPIs by which to judge the success of the project. There should also be an understanding of what happens after the pilot project if it is successful, and what constitutes success.

We hold the strong belief that corporates should always pay for pilot projects. Although it doesn't need to be at market rates, startups have limited time and resources, and they could be spending their time on other paying clients. If you want to focus their attention on making your pilot a success, pay for the project. This is also helpful if the pilot does not lead to a larger partnership, in which case at least the startup was paid for its time and can walk away with no, or at least fewer, hard feelings to minimize the impact on the corporate brand. This also builds credibility for your company with VCs, who hear about these paid pilots and are more likely to send you top companies as a result.

A good example is Diageo, which runs startup pilots through a dedicated pilot team in the market where the technology will be trialed, with close involvement of a senior stakeholder. Each pilot has a pre-approved budget of $100,000. "If we like a startup, we can quickly move to a pilot study, see the outcome of the pilot, and decide whether to scale it or try something else," said Venky Balakrishnan Iyer, former global vice president of digital innovation and Diageo Tech Ventures.[10]

POCs, MVP, and JDAs – Oh My!

A partnership that has a technical focus usually results in an acronym of some sort: proof of concept (POC), minimum viable product (MVP), or joint development agreement (JDA). Product co-development usually includes the startup and the corporation jointly developing or integrating a specific product, with the intention of it being used in the market by one or both of the parties' customers.

These should be outlined by a clear document detailing mutual responsibilities, a pre-designated budget (usually coming from the corporate partner), a clear articulation of resources from both parties, a clear time frame within which either party can decide to terminate the partnership, and specific deliverables.[11] This can be called a variety of things, but it's usually one of these three acronyms:

Proof of Concept (POC)

This is a project to demonstrate the feasibility of an intended goal, such as a product's ability to do something specific. This is usually not a "live" product for customers to use, but demonstrates what is possible. This can be creating something new, or integrating something existing (e.g., a startup product with a corporate product) to show what it would look like together.

Minimum Viable Product (MVP)

This is a version of a product with just enough features to satisfy early customers and provide feedback for future product development.[12] This is intended to be tested with customers for feedback, but not for long-term usage.

Joint Development Agreement (JDA)

This outlines the terms for two or more parties to collaborate on the development of a specific product or technology. This tends to be driven by research and development (R&D) teams from the corporate side and is more research-intensive than the lean startup methodology employed by an MVP process. Intellectual property (IP) is an important factor in a JDA, so the document outlining the JDA terms should clearly state who owns what.

These three acronyms are very similar and often used interchangeably. The name doesn't matter as much as the clear and mutual understanding between both parties on what will happen, when, and by whom.

Go-to-Market Partnerships

Sales-focused partnerships are another great option. These take existing products through the existing corporate, and sometimes also the startup, sales channels together. These go-to-market (GTM) partnerships focus on driving revenue together where the partnership is stronger than selling individually.

This usually works better with growth-stage startups that are more equipped to sell things in the market because they already have their own customer base and sales team. However, it can also work with early-stage companies if their product is fully developed and ready for customer usage, even if their team and traction are still small.

The startup and corporate should define a clear sales process that includes defining the market segment, identifying target customers and the specific people who are key to the decision, qualifying leads, and going through the buying process together.[13] Often this will also include some training by the startup to the corporate sales team, so they can activate their sales channels and know how to sell the product without the startup being involved.

THE DEVIL IS IN THE (BORING OPERATIONAL) DETAILS

All of this sounds good in theory, but in practice it can be incredibly hard to implement in a large, complex corporate structure. There are cumbersome processes around legal and procurement that are well intentioned and important when working with other large organizations, but they simply do not work for startups.

Many challenges to the corporate process receive instant pushback from leadership backed by the traditional crushers of dreams that create the systems in the first place: legal, HR, procurement and accounting. These functions create important controls necessary to the operation of large global businesses; they also smother innovation in the crib.

When working with startups, *corporates must accept that different rules apply* and clear the path internally with colleagues in legal, procurement, compliance, accounting, and other relevant groups. A streamlined approach is necessary to make these partnerships work.

"What I've found is that someone at the company gets really excited, and then there's a lot of focus on getting a partnership done," says Jenny Fielding, managing director of Techstars–New York City and The Fund. "And then they realized that they hadn't checked with legal, they hadn't checked with procurement, they don't know where the budget is coming from." Fielding suggests that "just getting some of the fundamentals in place will make you a friend to founders as opposed to friction. I see a lot of that friction with corporates, but finding where the budget is coming from and preauthorizing that budget can be super helpful, as opposed to having to get everything signed off on afterwards."

This is very often the reason that partnerships fail or take too long, thus losing the initial advantage. Accelerator teams should work these details out before the program to ensure successful partnerships afterward. They will still be complex, and continually improving the processes will be an important part of making the partnerships work on an ongoing basis.

Procurement

Procurement departments need to simplify and standardize the onboarding process for startup partnerships. There should be a standard set of documents and lightweight versions of vendor onboarding processes that should take no longer than a couple of weeks to get through. At big companies, from our research and personal experience, the procurement process can take anywhere from 2–12 months. This is a killer to a partnership and ties the hands of both partners, who lose momentum and a competitive advantage in the market every day that goes by. Startups win by moving faster than their competition, as they are usually not the only ones addressing the problem. By the time a nine-month procurement process is complete, a competitor could have blown past them.

"When I was at a big company, I always used to say that procurement is where innovation goes to die," says Vijay Rajendran, head of corporate innovation and partnerships at 500 Startups. "If you've got to get five years of audited financials as part of the registration to the procurement system, then most startups can't do this. And most people in the position to partner with startups are going to say that it's not worth the time to make this work in terms of the existing structure we have."

Many standard big company procurement clauses are irrelevant in the case of a POC or early partnership, or they create legal obligations that cannot be upheld by a smaller startup.

Corporates need to rethink their procurement contracts and processes to make sense for startups. This does not mean eliminating essential clauses needed to do business, but rather, pruning unnecessary things while still protecting both parties. This should be a couple of pages maximum and can be renegotiated or put through a more robust process if the partnership expands beyond a certain time frame or metrics. A corporate accelerator that creates a streamlined process for partnerships can make the difference between success and failure. Startups can get stuck in the purgatory of traditional corporate decision-making processes, and will eventually run out of money or resources.

Streamlining long-standing procurement processes is not a simple undertaking, especially with a procurement team that is not used to working with startups. This is where your executive sponsors and CEO can be pulled in for great effect. If it is important to senior leadership, the procurement team will make it happen. If it's just the accelerator leader asking, it's much more of an uphill battle without the proper incentive structure.

According to EarlyMetrics, a research and ratings firm in the startup vertical, "Some corporates have started working on startup-friendly tools: Sanofi for instance, uses an SME Charter which provides a collaboration framework adapted to early stage ventures; the FAST Track by Airbus is also an innovative program created to put corporate managers at the disposal of interested ventures to design a solution mutually beneficial for the parties involved."[14]

"While we don't go in and rewrite the procurement manual, we do highlight these important areas for large corporations to get right and to recognize that this is part of the work, to go in and fix the systems and processes if they hope to have a good system that works for the business," says Rajendran of 500 Startups. "There's a lot of boring, not very cool things that you have to do in order to actually not get stuck later. Otherwise, if you skip over it in the excitement of launching things that are new and innovative, you find yourself trying to jog in quicksand later."

Legal, HR, procurement, accounting and other such functions create important controls necessary to the operation of large global businesses, yet they can also smother innovation in the crib. An accelerator leader's critical role, with the support of influential stakeholders, is to convince them to make the changes needed to partner effectively and efficiently with startups. Start with putting boundaries on the size and potential impact of the pilots and partnerships with startups – legal can get involved if the impact is designated to be past a threshold that is worth their time.

If all else fails, bring out the big guns – literally. The United States Department of Defense, potentially the most conservative, life-or-death decision maker on the planet, has streamlined its process for working with startups with great success – giving startups billions of dollars a year.[15] If they can do it, so can you.

Legal

Long contracting processes can kill startups, as they simply don't have the resources or capabilities to deal with such contracts. They also usually don't have in-house lawyers, so every revision is extremely expensive to a company with limited resources.

Although lawyers aren't known for their entrepreneurial thinking, we have seen many good in-house lawyers create standard templates for working with startups. If your in-house legal team does not have the right mentality to do this, you can work with your outside counsel. They should have prior experience working with startups, especially if there is investment and equity involved, because some well-intentioned corporate lawyers put in clauses that make sense to them but irreparably harm the startup in fundraising and other clients if the downstream implications are not fully understood. This has happened to your authors personally, but luckily we caught it before it became a problem.

The key standardized legal agreements your innovation team should pre-negotiate before the accelerator program are:

1. Nondisclosure agreement (NDA)
2. IP and data protection
3. Term sheet for participation in the accelerator (and investment, if it's included)
4. Memorandum of understanding (MOU) – as the partnership starts to develop, startups and corporates should write down the guidelines as they understand them; MOUs are not legally binding, but they help to align expectations and make it feel more "official"; this is also a document that startups can show their current or future investors to demonstrate progress
5. General partnership agreement – for legally binding, simple partnerships
6. Co-development agreement – for joint product development, should it take the form of POC, MVP, JDA, or other pilot
7. Sales channel partnership agreement – for go-to-market partnerships, and will likely include a revenue share agreement

Metrics

There should also be clear objective metrics and milestones, under a clear timeline. Setting KPIs further aligns expectations and makes it easier to understand if a partnership is working or not. If not, and one or both parties did not live up to their expectations, it makes it easier to end the partnership with fewer negative feelings.

These should also be monitored on a regular basis, so it's not a surprise at the end of the designated term when things don't go according to plan. A good strategy is to use the basics of Agile development and have a regular playback or stand-up to share information. This can be quick and informal, or formal and more of a report template, though the former is preferable to prevent unnecessary friction and administrative burden on startups. If you must do something formal, allocate a corporate resource to help collect and collate the appropriate date. Reporting obligations should not exceed what is truly necessary, otherwise processes will slow down and disagreements will fester.

SMART Goals

It is a good practice to use the SMART framework for achieving goals together: Specific, Measurable, Achievable, Realistic, and Time-Bound.

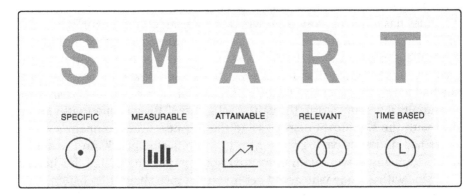

Patrick Riley, CEO of the Global Accelerator Network, recommends that "startups should get corporate sign-off on the specific, measurable and time-bound three-year, one-year, and quarterly objectives for the project they're embarking on together, making time to review and measure goals every quarter. The smaller and more tangible the goals are, the better."[16]

Governance and Decision Rights

It is important to formalize who makes decisions and when other people need to be involved in a decision. This helps, because a startup will almost always move faster than the corporate partner, so an understanding here makes it easier for them to move fast and pull the corporate in when they need to be involved. This also helps the corporation move faster and identify when they are the bottleneck.

Payment

As much as you may want to avoid it, you need to have a good relationship with your finance and accounting teams to figure out payment terms that work for both the corporation and the startup. This means you will need to figure out how to pay the startups sooner than the typical corporate payment terms.

Big companies usually don't have issues with cash flow, but startups usually need shorter payment cycles to stay afloat. If the corporation is a customer of the startup, they simply can't endure 90-plus-day payment terms, and more importantly, will focus their energy on clients and partners who have more liquidity in their contracts as a necessary survival mechanism.

Jules has a horror story from when she was an entrepreneur, when one of her largest corporate customers required 180-day payment terms and was always late to pay even then. Covering the cost of goods sold without realized revenue for more than half a year almost took down the business, and she had to rely on expensive factoring to maintain a survival-level cash flow. Eventually it was not worth the pain, so she "fired" the customer rather than deal with the significant disruption to the business. This company's direct peers had no issues paying sooner, so it also reflected poorly on the ability of the company to work with innovative startups and she shared this honest feedback with anyone who asked her for a reference about this customer.

We understand that this can be difficult for a corporation to do, but it is important for innovation programs to pre-negotiate this with your finance department. Although expediting payment terms can be a challenge for large, complex organizations with certain embedded processes, there are usually workarounds. For example, for a defined pilot or anything time-bound, you can pay up front in one payment, rather than wait until the project is complete. Again, this is an area in which senior executive support can move mountains.

BEST PRACTICES FOR CORPORATE-STARTUP COLLABORATION

Partnerships between big companies and startups is no easy task, but it is possible. Based on our research and experience, we've collected the best practices to keep in mind when enabling partnerships.

Align Expectations

The first step in making corporate-startup partnerships work is to align expectations. This includes a mutual understanding of the goals of a partnership and a clear timeline and agreement on resources needed to achieve it. There should also be a way to break off the partnership if it is not working for any reason. It's also important to communicate perceived strengths, weaknesses, motivations, and values. This allows startups and corporations to understand their respective "whys," so they can work together to achieve something greater than either of them could do alone.

To assist with aligning expectations, transparency is important, even if it's uncomfortable. For example, if a corporation's goal is to test a partnership then acquire the startup quickly if it works, this should be discussed as an option. It's better to know at the outset than for both parties to spend time and money on something with the expectation of different outcomes.

Connect to the Right People

The massive, matrixed organization and grandiose titles (what does a senior vice president do, anyway?) make it difficult for startups to connect with the right department and individuals who actually have decision-making power within a large corporation. A key challenge for startups working with big corporations is figuring out, then gaining the attention of, the decision makers and the economic buyer for their partnership to work. This is where an innovation team or "interface" platform can be helpful.

If these decision makers start as mentors, that is the ideal situation and a key value add of the corporate accelerator program. They can take over the relationship after the program ends, and accelerator leaders should manage expectations that they are expected to do so if all goes well. Have a conversation beforehand with both the decision maker and the startup, ideally together, at the beginning of the program to discuss what success looks like. Specifically, what needs to happen in the next three months to lead to a partnership after the program. And what does that partnership look like? Hold people accountable.

Access to Resources

Big companies are slow and complex, and startups usually need access to some things within this organizational structure to be successful. These resources are usually what's exciting about the partnership in the first place, giving the startup an "unfair advantage" by tapping into corporate sales channels, data, IP, and expertise. Access could be an account for a particular technology (e.g., cloud credits), a customer, data (e.g., customer usage data), a form or process to clear blockers (e.g., approval to use the logo in marketing), or a person to approve something specific (e.g., a senior business unit leader to approve messaging). These can also be financial resources, if that is part of the contract. Without quick access to these resources, the partnership momentum can slow down and cause unnecessary frustration. There should be one point person at the corporation who the startup can work with to identify and access these resources.

In particular, according to corporate accelerator as a service (CAaaS) company Plug and Play, "many startups need corporate data in order to gain insights about customers and how the corporation can more effectively conduct its operations. Given the need for data and the lengthy security protocols that startups must go through in order to acquire it, partnership processes would be streamlined if corporations created a model data set that potential startup partners could use to test their solutions. This would shorten the security protocols that corporations use and save both parties time and resources necessary in working with corporate data."[17]

Accept Failure

Most startups don't succeed, and many partnerships do not succeed. Nor should they. Innovation is all about taking risks and learning, so when a partnership unearths something that fundamentally doesn't work, either on the product, the partnership structure itself, or the fit between the startup and the corporate, then the partnership should end. Although startups are usually aware of this, corporates are often not used to accepting failure and fear that this result will reflect poorly on them. This is not the case, and, in fact, if there are no failures in partnerships over the course of many attempts, it usually means that the corporation is not taking enough risks or not being ambitious enough in the goals. Have clear milestones for the partnership, where there is a gating function and the partnership can end, or be renegotiated, if it's not working rather than become a zombie that is not working but won't die.

Move Fast(er)

Speed is one of the biggest differences between a startup and a corporation. Startups move fast, corporations don't. Corporate teams need to set the expectation with stakeholders that they will be working in a different way on these partnerships, and that speed is critical. "Fast" for a corporation is measured in quarters. But for a startup, speed is measured in weeks, or even days. In today's ever-changing environment, real speed can be the difference between becoming a market leader and being left behind.[18]

Reframe the Value to the Business

Innovation can sometimes be overlooked as a serious business initiative, sometimes falling into the category of marketing or corporate social responsibility. However, innovation is business critical, and this message needs to be articulated to the rest of the company. Many times the company outside the innovation team does not see the value of startup partnerships or the work of the innovation team. They may be single-mindedly focused on executing in the traditional way they always have, and do not have incentives to innovate or see the value in doing so. This can allow internal politics to undermine the innovation team's work and prevent any real chance of a partnership being successful.

It can be a slow process to get detractors on board, but it helps to demonstrate the value of accelerators by consistent internal communication and providing immediate value. For example, most big companies have internal research arms to identify market trends and other business intelligence. One way is to use the insights from the startups in the program, and even the ones that are from your pipeline, to identify market trends as business intelligence.

According to the research from professors Julia Prats and Josemaria Siota at the IESE Business School, "When this problem arose at one of the world's top five healthcare companies, the CINO [chief innovation officer] did two things. First, she elevated the value of the corporate venturing unit to the rest of the company by making it a market trends detector. Along with developing new products, she required it to identify external threats, analyze solutions devised by rival companies, and target growth opportunities for the firm's main businesses. Second, she allocated the costs of developing proofs-of-concept equally between the parent company, the corporate venturing unit, and the business unit that stood to benefit. The CINO's decisions won over the directors of the business lines. They realized they could devote more time to developing their products and services, knowing that the venturing unit was providing them with the latest marketplace intelligence. Also, sharing in the costs of the corporate venturing encouraged other units to contribute to its success."[19]

Business Unit Integration

The innovation team cannot own partnerships indefinitely, because they are usually not operating business units within the corporation. The partnership must eventually land within the appropriate business unit or other operational team that makes sense for the partnership. The sooner the partnership can be integrated with the business unit (BU) the better, even starting at the selection process before the accelerator begins. An innovation person can continue to be a point person or friendly support structure for the startup, but moving it over to the BU as quickly as possible is critical. This, of course, only works if the BU is on board and has allocated the appropriate resources to make it work.

Mutual Respect – What's in a Name?

It's important to develop a relationship in which both parties respect what the other brings to the table. Just because a corporation is big doesn't mean it has all the power in the relationship. Corporations and startups need each other, so acknowledge it and treat each other with respect.

One manifestation of this, which is a personal pet peeve for Jules, is using the word *vendor* to describe the startups. Typically, a vendor is someone who sells a product. Although this may be true at the most basic level, this is not a simple transactional relationship of the startup selling its product to the corporation. It can do this through typical sales channels without the need for an accelerator or innovation team to be involved. If the innovation team is involved and working on a partnership, there is mutual value, so the word *vendor* does not apply. Develop mutual respect for each other and refer to startups as the *partners* they are.

Set an Autopilot

A final best practice works for both corporate sponsors and their startups: set an autopilot. What we mean by this is to provide for and prepare for a communications breakdown. Remove critical path responses from the corporation as an obstacle to making things happen. One of the ways startup partnerships die is not through action but through inaction and neglect.

A common corporate culture response to change agents is to simply ignore them until they go away. By removing unnecessary approvals from the process, one often unrelated party in an unrelated area (looking at you accounting and legal) can't hold up a check or a sign-off by default. Action can always be taken, but make the default of a pilot program forward motion for the business unit to test and deploy.

Examples of this are small but important. Contracts can auto-renew for a rolling 90 days – safe for the company and life-saving for the startup. Consult and inform key stakeholders and allow input, but don't condition next steps on responses and approvals. Create an environment where the default is action.

CULTURE CHANGE, ONE STEP AT A TIME

Enabling partnerships at big companies means making changes to long-standing processes and mindsets. While this often feels like a perpetual uphill battle, they are slowly causing cracks in the stodgy corporate culture and moving to a place that embraces innovation. Every small win, even in a place that may seem boring or inconsequential, is a step in the right direction.

"Transformation is a loaded word. At the beginning, we're just trying to affect some kind of change, shake things up, whether it is achieving a pilot, or whether it is learning and exploring," says Rajendran of 500 Start-ups. "Ultimately, we're forcing people to do new things. And that is particularly true if you end up changing a policy or process. Those are shifts in behavior that are the seeds of cultural change if they compound over time. Whether it's this epic journey towards digital transformation that everyone has spent the last decade on, or something else, it comes down to changing culture in order to affect change that is really meaningful for an entire organization."

BLAZE YOUR OWN TRAIL

Wowza! Ava Lopez realizes that she has a lot of work to do before she can launch this accelerator. She gets to work starting the conversations with legal, finance, and procurement, and collaborates with them over several months to get some simplified processes in place. She works with her advisory board to map out MVP and partnership agreements and runs them past all of the business unit leaders who will likely be involved in the accelerator to get their buy-in. While not perfect, she believes she has arrived at a place that has the potential to work. (Fingers crossed!)

Every partnership takes on its own unique shape and form, and with some of these simple improvements we hope to see more successes resulting from corporate accelerator programs. This is an opportunity for leaders to blaze their own trail and contribute to the community of accelerator leaders who are diligently working to produce results. Sharing what works with your peers and discussing how to continuously improve as an industry will make us all better off.

AFTER THE PROGRAM

CHAPTER 16

POST-PROGRAM PORTFOLIO MANAGEMENT

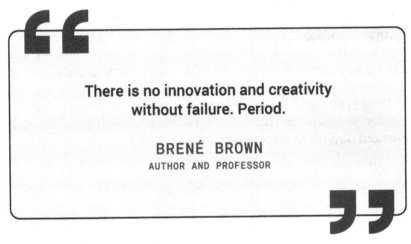

> There is no innovation and creativity without failure. Period.
>
> **BRENÉ BROWN**
> AUTHOR AND PROFESSOR

Source: May 15, 2013, The Wholehearted Life: Oprah Talks to Brené Brown. Harpo Productions Inc. Retrieved from: https://www.oprah.com/spirit/brene-brown-interviewed-by-oprah-daring-greatly/4.

There is a high rate of failure for both startups and accelerators, so if you get to a point where both are working, or at least surviving, congratulations! The best use of your time now is to support and nurture the subset of potential winners who make up the vast majority of your financial and strategic returns. All startups are not created equal. The ones that win tend to win big, and it is in everyone's best interest to focus time and effort there. These are the ones that will give your program a winning reputation, and in turn will help recruit more winners, which will continue to build the brand and reputation of your program in a virtuous cycle.

However, it is common for accelerators to stop their efforts after the program is over. From our research and personal experience, the number one reason that corporate accelerators fail to meet their strategic goals is the lack of follow through post-program. It's usually not the curriculum or even the company selection that prevents successes, it's the lack of ongoing support for a fledgling startup or relationships that have a seed of potential success, but need to be nurtured and cultivated after the program is over to achieve their potential.

This can be addressed with a comprehensive post-program support infrastructure, specifically around portfolio management. Without this post program support, all the hard work and momentum created from the accelerator program is put at risk. It may seem obvious, but the first step is to make a conscious commitment to investing time, capital, and resources to post-program portfolio management. Innovation takes time to develop, and startups need time and resources to achieve their vision. What's the point of an accelerator program if you just drop the startups and the budding partnerships into oblivion after the program?

If there is one major recommendation we have for almost all corporate accelerator programs to improve, it's to think through this post-program support and commit enough resources to do it properly.

WHY INVEST IN POST-PROGRAM SUPPORT?

It is a misguided, we might even say lazy, program that ends after demo day. The startups do not stop their business after the program and neither does your company! There are many reasons to continue the support for participating startups even after the program is over.

Improved Performance

The benefits of actively managing your portfolio are compelling. From a financial perspective, The Ewing Marion Kauffman Foundation found that the average exit multiple from investor active contact and support – defined as one to two times a month – is 3.7x, compared to the average exit multiple of 1.3x from passive contact – defined as one to two times a year.[1] Most corporate accelerator programs fall into the latter category, if they remain in contact at all.

From a partnership perspective, there will likely be some partnerships resulting immediately from the accelerator program, and corporates tend to focus exclusively on those. However, there are many participating companies that may be good partners down the line as circumstances change, such as when the company pivots, gains more traction, or the corporate business unit (BU) goals or team change to be more receptive to an innovation partnership. Actively managing the portfolio ensures you are aware of and, more importantly, part of those successes and can claim them as wins for the accelerator team.

Business Intelligence

Because the accelerator team has already done the hard work of developing relationships with a handful of curated startups that may achieve strategic goals for your business in some way, the easiest way to provide value back to the corporate parent is to continue to track the startups, and the markets they operate in, as they grow and scale or fail. This market intelligence (our pulley simple innovation machine of knowledge) is highly valuable, especially in aggregate as the portfolio grows and you are able to see trends and prevent future mistakes. This intelligence makes accelerator leaders look good, and provides real value to the corporation. If resources are a challenge, work with the internal market intelligence units, corporate development teams, or whoever else tracks market trends at your company. They usually pay significant fees for databases to track trends, but the information from your portfolio is not available anywhere else and is curated for your company. These teams will be motivated to help.

Reputation

The crux of anything in the startup world is having access to the best startups, and being a small part of the journey of the few outliers who achieve outsized successes. This is only possible for corporate innovation programs if they have a strong reputation in the startup world.

Reputation is a funny thing. One bad move can damage years of building a reputation. Especially in the startup and VC world, credibility and relationships are built over years, if not decades, of engagement. Startups and investors need to make major, company-changing decisions with imperfect information. They learn to trust their instincts and the people around them who have a track record of success, but this trust is hard earned and easily lost. Corporates are not typically well respected in the startup and VC world from an innovation standpoint because they are not invested in these same types of long-term relationships. While big companies may be seen as customers, there is some skepticism around partnership. In fact, many startups are created to destroy the corporate incumbents.

It is also difficult to manage a corporate's reputation in the startup world. The bigger the company, the more people there are out in the market talking to startups. The message probably isn't consistent, and some of your employees don't know much about your innovation strategy, so while well intentioned they are sending mixed, and often dangerously inaccurate, messages to the market. An active post-program support plan and engaged portfolio management may not prevent other people in your company from doing dumb things to damage your reputation in the startup world, but it goes a long way to help and continue to build a positive brand (our inclined plane simple innovation machine) adding value to startups.

It's worth considering the impact on your own culture as well. Failure to follow through tells your internal teams that even expensive investments in equity and programming for startups in the accelerator will be squandered; why then should they invest their own time and risk their careers if the company won't follow through on innovation?

WHY DON'T ACCELERATORS DO PORTFOLIO MANAGEMENT?

The root of the problem is that the accelerator teams do not usually have dedicated portfolio managers on their team to tend to the portfolio after the program is over, and thus lose regular contact with the graduates. Once you lose contact with a company, it's nearly impossible to help, even if you wanted to.

There are many reasons a corporate accelerator team may not actively manage a portfolio after the program is over. As strategic investors, helping the companies and even keeping track of them may not be considered to be business critical unless there is a partnership. There is no real motivation to help the startup succeed for the sake of it, even if they have some potential financial upside from equity ownership. Any upside would simply be too small for the corporate to spend much time or energy on this.

The focus of most accelerator teams is on implementing the program itself. For the typical small team that runs these programs, the process of recruiting, developing, and implementing the curriculum, organizing the demo day, and managing a wide variety of internal stakeholders is time consuming and exhausting. These teams' skill sets are usually also more aligned with program management and event planning, as that's what it takes to run an accelerator program.

Managing a portfolio of investments well is a very different skill set and not one that most accelerator teams have, though we argue they should. To ensure strategic goals, this is one of the most important parts of the accelerator. The point of an accelerator is not the program itself; it's using the program as a filter to find the best-fit startups for partnerships, market intelligence, product usage, or achieving other strategic goals. Without portfolio management, corporates are missing a massive opportunity. There are easy ways to improve this, but we cannot stress enough the benefits of portfolio management and encourage all corporate accelerators to include this in your planning and budget.

AFTER THE PROGRAM ENDS

After the accelerator program ends, your work is not done! Although it may seem like a whirlwind and your exhausted team is ready to take a vacation and not think about accelerators for a while, the downtime in between programs is when important work happens. Take a break for a week or two to give the team a rest, then come back refreshed and start on portfolio management.

Post-mortem

It is important to evaluate the program in an honest way so that you can continue to improve it. A classic principle of design thinking and lean startup methodology is to schedule a post-mortem or retrospective after the project or sprint ends. This brings your team and preferably also the key stakeholders together to review what happened in the program, take a hard look at what worked, what didn't work, and what you learned. It is important not to put any blame on any particular person or action; simply learn and continuously improve the program to get better every time.

There are many different frameworks for this type of session, but we prefer a no-frills approach that simply outlines what happened, what went well, what did not go well, and how you'll adjust in the future.

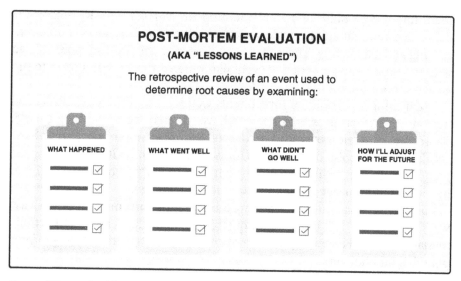

Most accelerator programs take at least three cohorts to get their bearings and refine their model, some take even longer and most are constantly evolving. Regular post-mortems can expedite this process and make your program more effective faster.

Feedback Surveys

While it is wise to conduct surveys throughout the program, it is the most important to do one after the program ends. This should be immediately after the program ends, and we also highly recommend doing one three to six months later. This checks to see if the strategic goals that you thought were being met are actually happening after the high of demo day and any initial buzz dies down.

A feedback survey should be sent to all participants and should be anonymous, including strong encouragement to share constructive feedback with the intention of improving the program. Sometimes start-ups are hesitant to share negative feedback because they do not want to risk a potential partnership with the corporate, so make it a safe and secure environment to share helpful feedback, both positive and negative.

The mentors and other stakeholders should also be asked for feedback, as they will have a different perspective based on their participation that can be very useful.

Alumni Programs

One of the most valuable resources of any accelerator program is the network of alumni. This ecosystem is worth investing time and energy to cultivate. Once they are alumni, the startups may continue to develop and scale, or they may start new businesses.

Especially after a few batches of accelerator programs, with some successes under your belt, this network of alumni can be extremely powerful as a recruiting tool, source of mentors and speakers, and general advocate for your program in the market. It is important to cultivate and keep actively engaged in the alumni community.

This can be as simple as setting up a Slack channel or WhatsApp group for the alumni, but it does require attention and curation. A regular method of communication is table stakes. Alumni management can also include a series of networking or educational events and is a good way to continue engaging corporate executives with the startup community, as well as maintaining and growing a top-notch mentor community, so make sure all key stakeholders are involved.

One of the best ways to work with key members of the alumni community directly is to bring success stories and experts back into the mentor network and advisory roles, place talent in new companies, and share leads and contacts with the newest members of the community. Invites to demo days and other invites may evolve into full weekends or getaways (often sponsored) to provide bonding time for founders from different cohorts and create a further bond.

Until the program is mature, this is not a full-time job, but corporate accelerators should allocate a portion of someone on the team's time to manage the alumni network. Eventually hiring a head of community or similar role is an effective use of resources.

Ecosystem Support

Accelerators have a lot of resources for startups when they are in the program, but startups still need these resources to grow their business after the program is over. It can be a massive value add to startups if there is some ongoing continuity in resources that support them after the program ends. This can be public relations (PR) and marketing resources, development resources, access to products, data, IP, or anything else that aligns with the strategic goals of your program.

According to a report from the Aspen Institute,[2] the types of post-program support offered to entrepreneurs include the following:

- Public-relations opportunities
- Connections with investors
- Board participation
- HR/recruitment support
- Regional meetups
- Online communities listing funding and promotion opportunities
- Office space

The type of support can vary, but setting up some sort of post-program alumni network to continue cultivating and supporting the ecosystem can be high value and dramatically improve the reputation and outcomes of the program.

PORTFOLIO MANAGEMENT BASICS

Portfolio management is critical but is often a new concept for most corporate accelerators. Although it can be improved and expanded over time, there are some simple basics of portfolio management that can have a high impact.

What Is Portfolio Management?

Portfolio management is the art and science of selecting and overseeing a group of investments that meet the long-term financial or strategic objectives and risk tolerance of the investor. For corporate accelerators or VCs with a portfolio of privately held startups, this means developing and maintaining a relationship with the founders, supporting their growth, and reporting on the relevant data as an investor to your key stakeholders.

Reporting: What to Measure?

To properly manage a portfolio, you need to have access to key data from each company. The adage of what gets measured gets managed holds up. This includes, but is not limited to:

- Updated financial statements – including an income statement to see growth, as well as a balance sheet and statement of cash flows to understand cash position and runway
- Sales pipeline – so you know where to add value; this can be sensitive to share with a corporate, but a strong relationship and established trust with the startup helps
- Key metrics – depending on the business this will vary; for example, for software-as-a-service (SaaS) companies, customer acquisition cost: lifetime value (CAC:LTV) is an important ratio, as well as sales cycle length and churn; track what the startup is tracking themselves
- Fundraising plans – to help make introductions where appropriate and give the CVC arm an opportunity to invest

This level of reporting should be done portfolio-wide on a quarterly, if not monthly, basis. You can use a software tool such as Seraf for greater automation and analytical capabilities. It is highly recommended that you complete a more in-depth annual report to share with your stakeholders, as a VC fund would share with its limited partners (LPs).

Map Out the Portfolio

It is important to segment the portfolio based on needs. There is a big difference in how you manage a portfolio when you have an equity stake or partnership and when you don't have either.

One simple way to divide the portfolio and develop a support strategy is to focus on your ongoing relationship with the companies in the portfolio. The vertical axis is investment. If you invested or have an equity stake in the company, there are certain shareholder obligations (such as voting) that need to happen and you will likely also have to report on the valuation of the portfolio to the corporate development team (or whoever in the company owns minority investments). The horizontal axis is partnership. If there is a formal partnership developing, whether an investment is made or not, the business unit (BU) and innovation teams should be involved in some capacity (though more actively if there is an investment).

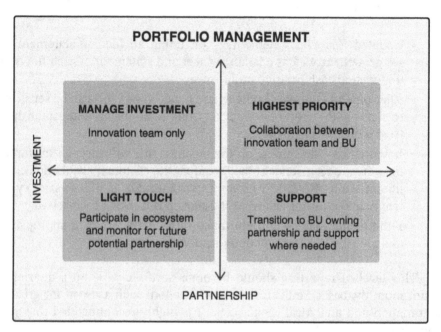

How Do VCs Do It?

As a benchmark, let's look at how venture capital investors do portfolio management. Venture capital investors actively manage the portfolio for two reasons. First, as financial investors, they receive better outcomes if they actively support their portfolio's success. Second, they must report back to their limited partners (LPs) on a regular basis, so they regularly collect data from the portfolio companies.

In fact, despite the moniker of "investor," most VCs spend the majority of their time on portfolio management. According to a classic *Harvard Business Review* article that still holds true today on "How Venture Capital Works," they estimate that 75% of a VC's time is spent on portfolio management activities including serving as director, acting as advisor, recruiting management, assisting in outside relationships, and supporting an exit.

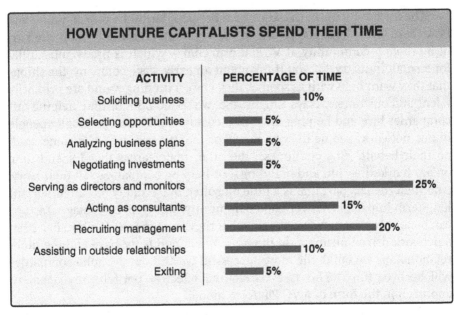

HOW VENTURE CAPITALISTS SPEND THEIR TIME

ACTIVITY	PERCENTAGE OF TIME
Soliciting business	10%
Selecting opportunities	5%
Analyzing business plans	5%
Negotiating investments	5%
Serving as directors and monitors	25%
Acting as consultants	15%
Recruiting management	20%
Assisting in outside relationships	10%
Exiting	5%

Source: How Venture Capital Works, Retrieved from: https://store.hbr.org/product/how-venture-capital-works/98611

Most VCs develop strong, ongoing relationships with their portfolio companies that can span decades over multiple companies. This starts with consistent communication. For example, Jules has a bi-weekly cadence call with most of her portfolio company CEOs from Mindset Ventures. This is a people business – you can only support the portfolio companies if you have a strong relationship with the founders and can help to positively influence the outcome of the company.

Lindsay Knight manages the Platform, or the "post-investment," team at Chicago Ventures, a $150+ million AUM (assets under management) VC fund that invests primarily in startups based in the central part of the United States. She works directly with the firm's 50-plus active portfolio companies on matchmaking talent, connecting to customers, marketing/communication/PR, building community, content, and events to help scale up and skill up more efficiently. "The term 'Platform' may be new in venture, but the work isn't. Helping companies operationally is what VCs have really been doing since the beginning of venture – it's part of the business," says Knight. "The person leading Platform has the 30,000-foot-view across the portfolio, and will build the structure for the firm to work alongside every single company in efficient but meaningful ways."

The formal Platform role became more popular in the past 10 years, and now there are at least 800 people in these jobs at VC funds – many are part of a growing community at VCPlatform.com – which is pretty substantial for a small industry. "If you think about an early stage company, the things that they want help with as soon as they close a funding round are primarily talent and customers," says Knight. "So, we spend a lot of time helping our companies hire and helping them find customers. Those are usually people in our network, people that we know, or that we can get to do some work on their behalf." She continues, "the other major areas that I spend time on are marketing, PR, and branding – or helping companies sell their story. And then the last part that is a little bit softer, but actually has an important long-term impact, is network and community. We think early stage startups can benefit from a network of peers that they can tap into. Venture has been a network driven business, so the more touch points we have and the more relationships we build, the more successful we and our portfolio companies will be over time." This is a classic and effective portfolio management approach in the form of a VC Platform model.

Most venture funds are doing this, but most accelerators are not. Although this is mainly to secure a financial return, the same principles apply to corporate investors who want to achieve a strategic return. Even with companies where a partnership does not currently exist, there may be an opportunity in the future. Even if there is not, the reputation and brand of a corporate stakeholder as an investor is benefited by helpful, active portfolio management. Portfolio company CEOs are often where VCs and accelerators get the best referrals for new startup deal flow. This applies to corporate accelerators as well, but if the corporate does not maintain a strong relationship with the founders, this channel is missing.

Should Accelerators Do It the Same Way?

Accelerators are not VC funds, and usually have strategic objectives, not financial objectives, for the participating startup. Although innovation teams may include a CVC team, they are usually more focused on strategic objectives than maximizing financial objectives. However, the way to achieve strategic goals is very similar. Connectivity to founders, active portfolio management, and long-term market intelligence from tracking companies over time are all useful to achieve your goals. Most accelerator teams lack sufficient internal resources to be involved in delivering valuable support to the portfolio after the program if there is no immediate partnership. This needs to change.

Who Should Manage the Portfolio?

We strongly believe that portfolio management is a key missing link to maximize the success of corporate accelerator programs. There are many ways to improve this.

One obvious way is to hire a dedicated portfolio manager on the accelerator or innovation team. This person should have experience managing a portfolio of startups, ideally at an accelerator or VC fund, and know how to support the companies while also knowing how to navigate the ins and outs of your corporation. We strongly advise not sending this to the corporate development team – while most big companies have experienced colleagues there who know how to manage a portfolio of investments, they are usually public company or much later-stage investments and we have seen things go awry here many, many times. Managing a portfolio of startups is very different, and requires someone who deeply understands the startup and VC world. This is a very hard role to hire for and retain, but with the right talent it can be one of the best options.

Alternatively, if your company has an active CVC team, they already manage a portfolio of startups. Whether they do it well is a question, but this is usually the best team within a corporation to take over portfolio management. However, the team should have a dedicated resource for the accelerator portfolio to ensure those companies are getting the right amount of attention. An accelerator portfolio tends to be a higher volume of smaller investments than a typical VC portfolio, so it takes a slightly different skill set and approach to do well.

Finally, you can outsource portfolio management to a third party. If you already have a third party lined up to manage the investments, which is a fantastic option if you don't have an internal CVC team, then this same entity should manage the portfolio. This can be an external VC fund or a specialist consultant who has a track record of success in this space. The trick here is to make sure this third party is connected to the right people at the corporation to support the portfolio companies with the right partnership enablement and introductions there.

Managing Through Leadership Changes

One critical topic to mention is how to manage a portfolio through leadership changes. The startup and VC world are based on long-term connections. When VCs invest in startups, they rarely leave their firms and abandon the portfolio companies. The incentive model for VCs only makes sense if the VCs stay in their jobs for many years and manage the portfolio to exit, which then allows them to recognize the upside of the investment.

In the corporate world, this is very different. The average executive changes roles every two to three years. When the accelerator team, especially the person who was managing the portfolio changes jobs, it can be very difficult for a new person to take on the responsibility without any friction. Often the portfolio companies are simply orphaned, which leads to all kinds of bad situations. This can be managed by either incentivizing the portfolio manager to stay in the role for the long term by providing, as VC funds do, upside that can be achieved when the portfolio companies exit. This is also another value add of an external portfolio manager who is incentivized by carried interest when the company is successful.

EXITS AND ENDINGS

Startups, especially if they are VC-backed, have a very specific trajectory as a business. The very definition of a startup is rapid growth, with the intention of achieving an exit within 10 years. This exit could be an M&A transaction, an IPO, or something similar.

Both the VCs and entrepreneurs themselves usually have exit strategies at the start of the business, and developing these relationships with potential acquirers early on is important. A big part of portfolio management as a corporate partner is to clear this path if your company is a potential acquirer. There are many nuances to this, and supporting an exit and being part of the deal is a particular skill set that requires an experienced portfolio manager to navigate.

Also, if a competitor to your company intends to acquire the startup, it is in your long-term best interest to support the transaction if you do not intend to buy the company yourself. If you build a reputation for blocking exits, no alumni founders or VCs in their right mind would recommend that startups participate in your accelerator.

If we leave you with any one message from this book, it's that an accelerator program is not just a three-month accelerator program. It is a filter for a pipeline of market intelligence, potential partnerships, or strategic relationships that need to be actively curated and managed over the long term. Having a comprehensive, thoughtful, and systematic post-program portfolio management initiative is the best way to capture the massive opportunity that accelerators present to achieve your strategic goals.

CHAPTER 17

PLANNING FOR LONG-TERM SUCCESS

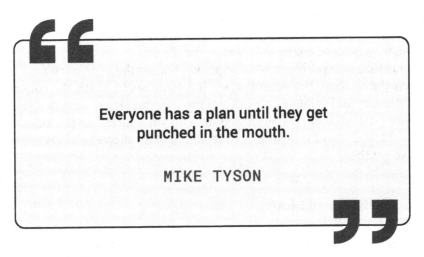

> Everyone has a plan until they get punched in the mouth.
>
> MIKE TYSON

Source: Mike Tyson

Congratulations on reaching the end of this journey. You've worked through the high-level strategy of why a corporate accelerator makes sense, and mastered the nitty-gritty details of how to recruit mentors and startups. You've decided on your programming and measures of success. You've even considered whether to bring in a partner from outside your company to help you establish the first few cohorts of your corporate accelerator or to run the investment and portfolio management.

Selling the vision to the senior executives, business unit leaders, and even the rank-and-file employees can be a challenge, but without them, getting momentum and traction for the program is impossible. You have a playbook in your hands, but as they say, the map is not the terrain. You need to navigate your own unique company and all of its idiosyncrasies to get the key stakeholders aligned with your vision, and this doesn't just happen once, it continues on an ongoing basis. Having a blueprint for action from this book, a benchmark for budgets and timelines, and a guide to ensuring goals and metrics of success are aligned will help, but if you're an innovation pioneer in your company, there are no trails to follow. You'll need to forge them yourself.

Building a corporate accelerator that can achieve the company's goals is within your reach if you can do these things. You can leverage your company's existing strengths and resources to help it avoid the fate of so many others who ignored change. As you make the rounds in your organization, you'll realize that people in the company often see the wave of change coming on the horizon, but don't know what to do about it. It's the culture of complacency and comfort doing things the way you always have that you are fighting. Win your battles one at a time with key converts to the innovation cause. Make it easy for them to see the potential for success and get engaged. You've got this!

THE JOURNEY SO FAR

The long process of planning and consensus building will kick off the official launch of your corporate accelerator. This is only the beginning, not the end, of your innovation journey. The initial launch will be followed by years of working with cohorts of founders and startups, and all the ups and downs that come with it. You'll be shepherding promising ideas into partnership opportunities and developing talent to help manage the accelerator and its emerging community of innovators and alumni. You will also be stimulating growth and innovation in your company, while changing its culture in the process. This is the fun part!

All of this will require new skill sets and, sometimes, new people. You may continue to grow with the accelerator or pass the baton to the next runner and return to another part of the company, bringing your newly refined ability to influence cultural change with you. This is an opportunity for the corporation, and also one for your career. Learning new skills and enacting change is never easy, but it can be very rewarding personally, professionally, and for the company as a whole. The journey starts with acknowledging that you need to adopt innovation into the company in the first place. As G.I. Joe told some of us as children, "knowing is half the battle." The other half is the hard work of execution. You've made it through the knowing and planning part of the journey. And the next stages will undoubtedly test you at every turn, but this is why you have this book to act as a guide. We've covered a lot of territory.

We started by introducing accelerators as a tool in the corporate innovation toolkit. You wouldn't be reading this if you weren't aware of the possibilities, but choosing the corporate accelerator as a tool to achieve your corporate innovation goals is a bold step. Although many have made this decision, not all have succeeded. Picking up this book immediately gave you a leg up on the competition.

We then reviewed innovation theory and practices to set the stage with popular frameworks used to bring innovation into the corporation. Working with startups through an accelerator or other innovation program has become much more understood over the last two decades. To begin with, accelerators are tools that fit right in with the classic *Innovators' Dilemma* as Clayton Christensen sees it. McKinsey's *Three Horizons* help you to manage the new innovation programs alongside existing core businesses. Methodologies such as *Lean Startup* and *Design Thinking* help you understand the processes that have been tested and proven to turn innovative ideas into startup realities. The concept of *Open Innovation* encapsulated the view of an enterprise with porous borders, having innovation flow in and out depending on where it can thrive best.

We then introduced the framework of a corporation as a complex machine that can be broken down into a collection of simple machines, which can each drive value for innovation programs. Thinking of innovation in terms of its core elements – or simple innovation machines – can identify the strengths and assets of the mature corporation and the areas where you have a unique advantage in the market. It allows a direct mapping of a set of goals to the accelerator's mission and planned impact. From the wheel to the wedge, the practical advantages of corporate accelerators can be fully understood. From this flows the structure of everything from recruiting the startups to the measures of their success.

The three accelerator archetypes gave us a way to align our goals with an accelerator program that can actually achieve them. Translating this into action means understanding the types of accelerators and the choices that need to be made to create a custom solution that's right for your organization. The exact structure and method of doing this will vary according to your specific why.

The most important thing for a corporation – the key thing that drives all the other decisions and choices in designing a successful corporate accelerator – is knowing why you're doing it. The goals for the corporate accelerator should align with the strategic goals of the company itself.

We then emphasized the importance of engaging with your key stakeholders, who need to be actively on board for the program to have a shot at success in the long term. Getting their buy-in can be a challenge, but is worth the effort. Some stakeholders will have ongoing roles in governance as well, and an investment committee will be needed to select the chosen startup partners. Keeping stakeholders in the loop regularly avoids surprises and promotes success. Pretending that there are no politics in keeping a long-term project like an accelerator alive doesn't work; communicate and provide your stakeholders with ammunition to support you more broadly within the organization. This communication also forms the foundation for broader cultural change, bringing innovation into the parent company one stakeholder at a time.

Talent and financial resources will be needed as you plan the launch of the corporate accelerators. It's important to have a clear understanding of the funding involved and the time span of commitment. For an accelerator program, this funding will likely be in the seven figures, and it needs to come with a multi-year commitment to learn and iterate, and to give the startups enough runway to grow and thrive before claiming a win or loss. Equally important is to staff the program appropriately. Innovation programs work best when it is a healthy collaboration of outsiders with expertise in the startup world alongside key people from the corporation who know the ins and outs of your particular business. We also articulated the many benefits of outsourcing a portion of the accelerator to experienced third parties, though the corporate team must still be highly engaged.

Once the planning is done, it's time to find the absolute best startups that meet your criteria and make it clear why they should join your program. Recruiting is a marketing process as much as a selection process, but having clear organizational goals will allow the investment committee to use agreed-upon criteria as they work through a process of selection. Finding the best startups that can bring outside innovation and talent into the corporate world is a real challenge. It's not simply a "field of dreams"; even if you build it, startups don't just come. The ones that would, well, they're not the ones you want. You'll need a promotion process to spread the word and generate interest, an application process with criteria to help you find the most promising candidates, and a selection process to pick the best startups for a long-term investment and operating relationship.

The corporate accelerator is looking for great startups, but so is every other accelerator and VC fund out there. The best startups have lots of options. To win this battle, corporate accelerators shouldn't try to outdo Y Combinator or Sequoia Capital. They should focus on what they uniquely bring to the table, namely, industry knowledge, access to expert practitioners in the field, and the possibility of a trajectory-altering pilot or partnership. A partnership that generates revenue for both the startup and the big company is the holy grail for a corporate accelerator's performance.

We walked through many different ways to make, or not make, an investment. For a startup choosing to work with a corporate, it's often the non-equity investment that is most compelling. While access to potential customers and opportunities to partner are compelling factors, an investment of some form is table stakes for running an accelerator, but can be done in a non-dilutive form such as a grant. When equity is involved, it becomes a long-term relationship with a lot of other complexities. This can align incentives and produce exciting returns, but it also requires significantly more resources to manage properly.

When the corporate accelerator launches, there's a sense of accomplishment and success when the first cohort gets started – a forward-looking sense of promise and possibility. It's important to ground this with metrics and measures that can track and reinforce this feeling of success over the longer term. As a common saying in the VC world goes, "lemons ripen early." Many of the initial startups will face the cold reality that they won't make it, which they tend to find out quickly. In other words, the failures come first. Since successes often take longer, make sure to have metrics that can act as a proxy for revenue growth or other important KPIs to ensure that your corporation sees enough value in the program to continue it and have time to achieve the long-term returns from the big winners. Innovation takes time.

By successfully engaging stakeholders and doing a lot of meticulous planning, the first group of companies is selected. Founders take over the accelerator space and the program begins. The acceleration part of the program is a mix of coaching, training, opening doors, and smoothing the way to success. It generally starts with a curriculum – a standardized set of training for the founders of budding businesses. Mentors and experts join to coach and offer lessons from their own experiences, and corporate mentors can ease the path to partnership. A final key element in the success of a corporate accelerator is follow-through, so active post-program portfolio management will maximize the impact of the hard work done during the program. Many leaders of corporate accelerators view demo day as an opportunity to kick the baby birds out of the nest, but nothing could be further from the truth. Follow-through is a key element to achieving successful outcomes.

EXPANDING ON YOUR SUCCESS

Once the first class has made it through the end of the program, it often feels like the journey has ended. demo day has gone off without a hitch, some companies have raised venture capital funding, and others are kicking off new partnerships. Although we wouldn't get in the way of a little celebration, this is also a chance to broaden your horizons. For many big companies, the successful launch of the corporate accelerator program can be the proof point for further expanding innovation efforts around the company. From small seeds mighty oaks do grow – this is only the beginning of your innovation journey.

An obvious area for growth is with the accelerator itself. Many first classes are tests and compromises. Future cohorts are a way to refine and perfect your unique accelerator model. In our experience, this takes at least three cycles to get right for most companies and never really ends. Adding additional business unit sponsors and expanding the program's reach within the company is another great area for growth. Invite key business unit stakeholder prospects – those you need but don't yet have on board – to key events like demo day or to participate in an advisory board or investment committee. Have them visit the accelerator and feel the energy. Discuss the startups that you couldn't bring on board that might have impacted their line of business – the ones that got away. Share the successful pilots launching as a result. When leaders see their peers benefiting, fear of missing out (FOMO) and personal choices will open up more opportunity within the company. Your early adopters' success will allow you to "land and expand."

Building additional accelerator programs is another way to leverage your original success. This can include different types of programs – for example, if you originally launched a venture accelerator, you could add a partnership or an ecosystem accelerator. Another possibility is to build a similar accelerator in a different vertical or geography. If you were focusing on AI at first, would it make sense to add a blockchain or big data-focused program? At multinational corporations, often the success of an accelerator in one location will get attention from other countries, who will reach out and want to launch a program of their own. In both of these cases, you already have the model. The first cohort is always the hardest; it is much easier to replicate it and train others to execute. We strongly advise keeping these under one management structure, usually an innovation team, to ensure consistency and effective sharing of resources. Adding accelerators creates a portfolio approach of diversification that allows the parent to tap into different innovation ecosystems or focus on different technology areas of interest.

Finally, there are a lot of other tools in the corporate innovation tool kit. An accelerator can be a great gateway toward broader organizational change and comfort with higher risk innovation initiatives. If a corporate accelerator is your first foray into an innovation program, a natural expansion could be to launch a CVC vehicle or an internal venture studio. Changing a company culture has to start somewhere. An initially lean accelerator team can grow into a broader initiative that manages the portfolio of investments in alumni companies or applies the accelerator model to internal ideas and teams. The possibilities are almost limitless.

With a successful accelerator program leading the way, bridging internal and external change with new tools becomes easier and easier. The more successes you have, the more credibility and budget come with it, which can lead to more successes. Once the path has been established to try new things, demonstrating actual business results, the appetite for innovation only continues to grow. The accelerator becomes the key that unlocks the door of corporate innovation. And with the pace of change only accelerating, it can be the key to a traditional company surviving and thriving.

EPILOGUE: A LOOK BACK

It's been nearly 10 years since Ava Lopez launched FabCo's first accelerator. She still feels an almost parental pride at every Demo Day as new startups keep the packed room of investors and stakeholders riveted with presentations on new innovations with unlimited potential for growth. She fondly remembers the days when she had to cajole and beg the business unit leaders for their time; now they fight to get attention from the accelerator team to serve their own needs. Some have even started their own customized accelerator programs under her guidance.

Ava leveraged the success of FabCo's first partnership accelerator to a global network of 12 accelerators tackling key areas and geographies of FabCo's business. She also launched a CVC arm and a series of venture studios, all of which operate under a powerful new innovation business unit that she runs, reporting to the CEO. She now boasts a team of more than 200 people worldwide, many of whom are former entrepreneurs but love the FabCo culture and are incredibly loyal.

The successes are almost too numerous to count, although of course she does count them in her annual report to the board of directors each year. Meanwhile, CEO Jordan Burns has been credited with one of the biggest comebacks of all time in the corporate world, doubling FabCo's revenue over the past decade. She said on her last earnings call that innovation initiatives account for nearly 40% of the company's growth.

Perhaps the most satisfying thing for Ava is a feeling that the innovative talents of existing employees have been unleashed – the internal company accelerator program she launched only two years ago is now producing as many promising partnerships as the startup accelerators. The external-facing program gets a little more attention after the successful IPOs of several companies from the initial cohort, and she can't help but be proud because she is still close with the CEOs of a few of them after nearly a decade of helping them navigate many ups and downs along the way through her comprehensive portfolio management initiative. The employees love working at FabCo and attrition has dropped dramatically. She feels that the culture has successfully changed, and that Freddie would be proud of his company all these years later.

The most exciting thing is that the future holds so much more to come! It's been great to be honored as an innovator by her peers, but Ava is much prouder when she hears how recruits are choosing to join FabCo because of its reputation as an innovator. After all, they are where the ideas will come from in the future – which seems to be getting brighter and brighter.

This future is in reach for every company out there, and a successful corporate accelerator can be your first step to get there. We wish you the best of luck on your innovation journey!

Endnotes

CHAPTER 1

1. Steve Blank, Why Companies Do "Innovation Theater" Instead of Actual Innovation, Retrieved from: https://hbr.org/2019/10/why-companiesdo-innovation-theater-instead-of-actual-innovation.

2. "CEO disruption," CB Insights, October 15, 2019. www.cbinsights.com/research/ceo-disruption-2/

3. "Growth & Innovation," McKinsey & Company, no date. www.mckinsey.com/business-functions/strategy-and-corporate-finance/how-we-help-clients/growth-and-innovation

4. "Three Years Later, U.S. Companies Continue to Struggle With Innovation, Accenture Survey Reveals," Accenture, March 21, 2016. https://newsroom.accenture.com/news/three-years-later-us-companies-continue-to-struggle-with-innovation-accenture-survey-reveals.htm

5. Valerie Mocker, Simona Bielli, and Christopher Haley, *Winning Together: A Guide to Successful Corporate-Startup Collaborations*, Nesta report, 2020. https://ec.europa.eu/futurium/en/system/files/ged/43-nesta-winning-together-guidestartupcollab.pdf (Page 8).

6. "The World's Most Innovative Companies," *Forbes*, 2018. www.forbes.com/innovative-companies

7. "50 Examples of Corporations That Failed to Innovate," Valuer newsletter, July 2, 2019. www.valuer.ai/blog/50-examples-of-corporations-that-failed-to-innovate-and-missed-their-chance

8. Scott D. Anthony, "Kodak's Downfall Wasn't About Technology," *Harvard Business Review*, July 15, 2016. https://hbr.org/2016/07/kodaks-downfall-wasnt-about-technology

9. "Global Innovation Management Market 2018-2022 - Changing Work Culture Propelling the $1.5 Billion Market - Research and Markets," Businesswire report, January 10, 2018. www.businesswire.com/news/home/20180110006097/en/Global-Innovation-Management-Market-2018-2022---Changing

10. "CB Insights Presents: Corporate Innovation Theatre In 8 Acts," CB Insights, December 16, 2015.www.cbinsights.com/research/corporate-innovation-theatre/

11. https://en.wikipedia.org/wiki/Innovation

12. www.merriam-webster.com/dictionary/innovation

13. www.drucker.institute/programs/drucker-prize/

14. Jill Lepore, "The Disruption Machine," The *New Yorker*, June 16, 2014. www.newyorker.com/magazine/2014/06/23/the-disruption-machine

15. "Why 60% Of Corporate Accelerators Fail After 2 Years," CB Insights, May 30, 2019. www.cbinsights.com/research/corporate-accelerator-failure/

16. Michael Brigl, Stafan Gross-Selbeck, Nico Dehnert, et al., "After the Honeymoon Ends: Making Corporate-Startup Relationships Work," Boston Consulting Group, June 13, 2019. www.bcg.com/publications/2019/corporate-startup-relationships-work-after-honeymoon-ends

17. Michael Brigl, After the Honeymoon Ends: Making Corporate-Startup Relationships Work, 13 Jun 2019.

18. Yann Pastor and Jason Bender, "Innovation led transformation: Reconnecting transformation with innovation . . . ," Deloitte, August 9, 2019. www2.deloitte.com/au/en/blog/consulting-blog/2019/innovation-led-transformation.html

19. Carmen Noble, "Clay Christensen's Milkshake Marketing," Harvard Business School Working Knowledge, February 14, 2011. https://hbswk.hbs.edu/item/clay-christensens-milkshake-marketing

20. Minda Zetlin, "Blockbuster Could Have Bought Netflix for $50 Million, but the CEO Thought It Was a Joke," Inc., no date. www.inc.com/minda-zetlin/netflix-blockbuster-meeting-marc-randolph-reed-hastings-john-antioco.html

21. David Jasper, "Talking blockbusters with 'The Last Blockbuster' filmmaker," *The Bulletin*, June 25, 2020. www.bendbulletin.com/coronavirus/talking-blockbusters-with-the-last-blockbuster-filmmaker/article_6810ed0c-b1a4-11ea-9563-2bd2186e954a.html

22. Beth McKenna, "The 10 Best Performing Stocks of the Decade," The Motley Fool, January 6, 2020. www.fool.com/investing/2020/01/06/the-10-best-performing-stocks-of-the-decade.aspx

23. "The 9 Industries Amazon Could Disrupt Next," CB Insights, no date. www.cbinsights.com/research/report/amazon-disruption-industries/

24. Naomi Eide, "AWS to encounter IaaS market 'erosion' as contenders mature," CIO Dive, July 29, 2019. www.ciodive.com/news/iaas-Azure-AWS-Google-Cloud-Alibaba/559716/#:~:text=AWS%20is%20the%20de%20facto,Microsoft%2C%2which%20has%2015.5%25

25. "The 9 Industries Amazon Could Disrupt Next," CB Insights. https://www.cbinsights.com/research/report/amazon-disruption-industries

26. Kate Schoolov, "Amazon is rapidly expanding its air fleet to handle more of its own shipping," CNBC, February 15, 2019. www.cnbc.com/2019/02/15/amazon-will-compete-with-fedex-and-ups-to-become-logistics-company.html

27. Ibid.

28. Driek Desmet, Ewan Duncan, Jay Scanlan, et al., "Six buiilding blocks for creating a high-performing digital enterprise," McKinsey & Company, September 1, 2015. www.mckinsey.com/business-functions/organization/our-insights/six-building-blocks-for-creating-a-high-performing-digital-enterprise

29. Scott D. Anthony, S. Patrick Viguerie, Evan I. Schwartz, et al., "2018 Corporate Longevity Forecast: Creative Destruction is Accelerating," Innosight, February 2018. www.innosight.com/insight/creative-destruction/

30. Richard N. Foster; Standard & Poor's. Retrieved from: https://www.innosight.com/insight/creative-destruction/

31. Jordan Bar Am, Laura Furstenthal, Felicitas Jorge, et al., "Innovation in a crisis: Why it is more critical than ever," McKinsey & Company, June 17, 2020. www.mckinsey.com/business-functions/strategy-and-corporate-finance/our-insights/innovation-in-a-crisis-why-it-is-more-critical-than-ever

32. Exhibit from "Innovation in a crisis: Why it is more critical than ever", June 2020, McKinsey & Company, www.mckinsey.com.

33. Sebastion Brunet, Miklos Grof, and Diego Izquierdo, "Global Accelerator Report 2016," Gust, 2016. http://gust.com/accelerator_reports/2016/global

34. "Why 60% Of Corporate Accelerators Fail After 2 Years," CB Insights. www.cbinsights.com/research/corporate-accelerator-failure/

35. Why 60% Of Corporate Accelerators Fail After 2 Years, May 30 2019.

36. Gaelle Brunetaud-Zaid, "Are you guilty of "cargo cult" thinking without even knowing it?" *Business Digest*, June 17, 2019. https://business-digest.eu/en/2019/06/17/are-you-guilty-of-cargo-cult-thinking-without-even-knowing-it/

37. Peter M. Worsley, "50 Years Ago: Cargo Cults of Melanesia," *Scientific American*, May 1, 2009. www.scientificamerican.com/article/1959-cargo-cults-melanesia

CHAPTER 2

1. Sheryl Sandberg, Chief Operating Officer, Facebook, Henry Blodget's interview with Sandberg at Business Insider's 2012 Ignition Conference.

2. www.goodreads.com/quotes/16419-know-the-rules-well-so-you-can-break-them-effectively

3. Retrieved from: http://web.mit.edu/6.933/www/Fall2000/teradyne/clay.html

4. "Cutting the Cord," *The Economist*, October 7, 1999. www.economist.com/special-report/1999/10/07/cutting-the-cord

5. Edmund L. Andrews, "AT&T Completes Deal To Buy McCaw Cellular," *The New York Times*, September 20, 1994. www.nytimes.com/1994/09/20/business/company-news-at-t-completes-deal-to-buy-mccaw-cellular.html

6. Mehrdad Baghai, Steven Coley, and David White, *The Alchemy of Growth*, Basic Books, 1999. https://books.google.de/books/about/The_Alchemy_Of_Growth.html?id=F5RxQgAACAAJ

7. "Enduring Ideas: The three horizons of growth," *McKinsey Quarterly*, December 1, 2009. www.mckinsey.com/business-functions/strategy-and-corporate-finance/our-insights/enduring-ideas-the-three-horizons-of-growth

8. How to Use the Three Horizons of Growth for Future Sensemaking.

9. Based on Enduring Ideas: The three horizons of growth by McKinsey quarterly, Dec 2009. Retrieved form: https://www.mckinsey.com/business-functions/strategy-andcorporate-finance/our-insights/enduring-ideas-the-three-horizons-of-growth#

10. Eric Ries, *The Lean Startup*, Crown Business, 2011. www.amazon.com/Lean-Startup-Entrepreneurs-Continuous-Innovation/dp/0307887898/

11. Steve Blank, "Why the Lean Start-Up Changes Everything," *Harvard Business Review*, May 2013. hbr.org/2013/05/why-the-lean-start-up-changes-everything

12. Alexander Osterwalder, *Business Model Generation*, John Wiley & Sons, 2010. www.amazon.com/Business-Model-Generation-Visionaries-Challengers/dp/0470876417/

13. *Source:* Why the Lean Start-Up Changes Everything, by Steve Blank, May 2013

14. Steve Blank, *The Four Steps to the Epiphany*, John Wiley & Sons, 2020. www.amazon.com/Four-Steps-Epiphany-Successful-Strategies/dp/1119690358/

15. Modified from Why the Lean Start-Up Changes Everything, by Steve Blank, Harvard Business Review, 2013. Retrieved from: https://hbr.org/2013/05/why-the-leanstart-up-changes-everything.

16. "What Is Agile? What Is Scrum?" Cprime white paper, no date. www.cprime.com/resources/what-is-agile-what-is-scrum/

17. Kent Beck, Mike Beedle, Arie van Bennekum, et al. *Manifesto for Agile Software Development*, 2001. https://agilemanifesto.org/

18. Max Rehkopf, "Kanban vs. scrum: which agile are you?" Atlassian Agile Coach, no date. https://www.atlassian.com/agile/kanban/kanban-vs-scrum

19. Tim Brown, "Design Thinking Defined," IDEO Design Thinking, no date. https://designthinking.ideo.com/

20. https://medium.com/@tejjwork/companies-usingdesign-thinking-c3a3dd 848a1d

21. "8 States That Prove Design Thinking Pays Off," ExperiencePoint, August 20, 2019. https://blog.experiencepoint.com/8-stats-that-prove-design-thinking-pays-off

22. Benedict Sheppard, Hugo Sarrazin, Garen Kouyoumjian, et al., "The business value of design," *McKinsey Quarterly*, October 25, 2018. www.mckinsey.com/business-functions/mckinsey-design/our-insights/the-business-value-of-design

23. Ravi Tejj, "Companies Using Design Thinking," Medium, no date. https://www.linkedin.com/in/tejj/ and Debbie Yong, "The Design Value Index Shows What 'Design Thinking' Is Worth," *Fortune*, August 30, 2017. https://fortune.com/2017/08/31/the-design-value-index-shows-what-design-thinking-is-worth/

24. "The Total Economic Impact Of IBM's Design Thinking Practice," A Forrester Total Economic Impact Study, February 2018. https://www.ibm.com/design/thinking/static/Enterprise-Design-Thinking-Report-8ab1e9e162289 9654844a5fe1d760ed5.pdf

25. J. Schmiedgen, H. Rhinow, E. Koppen, et al., *Parts Without a Whole? - The Current State of Design Thinking Practice in Organizations* (study report No. 97), Potsdam: Hasso-Plattner-Institut fur Softwaressystemtechnik an der Universitat Potsdam, October 2015. https://thisisdesignthinking.net/why-this-site/the-study/

26. Christine Murray Brozek, "Design-led firms win the business advantage," Forrester Consulting thought leadership paper commissioned by Adobe, October 2016. https://landing.adobe.com/en/na/products/marketing-cloud/350450-forrester-design-led-business.html

27. Design Thinking Resources, IDEOU. www.ideou.com/pages/design-thinking-resources

28. Sarah Benchaita, "IBM Tops U.S. Patent List for 2019," IBM News Room, January 14, 2020. https://newsroom.ibm.com/2020-01-14-IBM-Tops-U-S-Patent-List-for-2019

29. Modified from 2019 Top 10 US Patent Assignees https://www.ificlaims.com/rankings-top-50-2019.htm https://www.nasdaq.com/articles/patent-dominance%3A-top-5-companies-leading-the-charge-2020-01-17

30. Source: Open Innovation: The New Imperative for Creating and Profiting from Technology

31. Henry Chesbrough, "Everything You Need to Know About Open Innovation," *Forbes*, March 21, 2011. www.forbes.com/sites/henrychesbrough/2011/03/21/everything-you-need-to-know-about-open-innovation/#2bf940c275f4

32. Lauren Feiner, "IBM closes its $34 billion acquisition of Red Hat," CNBC, July 9, 2019. www.cnbc.com/2019/07/09/ibm-closes-its-34-billion-acquisition-of-red-hat.html

33. Benjamin Reid, "Open innovation: A brief history," *HR*, July 21, 2014. www.hrmagazine.co.uk/article-details/open-innovation-a-brief-history

34. https://en.wikipedia.org/wiki/Research_and_development

35. https://en.wikipedia.org/wiki/20%25_Project

36. "From AT&T To Xerox: 85+ Corporate Innovation Labs," CB Insights, July 27, 2020. www.cbinsights.com/research/corporate-innovation-labs

37. www.lockheedmartin.com/en-us/who-we-are/business-areas/aeronautics/skunkworks/skunk-works-origin-story.html

38. https://labs.fidelity.com/

39. "The 2019 Global CVC Report," CB Insights, no date. www.cbinsights.com/research/report/corporate-venture-capital-trends-2019 or Priyamvada Mathur, 3 things to know about CVC activity in 2019," PitchBook, August 22, 2019. https://pitchbook.com/news/articles/3-things-to-know-about-cvc-activity-in-2019

40. Jason D. Rowley, Inside The Ups And Downs Of The VC J-Curve, 20 Sep 2019.

CHAPTER 3

1. Halting Problem, "Facebook's New Motto: 'Move Fast And Please Please Please Don't Break Anything,' Medium, May 21, 2017. https://medium.com/halting-problem/facebooks-new-motto-move-fast-and-please-please-please-don-t-break-anything-8aefdd405d15

2. Halting Problem, "Microdosing Intern Has Bad Trip, Breaks Facebook," Medium, December 9, 2015. https://medium.com/halting-problem/microdosing-intern-has-bad-trip-breaks-facebook-b440c0026845

3. Dan Marcec, "CEO Tenure Rates," Harvard Law School Forum on Corporate Govenance, February 12, 2018. https://corpgov.law.harvard.edu/2018/02/12/ceo-tenure-rates/ and https://www.pwc.com/gx/en/news-room/press-releases/2019/ceo-turnover-record-high.html

4. "Growth & Innovation," McKinsey & Company, no date. www.mckinsey.com/business-functions/strategy-and-corporate-finance/how-we-help-clients/growth-and-innovation#)

5. Volker Staack and Branton Cole, "Reinventing innovation: Five findings to guide strategy through execution," PwC's Innovation Benchmark Report, 2017. www.pwc.com/us/en/services/consulting/innovation-benchmark-findings.html

6. Michelle Nickolaisen, "Examples of Simple Machines & Complex Machines," Sciencing, April 28, 2018. https://sciencing.com/examples-machines-amp-complex-machines-7221376.htm

CHAPTER 4

1. John Ream and David Schatsky, "Corporate accelerators: Spurring digital innovation with a page from the Silicon Valley playbook," Deloitte Insights, February 16, 2016. www2.deloitte.com/us/en/insights/focus/signals-for-strategists/corporate-accelerators-spurring-innovation-startups.html

2. Susan Cohen and Yael V. Hochberg, "Accelerating Startups: The Seed Accelerator Phenomenon," research paper, March 30, 2014. https://ssrn.com/abstract=2418000

3. Kirsten Bound, "The Startup Factor," Nesta, October 20, 2013. http://gust.com/accelerator_reports/2016/global/ and https://www.nesta.org.uk/report/the-startup-factories/

4. Paul Graham, "What I Did This Summer," blog post, October 2005. http://www.paulgraham.com/sfp.html?viewfullsite=1

5. Peter Edmonston, "Google's IPO 5 Years Later," *The New York Times*, August 19, 2009. https://dealbook.nytimes.com/2009/08/19/googles-ipo-5-years-later/

6. Jeff Grubb, "Amazon acquires Twitch: World's largest e-tailer buys largest gameplay-livestreaming site," GamesBeat, VentureBeat, August 25, 2014. https://venturebeat.com/2014/08/25/amazon-acquires-twitch-worlds-largest-e-tailer-buys-largest-gameplay-livestreaming-site/

7. Dean Takahashi, "Take-Two made $22M on its investment in gameplay livestreaming king Twitch," GamesBeat, VentureBeat, October 29, 2014. https://venturebeat.com/2014/10/29/take-two-made-22m-in-bank-on-its-investment-in-gameplay-livestreaming-firm-twitch/

8. Chris O'Brien, "Slack IPO starts trading at $38.50 for $23 billion valuation," VentureBeat June 20, 2019. https://venturebeat.com/2019/06/20/slack-ipo-starts-trading-at-38-50-for-23-billion-valuation/

9. Amit Chowdhry, "How Accel Made More Than A $4Billion Return On Investment From Slack," Pulse 2.0, July 1, 2019. https://pulse2.com/accel-made-more-than-4-billion-roi-from-slack/

10. Ari Levy, "Here's who is getting rich from Slack's stock market debut," CNBC, June 19, 2019. www.cnbc.com/2019/06/19/slack-debut-means-big-returns-for-accel-and-andreessen.html

11. "Corporate Accelerator," HowDo. https://howdo.com/corporate-accelerator/

12. Justin Peters, "How a 1950s Egg Farm Hatched the Modern Startup Incubator," *Wired*, June 28, 2017. www.wired.com/story/how-a-1950s-egg-farm-hatched-the-modern-startup-incubator/

13. Ibid.

14. Paul Graham, "How to Start a Startup," essay derived from a talk at the Harvard Computer Society, March 2005. www.paulgraham.com/start.html

15. Paul Graham, "Summer Founders Program," original announcement of Y Combinator, March 2005. www.paulgraham.com/summerfounder.html?viewfullsite=1

16. www.ycombinator.com/faq/

17. https://en.wikipedia.org/wiki/Y_Combinator

18. www.quora.com/Where-are-the-first-batch-of-Y-Combinator-now

19. Lucas Matney, "Y Combinator officially shifts its next accelerator class to fully remote format," *TechCrunch*, April 20, 2020. https://techcrunch.com/2020/04/20/y-combinator-officially-shifts-its-next-accelerator-class-to-fully-remote-format/

20. www.ycombinator.com/faq/

21. "CorporateAccelerators," HowDo. https://howdo.com/corporate-accelerator/

22. Angelique Moss, "Should you join a startup accelerator? Here's what you need to know," Hackernoon, April 3, 2018. https://hackernoon.com/should-join-startup-accelerator-need-know-cc95d823e388

23. Ream and Schatsky, "Corporate accelerators."

24. "A Guide To Corporate Innovation: 19 Strategies To Drive Innovation Now," CB Insights, November 9, 2018. www.cbinsights.com/research/corporate-innovation-strategy-guide/

CHAPTER 5

1. "Barclays expands Rise New York and launches Rise Growth Investment," Barclays, January 23, 2019. https://home.barclays/news/press-releases/2019/01/barclays-expands-rise-new-york-and-launches-rise-growth-investme/

2. https://urban.us/

3. www.urban-x.com/program/

4. "Verizon 5G First Responder Lab's Third Cohort Focused on AI," *Government Technology*, November 26, 2019. www.govtech.com/biz/Verizon-5G-First-Responder-Labs-Third-Cohort-Focused-on-AI.html

5. https://events.withgoogle.com/indie-games-accelerator/developer-stories/#content

6. https://events.withgoogle.com/indie-games-accelerator/benefits/#content

7. Taylor Soper, "Amazon and Techstars revamp Alexa Accelerator to help later-stage companies, unveil new cohort," GeekWire, June 17, 2020. www.geekwire.com/2020/amazon-techstars-revamp-alexa-accelerator-help-later-stage-companies-unveil-new-cohort/

8. Alexandra Whyte, "Disney revives the Accelerator program," Kidscreen, March 4, 2020. https://kidscreen.com/2020/03/04/disney-revives-the-accelerator-program/

9. https://sap.io/foundries/apply/

10. "MDR LAB is Back! Now With THREE Programmes," Artificial Lawyer, October 5, 2020. www.artificiallawyer.com/2020/10/05/mdr-lab-is-back-now-with-three-programmes/

11. "Orange Fab US announces new Fab Force corporate program model and welcomes new partner," Orange Silicon Valley press release, June 7, 2017. https://www.prnewswire.com/news-releases/orange-fab-us-announces-new-fab-force-corporate-program-model-and-welcomes-new-partner-300470422.html

12. https://harmonylabs.org/mission

CHAPTER 6

1. Start with Why: How Great Leaders Inspire Everyone to Take Action.

2. Luca Collacciani, "Why you should ask 'Why?' 3 times," LinkedIn, February 13, 2019. www.linkedin.com/pulse/why-you-should-ask-3-times-luca-collacciani/

3. Arnaud Bonzom and Serguei Netessine, "How do the World's Biggest Companies Deal with the Startup Revolution?" #500CORPORATIONS report, Insead, February 2016. http://cdn2.hubspot.net/hubfs/698640/500CORPORATIONS_-_How_do_the_Worlds_Biggest_Companies_Deal_with_the_Startup_Revolution_-_Feb_2016.pdf?t=1454307105225

CHAPTER 7

1. L. E. Preston and H. J. Sapienza, "Stakeholder management and corporate performance," *The Journal of Behavioral Economics*, 19(4), 361–375.
2. Alison Taylor, "Five-Step Approach to Stakeholder Engagement," BSR report, April 29, 2019. www.bsr.org/en/our-insights/report-view/stakeholder-engagement-five-step-approach-toolkit
3. Retrived from: https://www.ificlaims.com/rankingstop-50-2019.html; https://www.nasdaq.com/articles/patent-dominance%3A-top-5-companies-leading-the-charge-2020-01-17

CHAPTER 8

1. Money Money, Liza Minnelli by John Kander / Fred Ebb Money Money lyrics © Trio Music Company, Times Square Music Publications Company, Trio Music Co., Inc.
2. www.velvetjobs.com/job-posting/d10x-coach-and-entrepreneur-in-residence-eir-390667
3. "Design Principles for Building a Successful Corporate Accelerator," Deloitte, 2015.

CHAPTER 9

1. John Ream and David Schatsky, "Corporate accelerators: Spurring digital innovation with a page from the Silicon Valley playbook," Deloitte Insights, February 16, 2016. www2.deloitte.com/us/en/insights/focus/signals-for-strategists/corporate-accelerators-spurring-innovation-startups.html#endnote-4
2. http://history.techstars.com/

CHAPTER 10

1. Ruth Walker, "Build the plane while you're flying it," *The Christian Science Monitor*, March 24, 2016. www.csmonitor.com/The-Culture/The-Home-Forum/2016/0324/Build-the-plane-while-you-re-flying-it

2. West Stringfellow, "Corporate Accelerator," HowDo, no date. https://dev. webethics.online/howdo/corporate-accelerator/

3. John Ream and David Schatsky, "Corporate accelerators: Spurring digital innovation with a page from the Silicon Valley playbook," Deloitte Insights, February 16, 2016. www2.deloitte.com/us/en/insights/focus/signals-for-strategists/corporate-accelerators-spurring-innovation-startups.html

4. https://jlabs.jnjinnovation.com/vision

5. https://jlabs.jnjinnovation.com/vision

6. https://verizon5glabs.com/

7. https://verizon5glabs.com/

8. https://www.f6s.com/programs

9. Corporate Accelerator, Startupbootcamp, which runs accelerator programs around the world. https://howdo.com/corporate-accelerator/

10. Ross Baird, Lily Bowles, and Saurabh Lall, "Bridging the 'Pioneer Gap': The Role of Accelerators in Launching High-Impact Enterprises," Aspen Network of Development Entrepreneurs and Village Capital report, June 2013. https://assets.aspeninstitute.org/content/uploads/files/content/docs/ande/Bridging%20the%20Pioneer%20Gap%20The%20Role%20of%20Accelerators%20in%20Launching%20High%20Impact%20Enterprises%20.pdf   Also referenced https://howdo.com/corporate-accelerator/

11. Andrew Goldstein, Erich J. Lehmann, and Esther Prax, "Design principles of building a successful corporate accelerator," Deloitte Digital, 2015. www2. deloitte.com/content/dam/Deloitte/de/Documents/technology/Corporate_Accelerator_EN.pdf

12. Ibid., also referenced at "Corporate Accelerator," HowDo, no date. https:// howdo.com/corporate-accelerator/

13. "Corporate Accelerator," HowDo.

CHAPTER 11

1. "Flipping Te Power Dynamics: Can Entrepreneurs Make Successful Investment Decisions?" Village Capital, January 2019. https://newsandviews.vilcap.com/reports/flipping-the-power-dynamics-can-entrepreneurs-make-successful-investment-decisions

2. www.techstars.com/equity-back-guarantee-the-details

3. www.indie.vc/notes/v3-terms

CHAPTER 12

1. www.drucker.institute/thedx/measurement-myopia/

2. Some more detail on VC metrics can be found from the "Ultimate VC Metrics Cheat Sheet," EquityEffect, 2019, here: www.equityeffect.com/wp-content/uploads/2019/09/EE_The-Ultimate-VC-Metrics-Cheat-Sheet-hor-v2.pdf

3. Scott Kupor, "When Is a 'Mark' not a Mark? When Its a Venture Capital Mark" Andreessen Horowitz, September 1, 2016. https://a16z.com/2016/09/01/marks-offmark/

4. *McKinsey Quarterly* from October 2008, referenced in Jesse Niemenen, "50+ statistics on innovation – What do the numbers tell us?" Viima, October 10, 2018. www.viima.com/blog/innovation-stats

CHAPTER 13

1. Carleen Hawn, "The FIR Interview: Y Combinator's Paul Graham," GigaOm, May 2008, https://gigaom.com/2008/05/03/the-fr-interview-y-combinators-paul-graham/

2. Michael Brigi, Stafan Gross-Selbeck, Nico Dehnert, et al. "After the Honeymoon Ends: Making Corporate-Startup Relationships Work," BCG, June 13, 2019. www.bcg.com/publications/2019/corporate-startup-relationships-work-after-honeymoon-ends

3. *Source:* Michael Brigl, After the Honeymoon Ends: Making Corporate-Startup Relationships Work, 13 Jun 2019.

4. "What's Working in Startup Acceleration," Village Capital + GALI, March 2016. www.galidata.org/assets/report/pdf/GALI_digital_041816.pdf

5. Benjamin Hallen, Susan Cohen, and Christopher Bingham, "Do Accelerators Work? If So How?" research paper, April 3, 2019. https://papers.ssrn.com/sol3/Papers.cfm?abstract_id=2719810

6. Thomas Kohler, "Corporate Accelerators: Building Bridges between Corporations and Startups," *Business Horizons*, 2016. www.sciencedirect.com/science/article/pii/S0007681316000094

7. www.churchill-society-london.org.uk/EndoBegn.html

CHAPTER 14

1. Tobias Stone, "An Examination of Startup Accelerators Using Social Network Theory," University of Huddersfield doctoral thesis, 2018. http://eprints.hud.ac.uk/id/eprint/34731/

2. World Bank, "Nurturing Innovation: Venture Acceleration Networks," 2011. https://openknowledge.worldbank.org/bitstream/handle/10986/12519/689500ESW0P1250works0Report030Oct11.txt?sequence=2&isAllowed=y

CHAPTER 15

1. CB Insights, from presentation during the Collective conference in December 2019.

2. "Collaboration between Start-ups and Corporates: A Practical Guide for Mutual Understanding," World Economic Forum white paper, January 2018. www3.weforum.org/docs/WEF_White_Paper_Collaboration_between_Startups_and_Corporates.pdf

3. Arnaud Bonzom and Serguei Netessine, "How do the World's Biggest Companies Deal with the Startup Revolution?" #500CORPORATIONS report, Insead, February 2016. https://cdn2.hubspot.net/hubfs/698640/500CORPORATIONS_-_How_do_the_Worlds_Biggest_Companies_Deal_with_the_Startup_Revolution_-_Feb_2016.pdf

4. Michael Brigi, Stafan Gross-Selbeck, Nico Dehnert, et al. "After the Honeymoon Ends: Making Corporate-Startup Relationships Work," BCG, June 13, 2019. www.bcg.com/publications/2019/corporate-startup-relationships-work-after-honeymoon-ends

5. Julia Prats and Josemaria Siota, "How Corporations Can Better Work With Startups," *Harvard Business Review*, June 3, 2019. https://hbr.org/2019/06/how-corporations-can-better-work-with-startups

6. Brigi et al., "After the Honeymoon Ends."

7. Shameen Prashantham, "The Two Ways for Startups and Corporations to Partner," *Harvard Business Review*, January 30, 2019. https://hbr.org/2019/01/the-two-ways-for-startups-and-corporations-to-partner

8. Brigi et al., "After the Honeymoon Ends."

9. Prashantham, "The Two Ways for Startups and Corporations to Partner."

10. "Winning Together: A Guide to Successful Corporate-Startup Collaborations," Nesta report, June 2015. https://ec.europa.eu/futurium/en/system/files/ged/43-nesta-winning-together-guidestartupcollab.pdf

11. Ibid.

12. https://en.wikipedia.org/wiki/Minimum_viable_product

13. "Collaboration between Start-ups and Corporates: A Practical Guide for Mutual Understanding," World Economic Forum white paper.

14. Elia Pradel, "Startups & Corporates – Part 6 : Procurement and Startups, how to make it work?" Early Metrics, April 28, 2020. https://earlymetrics.com/series-start-ups-corporates-part-6-procurement-startups-make-work/

15. America's Seed Fund, www.sbir.gov/node/1695819

16. Pat Riley, "Building a Corporate-Startup Partnership? Here's What Will Help Make It Successful", Entrepreneur, July 5, 2019. www.entrepreneur.com/article/336034

17. Arjun Narayan, "Best Practices for Partnering with Startups," Plug and Play, July 30, 2018. www.plugandplaytechcenter.com/resources/best-practices-partnering-startups/

18. "5 ways your corporate innovation team can benefit from a startup accelerator," Highline Beta, 2020. https://highlinebeta.com/insights/5-ways-your-corporate-innovation-team-can-benefit-from-a-startup-accelerator/

19. Prats and Siota, "How Corporations Can Better Work With Startups."

CHAPTER 16

1. Angela Toy, "Portfolio Management for Venture Capital Success (The Three Cs in Print)," Jumpstart, May 17, 2019. www.jumpstartmag.com/portfolio-management-for-venture-capital-success-the-three-cs-in-print/

2. Ross Baird, Lily Bowles, and Saurabh Lall, "Bridging the 'Pioneer Gap': The Role of Accelerators in Launching High-Impact Enterprises," Aspen Network of Development Entrepreneurs and Village Capital report, June 2013. https://assets.aspeninstitute.org/content/uploads/files/content/docs/ande/Bridging%20the%20Pioneer%20Gap%20The%20Role%20of%20Accelerators%20in%20Launching%20High%20Impact%20Enterprises%20.pdf

Index

NOTE: Page references in *italics* refer to figures.

role of, in acceleration, 230–231

specialists as, 232–233

as stakeholders, 117

vendors as, 233–234

Metrics and key performance indicators (KPIs), 195–208

accelerator archetypes and, 77–81, 82, 83, 85–86, 88–89

customizing, 207–208

for equity returns, 200

financial metrics, 201–202

innovation needed for, 203–204

KPIs for mentors, 238

measuring success of innovation, 7–9, *8*

mission and, 204–207

for partnerships, 258

portfolio management basics, 277

for programming, 223

quantifying goals with, 197–200, *200*

strategic metrics, 202–203

"what gets measured gets managed," 195–196

See also Accelerator archetypes

Microsoft, 69

Mindset Ventures, 279

Minelli, Liza, 129

MINI (BMW Group), 81, 106–107

Minimum viable product (MVP), 24, 253, 254

Mischon de Reya, 97, 166, 182

Mission

metrics, KPIs, and, 204–207

understanding motivation for, 106–107

Models of accelerators. *See* Accelerator archetypes

Module-based approach, 216

Morris, Robert Tappan, 67–68

Motivation, 96–107

common reasons for, overview, 101

culture and talent as, 103–104

decision making and, 96–97

equity returns and, 105–106

fear of missing out (FOMO) vs., 106

financial vs. strategic returns as, 100–101, *101*, 105–106

goal setting and, 98

importance of understanding, 98–99

knowledge as, 105

mission and, 106–107

problem solving and, 97–98

reputation, brand, and marketing as, 102–103

sales as, 104

strategic investment and, 176–177

"why" as driver of decisions, 100–101

See also Goals

Mozilla Foundation, 93

N

Netflix, 9

Net present value (NPV), 23, 78

Newton, Isaac, 229

Nielsen, 203–204

Nomination process vs. open application, 160

Now/New/Next strategy (three Ns), 169

O

Office space

as investment, 179

programming and module-based approach, 216

programming and office vs. coworking space, 214–216

virtual programming vs., 216–217

Open application vs. nomination process, 160

Open innovation

accelerators, 34

corporate M&A, 35–36

corporate venture capital (CVC), 35

entrepreneur in residence (EIR) programs, 34

hackathons, 34

incubators, 34–35

innovation theory on, 29–31, *30, 31*, 33–36

pitch competitions, 34

startup partnerships unit, 35

Open Innovation (Chesbrough), 31

Openness, stakeholder engagement and, 126

Open source movement, 31

Option pricing model (OPM), 202